MAKING MUSIC MAKE MONEY

An Insider's Guide to Becoming Your Own Music Publisher

ERIC BEALL

BERKLEE PRESS

Editor in Chief: Jonathan Feist
Senior Vice President of Online Learning and
Continuing Education/CEO of Berklee Online: Debbie Cavalier
Vice President of Enrollment Marketing and Management: Mike King
Vice President of Academic Strategy: Carin Nuernberg
Editor of the First Edition: Susan Gedutis Lindsay
Editorial Assistant: Brittany McCorriston

ISBN 978-0-87639-210-2

Berklee Press

1140 Boylston Street
Boston, MA 02215-3693 USA
(617) 747-2146

Visit Berklee Press Online at
www.berkleepress.com

Berklee Online

Study music online at
online.berklee.edu

DISTRIBUTED BY

HAL•LEONA[RD]
7777 W. BLUEMOUND RD. P.O
MILWAUKEE, WISCONSIN

Visit Hal Leonard Or
www.halleonard.

To my wife Cheryl, who's been with me every step of the journey.
And to my parents, whose love and support made the journey possible.

Contents

Preface

So you've written a song. Or two. Or maybe even several dozen, or several hundred for that matter, all scribbled in a tattered notebook tucked away in your closet, or in files eating up space on your desktop. All of those songs, carefully and lovingly created, silently waiting on the answer to the inevitable question: What next?

Now assuming you've taken the time to read the title page of this book, you are probably well on your way to surmising the answer to this question (wonderfully perceptive and intuitive creatures, these songwriters are). Yes, you guessed it—what you need is: A PUBLISHER! You need an effective, diligent music publisher who will share your enthusiasm for your creations, organize those errant MP3s into a coherent catalog, dip into their deep well of contacts to put those songs into the hands of the right recording artists, music supervisors, and A&R executives, and who will then, with the tenacity of a loan shark, collect the inevitable flow of money that results. Simple, right?

Well, maybe. Having spent fifteen years as a professional songwriter, and having enjoyed successful and profitable relationships with several different music publishing companies, I would hardly be the one to tell you that such a goal is out of reach. As someone who has now spent more than twenty years on the other side of the desk, as a creative director for some of the music industry's most successful publishers, I would never minimize the value of working with a well-established music publishing company.

The purpose of this book is simply to let you in on a simple truth that has probably been lurking right under your nose. If it's a hardworking, well-organized, well-connected music publisher that you're looking for, look no further. You already have one. In fact, he or she has probably been around for some time now, having been with you since you penned your first potential hit. Your publisher is your greatest untapped resource, ready to take your *assets* (that's your songs) and put them into *action* (somewhere where they can be heard) to yield *income* (which is the goal here, remember). Whatever your publisher may lack in experience will inevitably be compensated for with an uncanny understanding of your work, and an unquestionable devotion to your career.

Songwriter meet your first, and quite possibly, finest publisher: You.

Okay, I know. It's not exactly what you were hoping for. You were expecting the high-powered, father-figure type, or maybe the nurturing Mother Hen, with deep pockets, a big office, and an invitation for you to a breakfast at the Sunset Marquis. Fair enough. Those characters do exist, and if you and your current publisher (that's you, pal) do your jobs well, you may someday meet that elusive music business icon. There is a paradox at work here. Until you take ownership of your own publishing company—which exists, at least in theory, from the day you complete your first song—you are unlikely to ever attract the interest of a major publisher, or, for that matter, an important artist, A&R person, or manager. In the beginning, there is you, and what you do will open the doors to all the other parties who will help to develop your career. When an aspiring writer asks me how to find a good publisher, I usually reply, "Become one."

The paradox extends even further. The truth is that the most successful songwriters in any large publishing company are those writers who have become successful music publishers on their own. They have learned by necessity how to pitch their own material, develop and administer their catalog, protect their copyrights, construct a solid business team, and establish a presence for themselves in the industry. Now, their publishing company is a solid independent business entity, and as such, it presents a larger music publisher with an opportunity for a real partnership: a co-venture with an already productive company.

This is the second paradox then. Not only are you most likely to find a publisher by becoming one; you will usually be most successful in working with a major music publisher when you reach the point of not needing one. Starting your own publishing company is not a choice to avoid affiliation with a larger music publisher. Rather, it is a proactive approach to putting yourself in a position where you can effectively work with another company. Only when you are able to confidently speak the language of publishing will you be able to get the best out of any publishing partner.

I'd love to say that I learned this lesson early in my songwriting career. But I would be lying. In truth, it was only when I entered the publishing world on the business end, thus coming into contact with a wide variety of writers much more successful than I, that the truth began to sink in. Songwriters like Steve Diamond, Billy Mann, Stargate, and Kara DioGuardi showed me what it means not only to be a creative force, but also to be an industry unto yourself. These are strategic, aggressive, knowledgeable people who bring the same vision and determination to running their publishing entity as they do to creating hit songs. No one asks these songwriters what they bring to the table. Everyone is too busy fighting for a seat.

From a corporation's standpoint, the advantage of going into business with a self-sufficient writer/publisher is obvious. Such a partnership allows a large company to build their roster and catalog of songs without significantly increasing the burden on their creative and administrative staff. The larger corporate entity can concentrate on those things at which it is most effective, while trusting that the writer's own publishing company is competently handling the day-to-day duties involved in developing the writer's career.

Let the whining begin:

"But being my own publisher will take time away from my writing."

"I'm no good at being a salesman. I'm a creative type."

"I don't have any industry contacts."

"I need advance money."

"Why should a writer sign with a publishing company if the writer is still expected to do all the work?"

Feel free to add more thoughts of your own. I can assure you, I am intimately acquainted with all of your objections. I have used them myself. And now, drawing upon the hard lessons of a twenty-year career in this business, I will share the one bit of insight I've picked up along the way: Sorry. Life is not fair, and show biz is one of the least fair sectors of life.

So there you go. If you like to wax nostalgic for a time when writers spent their time in solitude, quietly noodling away at their piano, while a fast-talking hustler with a heart of gold peddled their songs around town, I can only tell you that those days are gone. I would also suggest that you read biographies of some of the songwriting legends, like Irving Berlin, Berry Gordy, or Carole King. I suspect you'll find that those days never really existed at all. Successful songwriters have always been aggressive about getting their songs into the right hands, managing their career, and protecting their work. The sooner you accept that fact, the better. Smart businesspeople see the world not as it once was or as they might wish it would be, but as it really is.

Of course, there is some truth in the complaints I mentioned. Will being a publisher take time away from your writing? Yes. You will have to work harder. Aren't some creative people unsuited to "selling" their songs? Probably. But the number is far fewer than those who think they are unsuited to it. The publishing business is filled with former writers (David Gray, the executive VP of A&R at Universal Music Publishing Group, for one). The creative genes and business genes are not as mutually exclusive as we like to think. Don't you need industry contacts to be successful? Yes. So you will make them. You didn't have any friends in high school until you went there. You will only make contacts in the industry when you decide to become an active part of the industry.

And what about money? Of course you need it. We all need it. Even the big multinational corporations need it. Which is why they probably won't give you any until you show that you're already earning some.

When this book was first written, the music business was a much simpler place. Records were still sold in physical formats, labels were responsible for paying royalties, and radio was the primary exploitation venue available. Over the past decade, the music industry has been transformed by digital streaming, the rise of social media, the proliferation of new television networks, and court decisions that have muddied the already murky waters around the issue of what constitutes copyright infringement. Music publishers have been more affected than anyone by many of these issues and innovations, and in some ways, are still in the process of transforming their business to accommodate the new reality. We will look at all of the challenges publishers face in these areas, even when the solutions are still a work in progress.

But this book is not intended to be a comprehensive, technical how-to guide to starting your own publishing company. There are a number of those already on the market. Instead, I'll try to offer you an insider's view of the music publishing business, and offer some practical tips toward helping you effectively assume a role as your own best publisher. While this book is clearly directed toward songwriters, I also believe that it can be useful to any music business entrepreneur: manager, club owner, DJ, producer, promoter, and independent label owner. Anyone who regularly comes in contact with new songs and new writers should be considering establishing a music publishing enterprise. If done correctly, music publishing is a business that requires a relatively small upfront investment (no one's asking you to build a factory, after all) and offers a long-term business from which you can quietly collect income for many years to come.

Oh, and one more thing. For those readers who are old-fashioned enough to really love music, music publishing remains one of the few segments of the music industry still centered on "the song." Unlike the record business, in which most of the day can be spent mired in discussions about recording budgets, scheduling, tour support, radio promotion, distribution, publicity, you name it, music publishers actually get to spend a good part of their day listening to songs. For most of us who do this every day, that's what keeps us in the business: a love of songs and songwriters, and an appreciation of the power of a truly great song.

If you're a songwriter, you may already know the truth: the only way you will profit from your music is if someone hears it. In order for your song to move forward, you need someone behind it, pushing all the time, putting it in the hands of someone who will record it, perform it, place it in a television show or in an advertisement. This is the role of the music publisher: to make sure your songs have a chance to be heard.

What you may not have realized until now is that you, your song's creator, are also that publisher. During the course of this book, when I refer to a publisher, I'm actually talking to *you*.

You may never have lifted a finger towards getting your music heard. You might have no idea where to start. But by making it to page one of this book, you've already started. All that remains is to fill in the blanks in your knowledge. That's my job. So let's get to work.

PART I
START ME UP:
GETTING INTO
THE GAME

1

What Is Music Publishing, Anyway?

My family has a parlor game we like to play each Christmas. Picture the scene: Mom, Dad, Grandma, aunts and uncles, cousins and nephews, all gathered around the dining room table, as the annual holiday dinner begins. A moment of silence ensues, the joy of the season floods the room, and then it happens.

The Question.

"So Eric, tell us again. What is it that you *do* for a living?"

This has been going on for many, many years now. I've tried all the obvious explanations—company names, job title, reporting structure. It means nothing. I've tried analogies:

"A music publisher is to a songwriter what a book publisher is to an author."

"A music publisher is to a songwriter what an agent is to an actor."

Whatever. The truth is, to most of the world outside of the music industry, and a fair amount of the world inside the music industry, music publishing is a mystery.

This is not surprising. As attached as I am to my analogies, they're not all that accurate. Unlike a book publisher, a music publisher doesn't really manufacture anything; the music publisher owns the rights to the song, but not the CD or the MP3 on which the song is sold to the consumer. And unlike an agent with an actor, the publisher's real asset is the song, not the songwriter; a publisher owns the creation, not the creator. Confused? Yeah. You and my family.

So before you embark on your endeavor to make money from music—perhaps even to become your own music publisher, a quick history lesson is probably in order.

MAKING MUSIC MAKE MONEY

An Insider's Guide to Becoming Your Own Music Publisher

ERIC BEALL

BERKLEE PRESS

Editor in Chief: Jonathan Feist

Senior Vice President of Online Learning and
Continuing Education/CEO of Berklee Online: Debbie Cavalier

Vice President of Enrollment Marketing and Management: Mike King

Vice President of Academic Strategy: Carin Nuernberg

Editor of the First Edition: Susan Gedutis Lindsay

Editorial Assistant: Brittany McCorriston

ISBN 978-0-87639-210-2

Berklee
Press

1140 Boylston Street
Boston, MA 02215-3693 USA
(617) 747-2146

Visit Berklee Press Online at
www.berkleepress.com

Berklee Online

Study music online at
online.berklee.edu

DISTRIBUTED BY

HAL•LEONARD®
7777 W. BLUEMOUND RD. P.O. BOX 13819
MILWAUKEE, WISCONSIN 53213

Visit Hal Leonard Online
www.halleonard.com

To my wife Cheryl, who's been with me every step of the journey.
And to my parents, whose love and support made the journey possible.

Contents

Preface

So you've written a song. Or two. Or maybe even several dozen, or several hundred for that matter, all scribbled in a tattered notebook tucked away in your closet, or in files eating up space on your desktop. All of those songs, carefully and lovingly created, silently waiting on the answer to the inevitable question: What next?

Now assuming you've taken the time to read the title page of this book, you are probably well on your way to surmising the answer to this question (wonderfully perceptive and intuitive creatures, these songwriters are). Yes, you guessed it—what you need is: A PUBLISHER! You need an effective, diligent music publisher who will share your enthusiasm for your creations, organize those errant MP3s into a coherent catalog, dip into their deep well of contacts to put those songs into the hands of the right recording artists, music supervisors, and A&R executives, and who will then, with the tenacity of a loan shark, collect the inevitable flow of money that results. Simple, right?

Well, maybe. Having spent fifteen years as a professional songwriter, and having enjoyed successful and profitable relationships with several different music publishing companies, I would hardly be the one to tell you that such a goal is out of reach. As someone who has now spent more than twenty years on the other side of the desk, as a creative director for some of the music industry's most successful publishers, I would never minimize the value of working with a well-established music publishing company.

The purpose of this book is simply to let you in on a simple truth that has probably been lurking right under your nose. If it's a hardworking, well-organized, well-connected music publisher that you're looking for, look no further. You already have one. In fact, he or she has probably been around for some time now, having been with you since you penned your first potential hit. Your publisher is your greatest untapped resource, ready to take your *assets* (that's your songs) and put them into *action* (somewhere where they can be heard) to yield *income* (which is the goal here, remember). Whatever your publisher may lack in experience will inevitably be compensated for with an uncanny understanding of your work, and an unquestionable devotion to your career.

Songwriter meet your first, and quite possibly, finest publisher: You.

Okay, I know. It's not exactly what you were hoping for. You were expecting the high-powered, father-figure type, or maybe the nurturing Mother Hen, with deep pockets, a big office, and an invitation for you to a breakfast at the Sunset Marquis. Fair enough. Those characters do exist, and if you and your current publisher (that's you, pal) do your jobs well, you may someday meet that elusive music business icon. There is a paradox at work here. Until you take ownership of your own publishing company—which exists, at least in theory, from the day you complete your first song—you are unlikely to ever attract the interest of a major publisher, or, for that matter, an important artist, A&R person, or manager. In the beginning, there is you, and what you do will open the doors to all the other parties who will help to develop your career. When an aspiring writer asks me how to find a good publisher, I usually reply, "Become one."

The paradox extends even further. The truth is that the most successful songwriters in any large publishing company are those writers who have become successful music publishers on their own. They have learned by necessity how to pitch their own material, develop and administer their catalog, protect their copyrights, construct a solid business team, and establish a presence for themselves in the industry. Now, their publishing company is a solid independent business entity, and as such, it presents a larger music publisher with an opportunity for a real partnership: a co-venture with an already productive company.

This is the second paradox then. Not only are you most likely to find a publisher by becoming one; you will usually be most successful in working with a major music publisher when you reach the point of not needing one. Starting your own publishing company is not a choice to avoid affiliation with a larger music publisher. Rather, it is a proactive approach to putting yourself in a position where you can effectively work with another company. Only when you are able to confidently speak the language of publishing will you be able to get the best out of any publishing partner.

I'd love to say that I learned this lesson early in my songwriting career. But I would be lying. In truth, it was only when I entered the publishing world on the business end, thus coming into contact with a wide variety of writers much more successful than I, that the truth began to sink in. Songwriters like Steve Diamond, Billy Mann, Stargate, and Kara DioGuardi showed me what it means not only to be a creative force, but also to be an industry unto yourself. These are strategic, aggressive, knowledgeable people who bring the same vision and determination to running their publishing entity as they do to creating hit songs. No one asks these songwriters what they bring to the table. Everyone is too busy fighting for a seat.

From a corporation's standpoint, the advantage of going into business with a self-sufficient writer/publisher is obvious. Such a partnership allows a large company to build their roster and catalog of songs without significantly increasing the burden on their creative and administrative staff. The larger corporate entity can concentrate on those things at which it is most effective, while trusting that the writer's own publishing company is competently handling the day-to-day duties involved in developing the writer's career.

Let the whining begin:

"But being my own publisher will take time away from my writing."

"I'm no good at being a salesman. I'm a creative type."

"I don't have any industry contacts."

"I need advance money."

"Why should a writer sign with a publishing company if the writer is still expected to do all the work?"

Feel free to add more thoughts of your own. I can assure you, I am intimately acquainted with all of your objections. I have used them myself. And now, drawing upon the hard lessons of a twenty-year career in this business, I will share the one bit of insight I've picked up along the way: Sorry. Life is not fair, and show biz is one of the least fair sectors of life.

So there you go. If you like to wax nostalgic for a time when writers spent their time in solitude, quietly noodling away at their piano, while a fast-talking hustler with a heart of gold peddled their songs around town, I can only tell you that those days are gone. I would also suggest that you read biographies of some of the songwriting legends, like Irving Berlin, Berry Gordy, or Carole King. I suspect you'll find that those days never really existed at all. Successful songwriters have always been aggressive about getting their songs into the right hands, managing their career, and protecting their work. The sooner you accept that fact, the better. Smart businesspeople see the world not as it once was or as they might wish it would be, but as it really is.

Of course, there is some truth in the complaints I mentioned. Will being a publisher take time away from your writing? Yes. You will have to work harder. Aren't some creative people unsuited to "selling" their songs? Probably. But the number is far fewer than those who think they are unsuited to it. The publishing business is filled with former writers (David Gray, the executive VP of A&R at Universal Music Publishing Group, for one). The creative genes and business genes are not as mutually exclusive as we like to think. Don't you need industry contacts to be successful? Yes. So you will make them. You didn't have any friends in high school until you went there. You will only make contacts in the industry when you decide to become an active part of the industry.

And what about money? Of course you need it. We all need it. Even the big multinational corporations need it. Which is why they probably won't give you any until you show that you're already earning some.

When this book was first written, the music business was a much simpler place. Records were still sold in physical formats, labels were responsible for paying royalties, and radio was the primary exploitation venue available. Over the past decade, the music industry has been transformed by digital streaming, the rise of social media, the proliferation of new television networks, and court decisions that have muddied the already murky waters around the issue of what constitutes copyright infringement. Music publishers have been more affected than anyone by many of these issues and innovations, and in some ways, are still in the process of transforming their business to accommodate the new reality. We will look at all of the challenges publishers face in these areas, even when the solutions are still a work in progress.

But this book is not intended to be a comprehensive, technical how-to guide to starting your own publishing company. There are a number of those already on the market. Instead, I'll try to offer you an insider's view of the music publishing business, and offer some practical tips toward helping you effectively assume a role as your own best publisher. While this book is clearly directed toward songwriters, I also believe that it can be useful to any music business entrepreneur: manager, club owner, DJ, producer, promoter, and independent label owner. Anyone who regularly comes in contact with new songs and new writers should be considering establishing a music publishing enterprise. If done correctly, music publishing is a business that requires a relatively small upfront investment (no one's asking you to build a factory, after all) and offers a long-term business from which you can quietly collect income for many years to come.

Oh, and one more thing. For those readers who are old-fashioned enough to really love music, music publishing remains one of the few segments of the music industry still centered on "the song." Unlike the record business, in which most of the day can be spent mired in discussions about recording budgets, scheduling, tour support, radio promotion, distribution, publicity, you name it, music publishers actually get to spend a good part of their day listening to songs. For most of us who do this every day, that's what keeps us in the business: a love of songs and songwriters, and an appreciation of the power of a truly great song.

If you're a songwriter, you may already know the truth: the only way you will profit from your music is if someone hears it. In order for your song to move forward, you need someone behind it, pushing all the time, putting it in the hands of someone who will record it, perform it, place it in a television show or in an advertisement. This is the role of the music publisher: to make sure your songs have a chance to be heard.

What you may not have realized until now is that you, your song's creator, are also that publisher. During the course of this book, when I refer to a publisher, I'm actually talking to *you*.

You may never have lifted a finger towards getting your music heard. You might have no idea where to start. But by making it to page one of this book, you've already started. All that remains is to fill in the blanks in your knowledge. That's my job. So let's get to work.

PART I
START ME UP:
GETTING INTO
THE GAME

1

What Is Music Publishing, Anyway?

My family has a parlor game we like to play each Christmas. Picture the scene: Mom, Dad, Grandma, aunts and uncles, cousins and nephews, all gathered around the dining room table, as the annual holiday dinner begins. A moment of silence ensues, the joy of the season floods the room, and then it happens.

The Question.

"So Eric, tell us again. What is it that you *do* for a living?"

This has been going on for many, many years now. I've tried all the obvious explanations—company names, job title, reporting structure. It means nothing. I've tried analogies:

"A music publisher is to a songwriter what a book publisher is to an author."

"A music publisher is to a songwriter what an agent is to an actor."

Whatever. The truth is, to most of the world outside of the music industry, and a fair amount of the world inside the music industry, music publishing is a mystery.

This is not surprising. As attached as I am to my analogies, they're not all that accurate. Unlike a book publisher, a music publisher doesn't really manufacture anything; the music publisher owns the rights to the song, but not the CD or the MP3 on which the song is sold to the consumer. And unlike an agent with an actor, the publisher's real asset is the song, not the songwriter; a publisher owns the creation, not the creator. Confused? Yeah. You and my family.

So before you embark on your endeavor to make money from music—perhaps even to become your own music publisher, a quick history lesson is probably in order.

In the beginning, there was The Copyright. The idea of copyright law in the United States dates all the way back to 1790 and applies to any number of media: books, photos, inventions, and yes indeed, songs. Copyright law dictates that if you create it, you own it—and anyone that wants to use it must gain permission from you. When a songwriter writes a song, that song (or copyright) belongs to him or her, and all rights to use the song will require the permission and presumably the financial compensation of the songwriter. This basic principle of the copyright has held up pretty well since the eighteenth century, although the internet age has put it under fire as never before. We can only hope that it manages to hang on for at least a little while longer. If it doesn't, you and I both have big problems.

But back to the songwriter and his or her copyright. Into this happy union of Creator and Creation steps the middleman: The Publisher. Of course, the publishing business as it pertains to books has a venerable history, dating all the way back to the creation of printing technology in the fifteenth century. With all due respect to the hardworking monks who were writing out music back in the Dark Ages, music publishing has its roots a bit later, around the nineteenth century, when songs began to appear for sale to consumers in the form of sheet music. Then as now, the transaction was relatively simple: in order to make his or her song commercially available to the consumer, a songwriter would assign the "rights" to a publisher, who would then print up the sheet music, sell it (we hope), and then share the money with the songwriter (we hope).

Obviously, the sheet music business continues to be a viable business to the present day, and most of the large full-service music publishers have such a division within their corporate structure. But I want to be clear: the business of printing and selling sheet music is *not* the subject of this book. Not only do I know next to nothing about it, but what I do know would not lead me to suggest that a wise songwriter would try to act as his or her own sheet music publisher. Unless one really enjoys changing ink cartridges in the printer, I think the job of printing up music and selling it is probably better left to the experts.[1]

The subject of this book is contemporary music publishing, which is centered not around the sale of printed music, but on the sale or use of sound recordings. The process begins the same way: a songwriter creates a song (or "copyright") and then grants the rights to a music publisher. But now, the music publisher issues a license to a record company, which allows the company to sell a sound recording of the song in return for the payment of a royalty to the publisher. And of course, the publisher then shares that income with the songwriter.

---

[1] Though check out the print music self-publishing website www.arrangeme.com.

This writer-publisher relationship exists not only for those songwriters who have signed publishing contracts with big corporations or small independent companies, but also for songwriters who control their own publishing rights. If you're a songwriter who hasn't yet made a publishing agreement with someone else, you will get to wear two hats as you make your way through this process. When you're creating the song, you can wear your songwriter hat (think Stetson or maybe a beret). But when you are issuing licenses and collecting the money, it's time to put on your smart and stylish publisher hat. Even if the only songs you publish are your own, the fundamental activity of a publisher remains the same. You will issue licenses to those who wish to use or sell a sound recording of your song in exchange for a royalty or payment.

The royalty that is paid by the record company to the publisher and then to the songwriter is called a "mechanical" royalty, which refers to the fact that it comes from the sale of physical product like CDs or MP3 files, which are mechanically generated recordings. Mechanical royalties are one of the primary sources of income for most writers and publishers. But it is not the only form of income that the publisher derives from the copyright.

"Performance" royalties are payments made to the publisher by broadcasters, nightclub owners, department stores, you name it, in compensation for the licensing of public "performances " of the song. In short, this means that the songwriter receives a payment each time his or her song is played on the radio, television, on Spotify, in a concert hall, or even in a dentist's office. These payments are collected by the licensing organizations ASCAP, BMI, SESAC, or GRM, who then distribute the monies directly to writers and publishers based on the usage of any particular song (yes, they actually manage to keep track of that). Performance royalties are unique in that they are the only payments that flow directly to the writer without going through the hands of the publisher first. Every song's performance income is divided into equivalent "writer" and "publisher" shares. So a song that generates $10,000 in royalties for the writer will also generate $10,000 for the publisher, but the money is distributed directly to each party by the performing rights organization.

"Synchronization" fees (or sync fees) are a rapidly growing piece of the economic pie for music publishers. The term refers to music that is "synchronized" with a visual image, which is a fancy way of referring to songs that are used on television and in movies or advertisements. Unlike a mechanical royalty, which is a rate set by the U.S. government, or a performance royalty, which again is a set amount determined by the performing rights society, sync fees are negotiable. Sync fees range from very low or gratis to the absurd. (Note to file: if you make a low-budget film, do not plan to use "Shape of You" in the end credits). In most cases, a publisher is responsible for negotiating sync fees with the film or television company; the publisher is also responsible for collecting the money and distributing a portion back to the songwriter. What I like best about syncs is that they can provide a significant source of income for types of music that do not necessarily generate big sales numbers. The rock band Portugal the Man licensed "Feel It Still" to advertising campaigns for products ranging from iPads to vitamin water as well as five different television shows, and this exposure helped the single become the band's first entry on the *Billboard* Hot 100, going all the way to the number four.

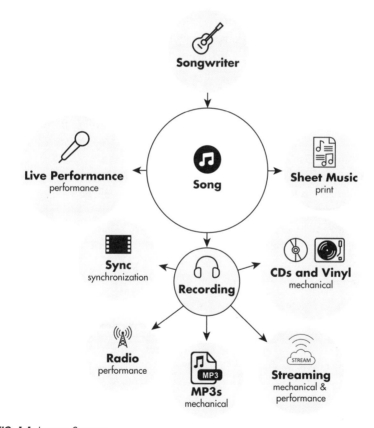

FIG. 1.1. *Income Sources*

In case your eyes are starting to glaze over at this point, which is usually what happens in my family at Christmas dinner, let's look at a simplified, almost-real-life example of the process in action.

The Creation

You, Talented Songwriter, have written a bona fide smash hit, touchingly titled "Your Copyright." At this point, you own the song and all the rights to it. But since you're only on the first chapter of this book, you're not quite sure how to properly publish the song. You need some help....

Enter Publisher.

Proving that you are not only talented, but also wise, you engage me, Music Business Weasel, to publish "Your Copyright," thereby granting to me the rights to license your new ditty. To keep this simple, we will suppose that you have granted me 100 percent of the publishing rights.

Welcome to the Record Business

Recognizing that "Your Copyright" is a song that will make an artist's career, a savvy record executive wants to record the song with Soon-to-Be-Very-Famous Artist. I, as the song's publisher, gladly grant the license to the record company, and the song is released. Of course, the song catapults STBVFA to fame, and the combined sales from the digital downloads and physical product comes to (for the sake of easy mathematics) one million units.

What's In It for Us

The current full statutory rate for a mechanical license is 9.1 cents per song, so the calculator tells us that the gross income that will be paid to me by the record company (remember, I'm the publisher) is $91, 000. Half of that amount ($45, 500) is considered the "songwriter's" share of the income. I then send to you an accounting statement, which details the sales of the record and the money that was paid to me, along with a check for the appropriate amount. I keep the other half of the money, which represents the "publisher's share."

It gets better.

Everywhere you go, you can't help hearing "Your Copyright" on the radio. This generates performance income, which is tracked by ASCAP, BMI, SESAC, and GMR. Remember, this money is paid in equal shares directly to the writer and the publisher by the performance society. So one happy day, while you are opening your mailbox to find a check from ASCAP, BMI, or SESAC, representing the writer's share of performance payments, I am receiving a matching check, which represents the publisher's share. Isn't this a good story?

And better . . .

"Your Copyright" is in the movies. Due to its now classic status, Hollywood Film Company wants to use the song as the theme of its big summer blockbuster. Again, as the publisher, it is up to me to negotiate the amount of the sync fee (think many 0s) and to collect the fee from Hollywood Film Company. And again, I will give you half of the money ("writer's share") and keep the other half ("publisher's share").

By now, it should be pretty obvious how a publishing company makes money. What may be less obvious is what a publisher is actually doing to earn that money, other than the vague "granting of licenses." What exactly does this "middleman" do to justify earning half the money generated by a song?

Plenty.

It is important to understand that the earlier example simply describes the flow of income from record company to publisher to songwriter. It does not describe the actual job of the music publisher, which is considerably more complex. There are five primary functions that are at the foundation of any effective music publishing operation, small or large:

- exploitation
- administration
- collection
- protection
- acquisition

Exploitation

In case you haven't noticed, songs do not generally find their own way into being recorded by a famous artist, into movies, or onto the radio. (Check the song files gathering dust in your iCloud for further proof of this.) For most songwriters, the primary value of a publisher is that of an ally in the never-ending struggle to get songs heard.

Please understand, the word "exploitation" has no negative connotations to a music publisher or a professional songwriter. In fact, it's just about the sweetest word in the dictionary. It simply describes the process by which a song finds some avenue to its audience, where it can begin to earn income for everyone involved.

Perhaps it's because this is what I happen to do for a living, but I believe that exploitation is the most important function of a publisher, and probably the most difficult to accomplish. For that reason, this book will focus disproportionately on the various opportunities and strategies for placing your music in money-making situations. It does not diminish the importance of any other publishing function to note that without exploitation, the other roles of a publisher are irrelevant. If the proverbial tree falls in the forest when no one's around, does it make a sound? I don't know. But I do know that a song that sits on a hard drive doesn't do much for anybody. A little exploitation never hurt.

In a large publishing company, the primary responsibility of exploitation will usually fall to what is termed the "Creative Department." These people, also referred to as professional managers or creative directors, are generally the ones stumbling into the office late, playing music loudly in their offices, running off to "pitch" meetings, or hanging out with the songwriters. It's a rough job, but someone has to do it.

Administration

Administration is the original function of the music publisher—the task of "administering" the copyrights. Simply put, this is the process of registering copyrights, issuing licenses, negotiating requests for reduced royalty rates, and sorting through the myriad of "paperwork" issues related to the use of copyrights.

As you'll see when we discuss this function in more detail, the administration of copyrights is a complex process that becomes more challenging as a publishing company grows. The more successful you are at exploitation, the more administration there is to be done. For this reason, many small publishing companies will do "administration" deals with a larger publisher. This sort of deal is generally a simple case of a smaller company shifting much of the paperwork burden to a larger firm. A large publisher might take on the responsibility of all administrative duties related to the smaller company's copyrights in exchange for a percentage (usually around 10 percent) of all the income generated by those songs.

It's never hard to locate the Administration Department in a music publishing company. Just follow the paper trail. When you find the offices with towering stacks of paper everywhere, you've entered the world of administration.

Collection

Music Business Weasel Says:
It's never easy to get paid.

Music Business Weasel

With songs potentially earning income in a vast variety of media, requiring royalty payments from any number of different record companies, sync fees from independent producers, film studios, and advertisers, and performance monies from licensing organizations all over the world, it can be more than a little daunting to keep track of who owes what, and where that money is supposed to go.

Needless to say, collection is a key aspect of the music publishing business. Remember, the publisher collects *all* the income generated by a copyright (except for the writer's share of performance payments, collected by ASCAP, BMI, or SESAC) and then distributes the appropriate percentage to the writer.

Any songwriter who's ever tried to decipher a royalty statement from a publisher will have some idea of the intricacies of this particular function. And any writer who has audited a publisher probably has some idea of how significantly small mistakes can add up.

Royalty by Source - Descending Total

Payee: REBH - Beall, Eric Summary

Royalty Period: 01 January 2019 to 30 June 2019

Page 1 of 11

Source	Mech	Perf	Digital	Synch	Sheet	Other	Total	Domestic	International
HFA - SPOTIFY - PREMIUM	0.00	0.00	1,913.48	0.00	0.00	0.00	1,913.48	1,913.48	0.00
HAL LEONARD PUB. CORP.	0.00	0.00	0.00	0.00	168.75	0.00	168.75	168.75	0.00
HFA - SPOTIFY - FREE	0.00	0.00	145.05	0.00	0.00	0.00	145.05	145.05	0.00
MCPS - Irish - Blanket	34.80	0.00	0.00	0.00	0.00	0.00	34.80	0.00	34.80
BMI - BET HER	0.00	18.94	0.00	0.00	0.00	0.00	18.94	18.94	0.00
YOUTUBE	0.00	0.00	18.12	0.00	0.00	0.00	18.12	18.12	0.00
JASRAC	3.77	9.34	0.38	0.00	0.00	0.00	13.49	0.00	13.49
HFA - APPLE MUSIC - INDV	0.00	0.00	12.22	0.00	0.00	0.00	12.22	12.22	0.00
COMP. & AUTHORS SOC. OF	0.00	9.20	0.00	0.00	0.00	0.00	9.20	0.00	9.20
NMPA P&U - SPOTIFY	0.00	0.00	8.07	0.00	0.00	0.00	8.07	8.07	0.00
GOOGLE PLAY - ALL ACCESS	0.00	0.00	6.81	0.00	0.00	0.00	6.81	6.81	0.00
PRS - BBC RADIO	0.00	6.80	0.00	0.00	0.00	0.00	6.80	0.00	6.80
BMI - MTV - CLASSIC	0.00	6.44	0.00	0.00	0.00	0.00	6.44	6.44	0.00
MCPS - NETFLIX GEOL	0.00	0.00	5.74	0.00	0.00	0.00	5.74	0.00	5.74
YOUTUBE PREMIUM - UGC - INDV	0.00	0.00	5.12	0.00	0.00	0.00	5.12	5.12	0.00
PRS - OVERSEAS INCOME	4.63	0.00	0.31	0.00	0.00	0.00	4.94	0.00	4.94
SPOTIFY - PREMIUM - UK	0.00	0.00	4.18	0.00	0.00	0.00	4.18	0.00	4.18
HFA - SONY MUSIC	0.07	0.00	3.98	0.00	0.00	0.00	4.06	4.06	0.00
HFA - APPLE MUSIC - FMLY	0.00	0.00	3.75	0.00	0.00	0.00	3.75	3.75	0.00
BMI - ENCORE - FAMILY	0.00	2.64	0.00	0.00	0.00	0.00	2.64	2.64	0.00
YOUTUBE - RED	0.00	0.00	2.57	0.00	0.00	0.00	2.57	2.57	0.00
AUSTRALASIAN PERFORMING RIGHT	0.00	0.02	2.51	0.00	0.00	0.00	2.53	0.00	2.53
BMI - PANDORA	0.00	0.00	2.29	0.00	0.00	0.00	2.29	2.29	0.00
PRS UK RECORDED	0.00	2.27	0.00	0.00	0.00	0.00	2.27	0.00	2.27
BMI - YOUTUBE	0.00	0.00	2.10	0.00	0.00	0.00	2.10	2.10	0.00
BMI - STARZ - KID & FAMILY	0.00	2.09	0.00	0.00	0.00	0.00	2.09	2.09	0.00
YOUTUBE - UK	0.00	0.00	1.98	0.00	0.00	0.00	1.98	0.00	1.98
iTUNES - GERMANY	0.00	0.00	1.61	0.00	0.00	0.00	1.61	0.00	1.61

IRVING MUSIC, INC.
2100 COLORADO AVENUE, SANTA MONICA, U.S.A. CA 90404-3504 Tel: 1888 474 4979

View or download your statements at www.royaltywindow.com
Or why not sign-up for our statement e-mail delivery service by e-mailing custservpubna@umusic.com

FIG. 1.2. A Page from a Royalty Statement

In a large publishing concern, the task of collecting the money is usually split between the Administration Department and the Royalties (or Accounting) Department. Royalty statements are traditionally issued to writers twice yearly—and when that happy season rolls around, you can spot the Royalty Department by the bags underneath their bloodshot eyes. Or the line of expectant songwriters waiting outside their offices.

Protection

It's a jungle out there. Once you begin to understand the value of a copyright, which can generate income over many, many years, you begin to understand the need to protect that valuable product. The publisher is responsible not only for exploiting a copyright, but protecting it from unwanted exploitation (which is usually when there is no appropriate compensation). This means resolving issues related to reduced royalty rates, unauthorized use of the song, unauthorized alteration of the song, and percentages of ownership between co-writers or co-publishers.

As many writers have learned, protection is not just a matter of protecting your song from those who might wish to infringe (read: steal) it. The accusations can easily flow the opposite way, with other writers accusing you of "stealing" their song. In these cases as well, it is a publisher's job to protect you and your copyright, whether that means negotiating a settlement, or if necessary, defending the copyright in court.

With the prevalence of sampling, some large publishers have now gone to the extent of establishing a Sample Department, which includes expert listeners responsible for uncovering any unauthorized "sampling" of their copyrights. Likewise, the policing of platforms like YouTube and TikTok requires publishers to carefully monitor a boundless sea of user-generated content for copyright violations. These days, you gotta watch your back....

Acquisition

You also have to look ahead. Publishers who want to grow their business beyond representing the songs of a single writer or band are always scouting for new talent, in an effort to keep up with the ever-changing tastes of the listening public. This function requires several skills from a publisher: the ability to accurately evaluate the skill of a developing songwriter or the commercial potential of a particular song, the savvy to know at what price new music can be acquired, and the persuasiveness to convince a songwriter to turn over control of his or her beloved copyrights.

Acquisition is usually a function of the Creative Department. It's a job that is at once the most tedious role in the publishing company, and the most thrilling. It means listening to a ceaseless supply of demo recordings (mostly bad), spending long evenings in dingy clubs (mostly dark and loud), and poring through pages of industry trade magazines (who every week find the Next Big Thing, which almost never is). It also means every once in a while finding an undiscovered song or songwriter that is truly unique or special— the rough equivalent of a very small needle in a very large haystack. The excitement of hearing a *hit* before anyone else, and having an opportunity to play a part in bringing that song into the world, is what keeps most of us in the business of music publishing.

Exploitation, administration, collection, protection, and acquisition. If you're a songwriter, I know what you're thinking. "What about that part that I like best? The part where publishers pay writers money they haven't earned yet . . . "

Ah, yes. The writer advance. While it is not one of the primary functions of a music publisher, the role of Songwriters Central Savings and Loan is one that has come to define the publishing business, particularly with respect to the large corporations that dominate the modern music publishing industry. For many songwriters, the music publisher is perceived primarily as a bank, willing to loan money in the form of "advances," which will then be repaid to the publisher from the songwriter's future earnings. Here's how it works.

When seeking to acquire a desirable copyright, or to sign a promising writer to an exclusive publishing agreement (which simply means that the publisher is acquiring rights to all of the writer's copyrights for a set period of time), a publisher frequently finds that personal charm, vague promises of stardom, and a couple of pricey lunches are not enough to close the deal. In order to convince the songwriter to grant the publisher the rights to the desired copyrights, the publisher must also fork up some cash.

As with almost everything in show business, the amount of the advance paid to a songwriter can vary wildly, from the paltry for a young, unproven writer, to the astronomical, for an established hit-maker or the hot new buzz band. In addition, a publisher may also agree to pay for other items, such as demo recording costs, travel, or equipment rentals. This will usually be labeled an "additional advance." But whatever the amount, a songwriter should remember that any advance is always recoupable. This means that the writer will not be paid a percentage of the income generated by his or her copyrights until the publisher has recovered the amount of the advance. An advance is not a wage or a fee paid to the writer. It is an interest-free loan against future earnings.

Music Business Weasel Says:
There are no money-back guarantees.

Music Business Weasel

A publisher must remember that an advance can only be recouped from future earnings. It will not be repaid by a writer whose songs fail to earn back the amount of the advance. If you're going to be in the banking business, then bankers rules apply: make your loans only to those people you are pretty sure can pay them back. The amount of an advance should reflect what you believe a writer, under reasonable circumstances, can earn from his or her songs. The advance should not be based on how badly you want to sign the writer, or what the writer needs, or what others in the industry would pay the writer. Because of their financial structure, large publishers can sometimes offer an advance that far exceeds what they believe a writer can actually earn. But if you are playing with your own money, prudence is always the better part of valor.

While it is not an integral part of the music publishing business, the writing of an advance check has become such an important part of the publisher's role that we could probably add one more function to the Big Five—let's call it *capitalization*. By advancing money on future earnings, a publisher is giving the writer the money he or she needs to survive and grow the business as they feel necessary. In this book, we will not devote a great deal of space to this particular function, as I doubt most readers are eager to begin handing out thousands of dollars in advances to their songwriting cronies. Nevertheless, it is important to understand that it is a strategy employed aggressively by all of the major publishers. It is also important to understand how you and your fledgling publishing business may someday be able to obtain access to that capital from a larger company wishing to enter into a partnership with you.

Pennies from Heaven

Given the music publisher's role as a "middleman" in the process of turning a song into a record, music publishing exists somewhat in the shadows of the music industry. And yet, at least until the Spotify era, the music publishing divisions of the major music corporations were often more profitable than their flashier, more media-friendly record label cohorts. Because of inequities in the economic framework of the digital streaming business, record labels have seen an explosive growth over the past few years that has eluded their publishing divisions. Nevertheless, music publishing remains a key component to the business structure of any major music company.

Sometimes ridiculed as a "pennies" business, publishing is a testament to the truth that pennies add up. If properly cared for, a classic song can continue to generate many pennies worth of income year after profitable year. As the amount of media opportunities for music exploitation continues to increase (think about the endless flood of entertainment programming coming out of Amazon, Netflix, Disney, and HBO, not to mention satellite radio, streaming services, and YouTube), music publishing is a consistently growing business, with revenues in 2019 of 10 billion dollars. (Source: *Music Business Worldwide*) While it may not get you the front-row seats at the Grammys, success as a music publisher can nevertheless be highly rewarding. Ask Berry Gordy, the legendary founder of Motown, who sold 50 percent of his publishing entity, Jobete Music, to EMI Publishing in 1997 for over $132 million. Or Bob Dylan, who sold his publishing catalog to Universal Music Publishing in 2020 for what was rumored to be over $300 million. And remember, these companies were started by individual entrepreneurs—songwriters who were prescient enough to build their copyrights into empires.

Now if you can explain all that to my grandmother, you're invited over for Christmas dinner.

2

Wait! This Doesn't Sound Like My Music Business....

Now that we've looked at the fundamentals of music publishing, you may be even more confused than before. The problem is not your difficulty in understanding the concept of music publishing. What's really confusing is trying to understand how it applies to the music business you're in.

The truth is, we are living in a time in which the music industry is being reinvented every day in a thousand different ways. Certainly, there are booming songwriting communities, particularly in Los Angeles, Nashville, and London, that still work in the traditional ways: finding out which big or soon-to-be-big artist is looking for songs, getting together with other songwriters to try to write for that artist, and collecting the income generated from radio, sales, and synchronization when those songs find a home. For those working in this traditional context, the explanation in chapter 1 probably sounded pretty familiar, and each of the five functions of the music publisher felt more relevant than the last.

But what if that isn't really the music business you're in? Let's say you're an artist who releases your own music independently. Or you're signed to a small label who simply splits the income with you 50/50 but has never heard of mechanical royalties. Or you're a producer who makes beats, or a topliner who sells your work online. Or you make music for a music production library for use in television or advertising. The explanation in chapter 1 might make sense in the abstract, but a bigger question is raised: "What does all this mean to me?"

Even within the more traditional sides of the music industry, the past decade has brought transformative changes in the way that songs generate income. Streaming on platforms such as Spotify and Apple have replaced physical sales and iTunes. YouTube and SoundCloud have replaced MTV and maybe even radio. In a time when everything is changing, music publishing must be changing too, right?

Actually, not so much. The underlying principle of music publishing is the simple idea of copyright: you created it, therefore you own it, and no one can profit from it without your permission. Because of this rock-solid foundation, the fundamentals have changed less than you might think. The legal principle of copyright doesn't go away just because someone created new technology or a different business model. If a song is created, then either the creator or the person/company to which the creator assigns control of the right to copy is the "publisher," even if they're not sure they know what that role entails.

No matter if the goal of a songwriter is to have his or her song streamed digitally on Amazon, pressed onto vinyl, performed in a Broadway show, or posted on BeatStars, whoever controls the copyright still needs to find those opportunities for exploitation, administer the licenses, collect the money, and protect the song. The challenge is understanding how to apply these functions to some of the new business models and digital service providers. For anyone who has followed the last decade in the music industry, it will not be surprising to learn that publishers are still figuring out how to do that.

Independents' Day

This is truly the age of the independent musician. Some are putting music out on their own label; others release music through an independent distributor or an indie label whose business model is based on a split of all income with the artist. For these artists, the appeal is not only the easy access to the market but also the simplicity of accounting. The money comes into the label or distributor; they take their cut and send the rest to the artist. No mess, no stress, and no publishing problems to sort through, right?

But what if the artist co-writes the songs with someone else—maybe even someone already signed to a publishing agreement with another company? What if the artist is part of a band, and only three of five members in the group are involved with the writing? What happens if one of those writers wants to assign their publishing to a larger company in exchange for an advance, or even sell out entirely?

Ah yes, music publishing rears its ugly head once again. If you are releasing your own music and not accounting for mechanical royalties, you're not changing the way music publishing functions. You're just choosing an alternative accounting method—one that's simple, but sloppy. Likewise, if you work with an indie label or digital distributor that consolidates all of your income into one payment, part of that money is for publishing income, whether or not you recognize it.

The key concept to understand, especially for those working in the independent world, is the distinction between a sound recording and a composition. For every "song" that you make available in the marketplace, no matter if it's on Spotify or a special issue vinyl album you sell at shows, there are always *two* copyrights, not one: the copyright on the master recording and the copyright on the composition.

The Copyright on the Master Recording

The copyright on the master recording applies to the actual recording of the song. It's a record of a specific performance by a specific artist made at a specific time. This became a pivotal issue during the great media war of 2019 between Taylor Swift and music business mogul Scooter Braun, which brought to public light the complicated relationship between artists and the ownership of the recordings they create. As those who followed the drama learned, the original master recordings for many of Taylor's biggest hits, from "Our Song" to "Blank Space," were not owned by the artist herself, but rather by the record company for which she recorded them at that time, which was Big Machine Label Group. This is fairly typical. The record company pays for the costs of the recording, pays the artist a royalty for what is sold, and in return owns the copyright for the master recording. Even though Taylor left Big Machine in 2018 to sign with Universal Music Group, the copyrights for those recordings from the earlier years in her career remained in the control of Big Machine.

When Big Machine's owner Scott Borchetta decided to sell the company's assets to Scooter, Taylor Swift went on a full-scale social media attack, venting her frustration that she had no control over her own recordings. This was probably aggravated by the fact that she received no share in Big Machine's rumored $300 million selling price. Immediately after the sale, Taylor announced her intention to rerecord her early albums, creating 2020-generation versions of the records that catapulted her to success a decade earlier.

So while Scooter Braun and his company Ithaca Holdings LLC would own the original copyrights, Taylor Swift would own the copyrights for the new performances, the ones recorded in 2020. At that point, there would be two master recordings of hits like "Love Story": the original 2008 version owned by Ithaca Holdings, and the new Taylor-approved and controlled version from 2020. For those who are already starting to get confused, you can take some solace in this: the copyrights that apply to the various "master recordings" actually have nothing to do with music publishing.

The Copyright on the Composition: "The Underlying Copyright"

The copyright on the composition (i.e., the "underlying copyright") is the one that matters to music publishers. For example, the song "Love Story"—that instantly identifiable combination of melody, lyric, and chord progression—is owned by the songwriter Taylor Swift and controlled by her very happy publisher, Sony ATV. Every version of that song, regardless of who owns the master recording, must be licensed by Sony ATV, and royalties must be paid to them for the income that any master recording generates. The song is the copyright that "underlies" all of the different recordings.

This is also why Taylor Swift's strategy of rerecording her early catalog could be so effective. As the songwriter, Taylor must authorize Sony ATV to license any use of her songs in the synchronization market (films, television, advertising). So she could simply instruct Sony ATV that the only uses she will permit are those using the Taylor-owned master recordings. At that point, Ithaca Holdings would be left with a collection of very important early recordings of a superstar that can't be licensed anywhere. Shake it off, indeed.

For each song, like "Love Story," there is one copyright for the composition (controlled by Taylor and Sony ATV) and one copyright for each master recording: one for the original 2008 master recording (owned by Ithaca Holdings) and one for the new master recording that Taylor intends to make. Controlling the copyright for a master recording is definitely not the same as controlling the copyright for the song itself.

The problem with some independent business models is that they try to converge these separate copyrights—master and publishing—into one. Under the assumption that the singer is also the songwriter, they make one payment to the artist for all the income (after the label takes its share) and ignore the need for mechanical licenses and the corresponding mechanical royalties.

If you are a solo artist, you write all your own songs, and you never record anything where another writer is involved, this probably works reasonably well—at least, in the short term. But if there are other writers participating on some or all of the songs, you are short-changing yourself or the other writers if you don't break the publishing income out separately on any royalty statements. If you're receiving airplay or streaming activity anywhere in the world, some money from the radio stations or streaming services is going directly to collection agencies in every country in the world for performance and mechanical royalties. You will not be able to collect the money that belongs to you as a songwriter unless you've done the administrative work of a publisher, by registering the song in each different territory.

The attempt to combine master income and publishing income almost never works out well. This is why most digital service providers now pay publishing royalties directly to publishers or collection entities such as the Mechanical Licensing Collective (for mechanical income) or ASCAP, BMI, or SESAC (for performances). Likewise, most independent distributors are now offering publishing "administration" services as part of their product offering, although assigning your publishing rights by clicking a box is not the solution I would recommend.

The ownership shares on many songs are too complex, the income is generated across too many territories, and the potential value of a publishing catalog is too significant to simply roll all the income into your digital distributor's royalty statement and just split the money among the people in the band. Even as an independent musician, sooner or later you will need to exploit your songs (whether it's your recording of them or an alternative version), register them around the world, collect the money that's being generated in each territory, and protect your song against copyright infringement. I'd say that makes you a publisher. If it looks like a duck and quacks like a duck, it is—even in this time of independence—a duck.

The Beat Market

One of the things I love about songwriters is the blend of infinite ingenuity and street-level hustle many of them bring to navigating through the maze of the music industry, trying to make it around a thousand closed doors. No genre better displays this unbridled entrepreneurial spirit than hip-hop, which makes it the best spot to see the future of music publishing, with all of its challenges and opportunities.

In their determination to get music out to the public as quickly as possible, most hip-hop producers treat music publishing as completely irrelevant. From its very beginnings, when songs like "Rappers Delight" were built on replayed versions of disco classics like Chic's "Good Times," all the way to songs like Travis Scott's "Sicko Mode," which lists thirty different songwriters, hip-hop has often operated outside of the standard structures of music publishing. Loops are taken from bits of existing recordings, hooks are lifted from well-known songs, beats are "sold" in online stores or from sample packages, and feature performances are added in exchange for one-time fees. In almost every sense, it is a publisher's worst nightmare.

But still, the laws of copyright win out. While hip-hop has repeatedly pushed copyright law to its limits, in the end, even this genre is forced to conform to the old principle of "you wrote it, you own it; everyone else needs a license." Sooner or later, samples taken from existing songs have to be cleared by gaining permission from the original publisher, in exchange for a percentage of ownership in the new copyright, a one-time fee, or a settlement payment in a lawsuit. New twists on familiar hooks, like "Wild Thoughts" by DJ Khaled, need similar permissions. A beat "sold" directly or through a website can be treated as an exclusive license or a buy-out, or done on a non-exclusive basis, which must then be licensed if it's used on a commercial recording. Any feature performance in which a rapper both performs on the record and creates his or her own rap must be either a "work for hire" or considered part of the new composition, with the featured rapper getting a share as a songwriter.

It's complex and sometimes ugly, but it's still music publishing. Any publisher working in hip-hop has sampled or been sampled, read and reread the fine print on a sample pack, negotiated featured artist agreements, and registered an endless array of derivative titles, one for each new feature. If this is your market, you can expect to negotiate split agreements more complex than an international peace treaty and see more legal battles than Judge Judy. You'll not only be a music publisher. You'll be a very busy music publisher.

Those who work in the mainstream pop or electronic dance music world face similar challenges. In addition to a frequent use of samples, loops, interpolations, and sound packages, this music is often composed through a process in which songwriters create a traditional song (melody/lyric/chord progression) and then send that off to a DJ/producer who subsequently adds the track (drums, bass, keyboards, thirty-second-note snare rolls). In return, the producer usually expects to share in a portion of the "new song." This invariably leads to a lot of soul-searching, contentious discussions of what constitutes a "song." In the end, there's usually a concession by the original writers to give up part of the ownership of the original song (because the DJ has three million Spotify followers, and you don't).

There are almost no set rules in these particular markets, because the people who work in them would figure out a way to work around them as soon as the rules were made. Everything is a negotiation. But as you'll see in parts II and III, negotiation is a fundamental part of the job of being a music publisher. Read those chapters well. They will be the story of your life.

Music Production Libraries

If hip-hop complicates the role of a music publisher, the music production library business simplifies it—maybe a little more than would be desirable. Music production libraries range wildly in size and business model, but in general, they provide low-cost music for synchronization uses, most often on a non-exclusive basis. This means that the same song could be used hundreds of times: on a sports broadcast, a TV show, a low-budget film, or an Internet advertising campaign. While some songwriters have their own production libraries, most songwriters who do this type of work are signed in some way to a larger company who represent a wide catalog of styles and moods.

These businesses have a music publishing aspect to them, but their model is more limited than a traditional publisher. They are certainly in the business of acquisition and exploitation, although their efforts tend to be almost exclusively in the area of synchronization. They do register songs at the performing rights organizations around the world. Likewise, they certainly collect income, though they do not always distribute to the writers, as the writers often receive only the writer share of performance income, which comes to them directly from ASCAP or BMI. While the need for protection in this line of work is far less than in the hip-hop world, music production libraries do fill that role as well, guarding vigilantly against unlicensed (or unpaid) uses.

The primary difference between traditional music publishers and music production libraries is that of focus. Unlike the traditional publisher, who tends to prioritize the development of "hit" songs that can then be licensed to the synchronization world for high prices, libraries focus on developing a wide client base (networks, ad agencies, branding companies, film studios) who will pay them a fee for permission to use any song in the library. Music libraries succeed based on *volume*—the granting of many small, non-exclusive licenses—while publishers generally aim to succeed on *value*—a smaller number of licenses granted with a greater degree of exclusivity for much higher prices. Nevertheless, the principles of publishing remain unchanged. It's merely a question of different business models to service the needs of different types of clients.

All the Music in the World at the Touch of a Button. Who's Paying?

Just as new business structures have been sprouting like wildfire in the music publishing sector, the distribution side of the music industry has seen even greater disruptions, all of which have had massive effects on the music publishing business—many of them negative. As most songwriters have realized as they stare in shock at their royalty statements, digital services like Spotify, YouTube, Pandora, and SoundCloud have had a transformative impact on music publishing.

To be honest, I can understand why many digital services relegated music publishing to a secondary concern as they launched their services in the early 2000s. Unlike a master recording, which can usually be licensed through one specific record company, obtaining a license for the song is an exceedingly messy business. Songs have multiple parties involved (each individual writer and their publisher), the publishers change frequently as songwriters leave one publisher for another or sell their copyrights altogether, and there is not yet a central database to find out who currently owns the copyright. If your goal is to quickly license all the music in the world and put it on your site, a messy business is exactly what you want to avoid.

Nevertheless, after a barrage of copyright infringement lawsuits, multi-million dollar settlements from companies like Spotify, and ultimately, the passage in the United States of the Music Modernization Act in 2018, digital services have been forced to acknowledge that music publishing is more than a minor inconvenience. When a song shows up on Pandora or Amazon, or a video goes up on YouTube, it's not just a recording by a particular artist that is being used. It's also the song itself. As always, this means that the music publisher who controls the copyright for the song has to grant permission and be compensated. While the war over what is a fair rate of compensation continues to rage, most digital services have put systems in place to license and pay royalties to publishers for the songs used on their service.

Here's how it works.

Interactive Streaming

We'll deal with the toughest one first. Anyone who follows the music biz knows that it has never been smooth sailing between the music business and the digital service providers (DSPs) who provide interactive streaming services—the ones in which the customer can choose to listen to specific tracks. Spotify has been the most contentious player in the game, and the struggle between music publishers and Spotify continues to grab headlines. YouTube and music publishers have had their battles as well, though that relationship seems to have gone from the heated arguments and wild accusation stage to the quiet bickering of an old married couple. Apple Music has been an exception, largely avoiding the rancorous conflicts with music publishers that have afflicted their competitors.

But for all of the fighting between the DSPs and the music industry, the reality is that most of the punches are being thrown over "how much" the digital services will pay. The right of music publishers to license the use of their songs on the digital services and the process by which they do that is accepted by everyone on both sides.

Spotify, Amazon, Pandora, Google, Apple, Tidal

To go back to the terms we introduced in chapter 1, it has been established that an interactive digital stream is both a "mechanical use" (because a stream is a mechanical reproduction of the song that replaces the need for a physical product or even an MP3) and a "performance" (because the stream is also a broadcast). This means that companies like Spotify and Apple must obtain mechanical licenses for each song available on the service and pay a corresponding mechanical royalty. At the same time, the services also need to obtain a performance license through ASCAP, BMI, SESAC, or GMR and pay out a performance royalty to those agencies, who then pass the money on to publishers and writers.

YouTube

YouTube adds an additional wrinkle by introducing the element of visuals. Thinking back to chapter 1, this visual element means there is a "synchronization" right involved, because the song is being synchronized to a visual image. Technically, YouTube would need a mechanical license (for the stream), a performance license (for the broadcast), and a synchronization license (for the use of the visual). Because synchronization licenses are the only licenses for which there is no set rate, it's obvious that life could get pretty difficult for YouTube. Imagine having to negotiate each use of every song in the background of a cat video.

To avoid such a nightmare scenario, YouTube, which is owned by Google, negotiated an agreement for the payment of a portion of the advertising revenue generated by any video that is monetized. (A video is "monetized" when there are advertisements running prior to the video.) If a publisher finds a video of its song on YouTube, it has the choice to monetize the clip and take a share of the income, or to take down the video entirely. The system requires an absurd level of policing, for which small publishers often call upon outside services like Audiam. But at least there is a pot of gold at the end of the rainbow for publishers willing to pursue the "protection," "collection," and "administration" roles with a vengeance.

TikTok

To see music publishers in full "protector" mode, just tune into the ongoing drama at TikTok, the latest entry in the digital music sweepstakes. Much like YouTube in its early years, TikTok launched with an almost complete disregard for copyright law; virtually every video constituted an infringement. At the same time, many record labels embraced the format because of the obvious promotional value and the potential to launch a viral hit.

But like police at a frat party, it was only a matter of time before the music publishers stepped in and threatened to shut things down. In 2019, the National Music Publishers Association encouraged the U.S. government to take action against TikTok, labeling it a copyright infringer that has failed to obtain licenses for many of the works used on the site. It is true that TikTok put preliminary agreements in place with a small number of publishers, probably thinking that those agreements would give them access to most of the songs that their audience was likely to use. But that sort of "close enough for government work" idea doesn't really fly when it comes to copyright. Even one song used without a license can become a million-dollar liability for the company doing the infringing.

Because TikTok is owned by Chinese company ByteDance, there's an extra added air of international intrigue with this particular case. But for the most part, it's a good example of publishers doing what they're supposed to do. They spot infringement issues, take action to protect their songs, and in the end, negotiate with these new services in order to issue licenses and generate income for the songwriters. From player pianos and the first days of radio broadcasting all the way to services like TikTok, the process has been much the same. Sure enough, by 2020, the National Music Publishers Association announced an agreement with TikTok that provided for a multi-year licensing agreement as well as compensation for the past unauthorized uses. Whatever technology dishes up, sooner or later, publishers have always found a way to monetize the use of their music. Hence the title of this book.

"That's all great," I can hear you saying, "but what about the 'how much' part? How much does the publisher and songwriter make from a stream on Spotify or view on YouTube?" That's a subject we'll dig into further a little later in this book. It's also one in which the answers are always changing. The payment formula, based on the service's revenue, the total number of songs streamed each month, and the price of a subscription is far too variable for me to give you a specific "rate" that you can expect to earn.

And even if I could, it could all change tomorrow....

The Music Modernization Act: Reimagining the Music Business

Depending on when you're reading this, the Music Modernization Act may be seen as a game-changer that saved the music publishing business, a folly that could never actually be realized, or a well-meaning attempt to induce order into the chaos of a music industry outpaced by technology. Hard to tell.

This legislation, passed by Congress in 2018, was driven by the National Music Publishers Association and the Songwriters of North America (SONA) to address the harsh effects of the new digital streaming environment on the music industry as a whole, but on music publishers in particular. Its grand innovation is the proposed creation of a Mechanical Licensing Collective, a sort of ASCAP or BMI for mechanical rights, which will be able to grant what are called "blanket" licenses to the digital service providers to use any music they wish, and which will be able to collect licensing fees from those services and redistribute the money to music publishers and songwriters.

As the Mechanical Licensing Collective starts its engines and rumbles into action in 2021, it will certainly change the role of music publishers in respect to their "administration" and "collection" functions, making it easier and faster for publishers large and small to license the myriad of services using music and to collect from them. Ultimately, the Music Modernization Act aims to change the "how" of music publishing: how songs are registered, how licenses are granted, how rates are negotiated, and how money is collected—with the goal of ultimately changing the "how much" side of the equation. The hope is that the bill will help publishers to both lower their administrative costs and raise the royalty rates being paid by the digital services.

Whatever changes the Music Modernization Act brings to the industry, it will not diminish the role of music publishers. If anything, the MMA is intended to reaffirm the fact that a songwriter has the right to control his or her work, license it, and be paid fairly for it. That principle is the basis for all music publishing, and it endures through every new business model or technological advance.

Music Business Weasel Says:
Songwriting without music publishing is a hobby.

For all the different types of "music industries" that exist in the 21st century, songwriting is not actually one of them. There is no business of songwriting; there never was. It's just something you do. At the beginning of the day, no song exists. Later that afternoon, a new piece of music has been brought into the world. But no money has changed hands. Songwriting only becomes a business when a song is released on Spotify, placed in a television show, played on the radio or in a bar, or used in a TikTok video. Suddenly, we're right back to the five functions of a music publisher. That's because songwriting is an art. Music publishing is the business of songwriting.

There's one clause in every music publishing or recording contract that's always amused me. It provides that whatever rights the music publisher or record label has, they apply to every technology known or unknown, as yet undiscovered, on every planet in every galaxy now known or unknown, etc., etc., etc. The language always struck me as a masterful bit of legal overreach.

But having seen the transition from vinyl records to CDs to Napster to MP3 and iTunes to YouTube and Spotify and undoubtedly to something else in the very near future, I'm starting to have more sympathy for the lawyers' attempts to cover every potentiality. This industry is constantly being remade, both by outside forces like technology as well as the creativity of its artists and the changing tastes of its audience. Music publishing's role, pure and simple, is to be sure that whatever happens, someone pays for the song.

If you want to hear the music, you have to pay the piper, whether through technology now existing or heretofore undiscovered, in galaxies now existing, or that come to exist in the future....

3

Start with the Song

Every great endeavor has to begin somewhere, and if you're going to launch your own music publishing venture, there's really only one thing that will get you started . . .

Songs. You need songs. Preferably good ones, and ideally, a healthy number of them. Because whatever you've got at the moment is your catalog. The first step toward becoming your own publisher is to come to grips with what will be the primary assets of your business: songs.

As I mentioned in chapter 1, this book will be directed primarily toward songwriters interested in developing their own publishing company. So I will assume that you already have a collection of songs sufficient to get you started in this game. If not, you may want to skip ahead to chapter 24 "Acquisitions: The Final Frontier." But make sure that you come back to this chapter, because taking stock of your catalog is never quite as simple as it seems.

The first question to consider is this:

Do You Own the Songs?

Of course you do. You wrote them, right? If you write a song, you own that copyright, both the writer's share and the publisher's share. You are not only the writer; you are also the publisher. But are you the only writer and publisher?

That gets a little trickier. If you wrote the song with someone else, you now own a portion of the song, which leads to a whole new set of questions:

What percentage of the song did you write?

Many songwriters assume that this is a matter of simple arithmetic: divide 100 percent of the song by the number of writers involved. That is to say, if there are two writers, each gets 50 percent of the song; if there are three, each of them gets one-third. Nice, tidy, and egalitarian. But not very realistic.

Imagine for instance that you wrote a song with the guy who has the recording studio next door. You wrote all of the lyrics, and three-quarters of the music. Your friendly neighbor programmed the drums and contributed a chord progression that eventually became the bridge of the song. Is your neighbor entitled to half of the song?

Maybe. As a songwriter, I prefer to stick with the easy formula and split everything equally (probably because it's the only way I can manage the math). But many writers would disagree, particularly in an instance as one-sided as the one above. There are many factors that could figure into this, including whether the lyrics and music were written after the drums were programmed (and thus, presumably inspired by them), the prominence of the bridge section, and the amount of guidance, suggestions, or hand-holding the co-writer provided while you were coming up with the bulk of the song. You should probably also consider the place of that co-writer in the music industry food chain. If he or she is a big fish (are there a lot of very shiny plaques on the studio wall?), or at least a bigger fish than you, I guarantee that the co-writer is expecting at least half of the song.

Writer splits are a touchy subject, and rarely as straightforward as they might appear. The hard truth is that the percentages on a song are entirely negotiable. I know of many writers who have wound up with two or three percent of a song, which definitely takes some of the thrill out of the experience if the song becomes a hit. The only way to deal with this issue is through an open and frank dialogue with your co-writer—sounds like marriage counseling, right? You must somehow, some way, reach an agreement as to what percentage of the composition is owned by each writer.

Then you *must* get it in writing in a "split sheet." A split sheet is a simple document that outlines the basic agreement between the writers regarding the ownership of the song. It should document the date the song was written, the writers involved, and the percentages controlled by each writer and publisher. It must be signed by each writer; each writer and publisher should maintain a copy. (You can find one version of a split sheet in appendix A.) The verbiage of the letter can vary, so long as it clearly states the correct shares of the song. The crucial point is that it must be signed by all writers, and you must keep a copy of it on file.

If you do not have split sheets for the songs in your catalog, you need to go back and get them. Yes, I'm aware that you and your co-writers are friends, and that you're all pretty laid back about this, and that this seems a little awkward, and you're sure everyone will be cool about it if something happens with the song. Trust me on this. I have seen twenty-year partnerships dissolve over petty split disputes. I have also learned that split discussions never become disputes until something good is about to happen with a song. The best time to have a discussion about percentages is before or during the writing session itself; the second-best time is immediately afterward. The single worst time to have the conversation is when it absolutely cannot be avoided, which is when someone has already recorded the song.

If your co-writer is signed to a larger publishing company, that publisher may have a split sheet that they use, which is perfectly sufficient. Likewise, if you're working with an artist signed to a record label, the label will likely send a letter clarifying the writer and publisher shares prior to scheduling a release. Some European writers prefer to simply use the song registration or deposit form at their performing rights society as a record of the agreed upon splits. This works only because most European societies require that the form be signed by all writers, whereas ASCAP and BMI do not. It doesn't matter who documents the splits, so long as all the writers sign and the percentages add up to 100. (I once waited months for a group of writers to settle the splits, but when they finally delivered the agreement to me, the shares added up to 112.75). However you do it, the first step toward organizing your catalog is determining exactly what percentage of each song belongs to you as a writer.

What percentage of the song do you publish?

Didn't we just talk about this? If you wrote 50 percent of the song, then you control your 50 percent of the publisher's share, right? Maybe. Let's go back to that hypothetical co-write with your neighbor. Was that co-write suggested or arranged by another publisher? If so, that publisher may expect a percentage of the publishing for anything written during those sessions. And what about your neighbor's recording studio? If he demoed the song at his studio, at his cost, then he may be expecting a greater portion of the publishing in return.

Or let's look at this from your side. Here you are, preparing to become your own publisher—ready to hit the streets peddling this new song like a professional, while your co-writer retires to the quiet privacy of his studio. Suppose you manage to place this song on a record or in a movie. Perhaps you should be asking to publish your neighbor's share. (This would give you 100 percent of the publisher's share of the song.) Come to think of it, that's a pretty good idea. Keep that one in mind.

Again, it is important that you never assume that you know the splits on a song, whether it concerns the writer's share or the publisher's share. I would never encourage you to try to take unfair advantage of a co-writer. That is a surefire strategy for a very short career. Nor would I suggest that you give up your own share of the publishing without reason. But song splits are always subject to negotiation, and you should not be hesitant about broaching the subject. Be sure that the publisher's share, as well as the writer's share, is clearly delineated in the split letter.

Are you sure that you own the songs?

Let's dig a little deeper. If you wrote the songs by yourself, was there anyone else in the room at the time, perhaps engineering or helping program the track? While you may be quite confident that their input wasn't really part of the writing process, they may be less sure.

How about samples? In many instances, clearing one well-known sample or interpolation from a major artist can require giving up 75 percent or more, sometimes even 100 percent, of the new copyright. (An "interpolation" is the appropriation of another song's melody or lyric, without the use of the original sound recording as in a sample. A good example would be the use of "My Favorite Things" in "7 Rings" by Ariana Grande.) This is not necessarily an argument against samples or interpolations, which are simply a part of the modern songwriting landscape. Nor would I necessarily say that you need to clear all samples immediately. Generally speaking, you can clear a sample once your song is slated to be released commercially. But be aware that if you've stuck a nice big chunk of a classic record into your "new" song, you own a lot less of that song than you think you do. You might not own any of it at all.

And then of course, there's every songwriter's worst nightmare. "Does this song sound like something familiar to you?" The subject of copyright infringement generally conjures up an image of nefarious behavior—a scoundrel listening through the keyhole as you compose your masterpiece, only to steal it out from under you. In my experience, most copyright infringement cases in the songwriting business are entirely unconscious. They are a matter of a writer unknowingly reprising a song lodged somewhere in his or her subconscious. It happens.

I know of one songwriter who waited years for a breakthrough hit, finally finding himself with a potential number one record. On the day that the song hit the top of *Billboard's* Hot 100, he received a call. He was being sued for copyright infringement by a superstar artist, who not coincidentally happened to be the writer's childhood idol. Of course, the writer had spent a lifetime absorbing this superstar's music, listening until he knew each song by heart. Unfortunately, he didn't recognize until that moment that he had just rewritten one of his hero's classic songs. This is to be avoided.

While you can never entirely safeguard yourself against copyright owner-ship issues, it is essential that in your role as publisher, you try to loosen some of the personal attachment you have to the songs in your catalog and examine any concerns carefully. This is particularly true as it pertains to infringement issues. Don't fool yourself. If something sounds like it might be a problem, it probably is. Many copyright issues can be resolved through negotiation, but you must deal with it sooner rather than later. It's all part of understanding your catalog.

If it seems like I'm harping a bit on this issue of copyright ownership, that's because I am. I've had the experience of working with a large catalog of songs, in which there are constant questions about writer and publisher percentages. I also know from experience that nothing quite makes your day like finally nailing down a commercial release for one of the best hidden gems in your catalog, only to find that you don't own the song at all. In the best cases, you will have just done someone a big favor, which will earn you some good karma but not much else. In the worst cases, you will damage your relationship with the record company, film studio, or advertising agency to whom you pitched the song, and you could find yourself in court with the song's real publisher. This is a business, and the first order of the day is to know exactly what you've got to sell.

Of course, there's more to understanding your catalog than just the ques-tion of ownership. The other question that comes immediately to mind is:

Are These Songs Any Good?

Ouch. That cuts a little close to the bone, especially if you wrote the songs. But if the first thing you must establish as a publisher is ownership of your catalog, then certainly the second thing is objectivity about your catalog. Perhaps the greatest benefit to becoming your own publisher is to acquire some degree of objectivity about your own work, and for a few moments at least, be able to stand on the outside of the writing process and make judg-ments regarding how your songs will actually function in the industry.

When I first made the transition from writer to publisher, the one question I heard over and over from my songwriter buddies was, "So what's it like on the other side of the desk?" The answer was that I could now see much more clearly how rare a real "hit" song really is. A songwriter who creates three or four genuine "hits" over the course of a twenty-year career probably belongs in the Songwriters Hall of Fame. Of course, writers don't usually think about this. If they did, they'd have a hard time getting out of bed every morning, much less writing a song. But when you become a publisher, you know the truth.

The truth is this: the catalog of any successful songwriter or publisher is inevitably a mixture of about 5 percent genuine, grade-A "Hits"; 45 percent "Good, Not Great" songs, and 50 percent "Misses." If you've written fifty songs and you think you have five or ten hits, you're fooling yourself. Remember, the goal here is *objectivity*.

Success in the publishing business depends largely on learning to maximize the value of not just the top 5 percent, but also the 45 percent of the songs that lie in the middle ground. As for the 50 percent of the songs that just plain miss their mark, there's not much you can do with those. Those songs are why every publisher needs plenty of big, empty file drawers in their office.

Let's take a good objective look at the catalog you're working with.

The Top Drawer

Can you spot the "hits"? Let's hope so. A hit song is a hard thing to define, but if nothing else, it should be obvious enough to stand out amidst the other songs in the catalog. The actual science of what makes a song a hit is something that we'll discuss at length later on in this book; for now, we'll stick with the basics.

If you're a performer, what song do you open or close with? Which one can silence a noisy audience? Which one do people request? If you had an opportunity to play one song for someone who could truly make a difference in your career, which song would you play? Those songs are your hits.

Is this a difficult choice? If it is, then chances are, you don't really have any hits in your catalog. Fine. Remember, the objective here is to be objective. Frankly, if you are a relatively new writer, you probably don't have a hit song in your catalog—yet. Focus instead on those three or four songs that you think are the strongest—that best represent what you do. Those songs go in your top drawer.

The Middle Drawer

Now think about the next category: Good, Not Great. These songs are your real challenge as a publisher. In order to have significant success, you need to learn to get the B-level songs in situations where they can generate income. They may never become hits (although with a little luck and timing, it can happen), but they can sometimes make it onto albums and television shows, into advertisements or a low-budget movie. As you narrow down the songs that fit into this category, here are a few things to consider:

Tempo

As a general rule, up-tempo songs are always more viable than ballads. Think about it—most albums have ten to twelve songs, out of which perhaps three or four are ballads. Every radio station plays at least three or four up-tempo songs for every ballad. Consequently, most labels release two or three up-tempo singles off any album, and only one ballad. If your catalog is made up predominately of brooding, downtempo material, the numbers are stacked against you.

When you get into the world of television, movies, and advertising, the advantage for up-tempo songs becomes even more pronounced. Action sequences, montages, and comedic scenes all require up-tempo material. In many instances, tempo can become the primary concern for directors and music supervisors.

One of the first steps in assessing your catalog should be to take note of all the up-tempo material, particularly songs that are 116 beats per minute or above. In most cases, an "up-tempo" song is defined not by the number of beats per minute so much as by its aggressive, rhythmic feel. This is especially true of urban material, where even the most up-tempo hip-hop or trap song rarely gets above 100 bpm. In styles like trap, dubstep, or future bass, it can be somewhat subjective as to what the "beats per minute" of a song even is, as the rhythmic feel can double the time or cut it in half even within the same song. But generally speaking, songs that are in the 116 bpm and faster category are rare, and can be very useful in instances where the need for tempo is of utmost importance. Unless the song is very weak, anything in that tempo category should probably go in the middle drawer.

Lyrics

Any lyric that breaks a bit from the typical love song mold should also be a part of your active catalog. Songs with inspirational lyrics (think "Firework" or "Hall of Fame"), controversial lyrics ("This Is America"), or even just silly, non-romantic lyrics ("Old Town Road") tend to stand out in a sea of songs about lost loves and broken hearts. Moreover, they are vastly more appealing to music supervisors and advertising agencies. You need some of these to work with.

Demo Quality

The production quality of a song demo is always a factor in assessing a song's value to the catalog. While you should avoid judging a song by its demo, you do have to be aware that it's easier to get a cut with a record quality demo than with a badly recorded guitar/vocal work-tape. This is especially true when it comes to pitching songs for television projects, where you can often get a great sounding demo placed directly in the show (which means you collect the master license fee, in addition to the publishing sync fee).

The Bottom Drawer

What about those songs that haven't quite found their way into either the "Hits" category, or the lesser, but still honorable "Good, Not Great" category? How about that cathartic, five-minute, intensely personal ballad that you never had a chance to properly demo but that still means so much to you? Sorry. The good news is, I'm not telling you to throw it out.

I am telling you to put it in the bottom drawer. Regardless of how special the song is to you, it is part of your inactive catalog. You probably won't need to get at it very often. I know this hurts, but take solace in the fact that every writer has "misses," and many of the songs in that category are some of the songwriter's personal favorites. But now we are thinking like publishers, and, for better or worse, those lengthy, introspective, personal musical statements simply aren't very useful to us. To call something a "miss" as opposed to a hit is not an artistic judgment; it is a commercial one. Publishing, after all, is a commercial business. To be effective, you need to invest your efforts in those songs most likely to yield a return.

Still, hope springs eternal. This is why you never throw a song away (that's a writer's role, not a publisher's). While the bottom drawer is not choice real estate, it isn't equivalent to being tossed out into the street either. Periodically review this part of your catalog, as you may find that you've judged some songs too harshly, or that the musical fashion has changed and something once hopelessly dated is now back in vogue.

More importantly, you will have instances where that song at the back of the drawer is the ideal pitch for a very specialized project. I can recall pitching songs for an advertising project in which the crucial selling point was the presence of the word "smile" in the song's chorus. When you get those sorts of calls, you need all the catalog you can get your hands on, and that bottom drawer can take on a new allure.

Can You Find the Songs?

As you begin this process of carefully sifting through each song in your catalog, you may already be noticing the third quality that you as a publisher must bring to bear on the stack of music in front of you. After ownership and objectivity, you must establish *order*.

Don't ask me why, but when I started writing songs, I had hundreds of digital tapes, most of them with only vague scribbled notes on the J-card to indicate what material they might actually contain. I would spend the first hour of every day just trying to find the track on which I was supposed to be working.

But of course, those were the dark ages, before one's whole catalog was nestled securely on a hard drive or somewhere in the Cloud. Now of course, it's easy for writers to know exactly what they have in their catalog. Except they don't. Inevitably, writers come to meet with me, search their computer for the song they want to play, and.... Oops. Sorry, that's the instrumental version. Or the initial rough demo. Or the one before they replaced the singer. They try again, and again. "Wow—I thought I brought this version. Let me email my co-writer, maybe they can send it right now . . . " they say, as I quietly return messages on my phone.

As a songwriter, how would you feel if every time you called your publisher about a specific song, she spent fifteen minutes looking through her database . . . "Umm, here it is . . . no, wait, that's someone else's song . . . I know I've got it somewhere, just hang on . . . are you sure you sent it to me?"

You see what I mean. What may be a mere eccentricity in a songwriter is something more problematic in a publisher. It is incompetence. Now that you are joining the publishing ranks, order is in fact the order of the day. So prepare to meet the metadata, because we are about to get organized.

There are a myriad of different ways to organize your catalog, ranging from a file drawer and some index cards, to comprehensive programs like DISCO. We'll discuss these in more detail in chapter 7. For now, let's just deal with the simple stuff. Each MP3 or WAV should be named clearly and correctly and stored somewhere on your computer (or in an external storage system) along with all of the necessary information about the song. How you choose to go about this is up to you. If you can't think of anything better, you could just use Dropbox and fill out a Song Submittal Form for each song. You can see an example of in appendix B. This form requires the following information:

- title
- writers (be sure to note whether or not you have a signed split sheet on file)
- publishers
- date written and/or recorded
- studio
- engineer
- status—is this a master, a rough mix, a work tape?

If this business of labeling and sorting and documenting feels like overkill, it probably is. But when you get to the chapter about lawsuits, particularly relating to ownership of the copyright, you'll understand why it's helpful to have a record of dates, studios, and engineers for each song. If this all seems like a lot of paperwork, you're right about that too. That's what publishing is.

In case you've missed it, the point of our whole discussion of catalog comes down to this: if music publishing is your business, then songs are your assets. Yes, they are works of art, and a means of personal expression, and entertainment, and a magical means of communication across social and political barriers that can make the whole world join hands and sing. But to a publisher, they are assets—not unlike inventory to a store, or airplanes to an airline. And if that's the case, then they should be treated with care. You must know what songs you have *ownership* in and how much of them you own. You must bring some *objectivity* to the management of your catalog. And you must establish *order* within that catalog, so that each song is properly identified, easily accessible, and part of a coherent cataloguing system.

It's a little like cleaning your apartment. Inevitably, you find a few things that you didn't remember you had and a few things that aren't yours at all. You realize that some of your stuff is a lot more valuable than other stuff. Eventually, you get enough things stacked on the shelves or packed into drawers that you can actually find what you need when you need it.

Think how good it will feel when you finish.

4

The "F" Word: Focus

There's one more quality that you need to bring to bear on your catalog: focus. It's so important that it gets its own chapter.

For some writers, artists, publishers, or entrepreneurs in the music business, the decision to focus their career on a particular genre or subgenre of music is one they hardly remember making. There may be only one style of music with which they really identify, or in which they feel their talent can fit. In many ways, these are the lucky ones. They are specialists without ever having chosen to be so. This doesn't necessarily mean that they don't understand or enjoy music outside of the genre in which they work, but it does mean that they don't feel compelled to personally create or sell *every* type of music that they enjoy.

And then there are the generalists. Blessed with a vast range of musical interests and a confidence to match, they're sure that their career should encompass everything from jazz to hip-hop, with some country songs and a bit of chamber music just to keep life interesting. You don't need to go very far into a conversation to recognize a generalist....

Music Business Weasel: "So, tell me, what sort of music do you write?"

Songwriter: "Oh, geez . . . that's a tough one, you know. I mean . . . I can write everything."

Uh oh. First off, let's get real. Nobody can write "everything." Nobody. Except maybe Mozart or Prince. But even the versatility of someone like Prince was based more on his ability to adapt or arrange his songs in a variety of styles, rather than actually altering his own songwriting approach. The same is true of Max Martin. While he has had hits in virtually every genre, most of these songs are essentially "Max Martin"–style songs, adapted to fit different markets.

One other thing to notice about Prince and Max Martin: they didn't start out that way. In the early years of his career, Prince was very much a part of the Minneapolis school of R&B, which he in large part created, but which later included Morris Day and the Time, and of course, Jimmy Jam and Terry Lewis. It was only after he achieved superstar status that he began to branch out into more experimental rock and jazz areas. Everybody comes from somewhere; nobody comes from everywhere. You cannot lay a foundation for your publishing company with a catalog that does "everything."

I once heard Monica Lynch, the former president of Tommy Boy Records and a very savvy music business executive, make this point in a forum attended primarily by developing writers and artists. She simply said that she was not interested in meeting with anyone who claimed they could do "everything." This was not well received. A murmur passed through the audience. How dare she seek to limit their creativity? Isn't that exactly what's wrong with the music industry, with its focus on markets, and formats, and target audiences, yada yada yada?

For whatever reason, many musicians, writers, and artists take a misplaced pride in their own versatility. They are so sure that they can play any type of music, sing any song, write in any style, or record an album that covers the entire range of American popular music that they miss one important thing:

It doesn't matter. No one cares.

Music Business Weasel Says:
Versatility is important only to session musicians, jingle writers, and wedding bands.

Everybody else needs to *focus*.

What does focus mean to a publisher? It means that as a start-up publishing company, your catalog should be made up primarily of songs in one particular musical genre. This is your focus. A catalog spread over two styles is workable, if the two styles are at least somewhat compatible. For instance, country and pop would be a better combination than country and techno. Within that stylistic focus, variety is both necessary and desirable. You need a selection of songs: up-tempos, ballads, mid-tempos, male songs, female songs, group songs. The idea here is not to limit anyone's creativity. The idea is to harness that creativity and direct it down one specific path.

Of course, there will always be some songs that fall outside any of your usual musical boundaries. Fine. Have fun with them. The idea of focus in business is no different than the idea of focusing your eye. The point is not to eliminate everything else from your view but simply to direct your eye toward the most important thing. Experimentation is essential and can sometimes lead to the discovery of a new focus, more viable than the previous one. Fine again. Then change your focus—but don't lose it. If someone asks what sort of music you publish and it takes you more than twenty seconds to answer, reread everything I just said. And then continue.

Three Things That Focus Will Do

Focus will give your publishing catalog an *identity*. Any business, in any industry, needs to establish some sort of identity in the minds of its customers. Call it branding or "finding your USP" (unique selling point) or whatever you like. The fundamental objective is to give your company a specific presence in a crowded marketplace. There is probably no more crowded marketplace than that of the contemporary music industry, with hundreds of established songwriters and publishers, not to mention thousands of mostly unknown companies, all vying for the same opportunities. Why does an A&R person need to speak to you, specifically?

When our friend the Music Business Weasel makes the standard inquiry, "What sort of music do you do?" this is what they are really asking, in their own moderately polite way: "Who are you?" "Why should I speak with you?" "Do you have anything I need?" If the weasel's opening gambit confounds you, or if you chirpily reply that you handle "everything" (which isn't really much different than not responding at all), you have lost the opportunity to answer these questions. You will probably not get another chance.

Because the music publishing business is not oriented toward the general consumer, but rather to other industry professionals, it is not a business in which massive marketing campaigns are a primary means of establishing a brand identity. Rather, music companies are defined first and foremost by the sort of music that they sell. The more specific the musical direction, the stronger the image that they can establish in the industry.

Versatility is not a highly valued skill in the commercial music business. Music is a specialized business that rewards specialists, not generalists. When you are dealing with an A&R person or a music supervisor, they want to believe that you have a particular expertise that you are selling them, just as they consider themselves experts in their particular field of music. If they inquire about your catalog, and you reply that you specialize primarily in

Southern hip-hop, or electronic dance music, or Christian metal, you have immediately given your company an identity in their mind. Likewise, you have established yourself as having some particular expertise.

But what if the A&R person is looking for Southern hip-hop and you tell them that you handle Christian metal? Isn't that going to turn them off? Sure it will. Having an identity means turning some people off. Sometimes it means turning a lot of people off. This is the same thing that gives you credibility with the people in your genre. A Christian metal band that tried to sideline as a hip-hop act would not reach a wider audience. They would alienate their core audience.

In fact, you will find that very few music business professionals are put off by learning that you don't handle the sort of music they are looking for. Instead, they recognize that they are talking to another professional who has the discipline and good judgment to stick with what they do best. If what you do doesn't fit what they need, most people in the industry will try to lead you in the direction of the person who would be your customer—whether it's putting you in touch with the appropriate A&R person in their company, or a project that they've heard about, or a friend of a friend who might be helpful. If your company has a clear direction, there is at least a chance that they can help you down the path. If you're going everywhere at once, no one can show you the way. And no one will try.

Which leads to the next thing that focus will do. It will give you a *community*. No man is an island. If it takes a village to raise a child, it takes a whole town to make a business. Ask any neighborhood bodega owner: if you wanna be in business, you gotta be part of the community.

Probably because we spent too many of our formative years locked away in solitude—listening to records, practicing our instruments, penning heart-wrenching poems of love and longing—many musicians and songwriters tend to be loners. Now that you're a publisher, it's time to become a team player. If you're wondering who your team is, a little focus will bring them into view.

By establishing a clear stylistic direction for your publishing venture, you become a part of that particular musical community, which includes other musicians, writers, artists, publishers, press, fans, promoters, radio programmers, and anyone else who shares a similar direction. This has been a constant theme in the history of American pop music: a musical community gives birth to a specific style, which, as it catches fire, brings to prominence a whole group of related artists, writers, producers, and companies. Think of the Memphis rockabilly community that spawned Elvis, Jerry Lee Lewis, and Johnny Cash; the Detroit scene that led to Motown or a later one that created the Detroit techno movement; or the Seattle rock scene that spawned

Nirvana and Pearl Jam. Think of the Brill Building, the "Sound of Phila-delphia," or West Coast rap. Most recently, consider the Toronto scene that launched Drake. Artists, writers, and companies do not develop in isolation. They grow in clusters, supporting, competing, and learning from each other. But until you focus your business on one particular musical territory, you will find yourself in no man's land—never really at home anywhere.

When I first moved to New York in the 1980s to become a songwriter and producer, I had the good fortune to come into contact with a small group of other songwriters who were also in the process of launching their careers. The group included Alexandra Forbes ("Don't Rush Me" for Taylor Dayne), Shelly Peiken ("Bitch" for Meredith Brooks, "What a Girl Wants" for Chris-tina Aguilera), Jeff Franzel (Shawn Colvin, *NSYNC), and Barbara Jordan (former Berklee faculty and founder of Heavy Hitters Music). While none of us were exactly the same in our musical style, we were all oriented primarily toward writing the sort of mainstream pop material in vogue at that time.

We initially got to know each other through what we called "song parties," at which we would meet to trade leads about who was looking for material, listen to and critique each other's new material, and, of course, trade industry gossip and horror stories. These get-togethers inevitably led to collaborations and friendships, and an ever-expanding network of other writers, musicians, demo singers, engineers, and record executives.

Before long, a fledgling musical community was thriving. If there was an A&R person that I hadn't yet met, inevitably an introduction would come through someone else in our group. If someone else needed a recommenda-tion for a demo singer, or a musician, I might be able to provide one. This is what friends do.

We were also competitors—all chasing after the same cuts, working on the same projects, and cultivating relationships with the same industry contacts. This is what businesses do: they compete, openly and without apology. And this too is a benefit of being part of a community. Competition inevitably makes everyone raise the level of their game.

As any good capitalist knows, healthy competition breeds innovation, better service, and a rising standard of quality. A lack of competition creates your cable company.

It's easy to see this fierce but friendly, "anything you can do, I can do better" attitude within many of the hot hip-hop production companies, like Quality Control in Atlanta., in which the competition within the company continues to push the producers, writers, and artists to be aggressive and innovative. It all starts with defining the musical boundaries of what you do—finding a place you and your business can call home.

But it goes even further. Once you've established an identity for your company and have become part of a musical community that can help to support and nurture your work, you still need to come up with a realistic plan of attack. Focus is also the key element to developing a *strategy* for your business. We're in Business Management 101 here, and if you've been at this for any length of time, you've probably already noticed a basic principle in action:

Until you can clarify exactly what you are trying to accomplish, it is very difficult to figure out how you're going to do it.

We can start by establishing that the fundamental job of a publisher is to find opportunities for their songs to be used in ways that can generate income, whether by getting them commercially released, performed in public, or placed in films, games or advertisements. This likely means you'll need to develop relationships with people who need songs, whether it's artists, record label A&R staff, managers, music supervisors for television and films, or advertising agencies. At the same time, the publisher needs to do the necessary paperwork to ensure that the income generated by those opportunities flows accurately back to the publisher and songwriter. This means working with performing rights organizations like ASCAP and BMI and other collection companies (which we'll discuss in detail in subsequent chapters), as well as issuing licenses to all those people who want to use your music. That's a lot of people to know and a lot of knowledge to assimilate, especially when the business is growing and changing all the time.

You will never know everyone or everything in every sector of the music business. The great news is, you don't need to. As soon as you focus your efforts on one particular segment of the music industry, you only need to know those people who are relevant to what you do. This is a lot easier. You now have an area of expertise, and your role is to make sure that you are fully versed in the information that applies to that particular genre. This means knowing the most important record labels or production companies, the most influential managers, attending the conventions catering to that segment of the industry, being familiar with the up-and-coming artists and producers, and staying on top of the emerging business and musical trends.

It also means studying and understanding the business strategies that have worked or might work in your field. For instance, pitching songs with a very simple, stripped down demo is probably a somewhat viable strategy if you're writing toplines for the world of electronic dance music. If you're a producer pitching songs to the urban/pop world, pitching such a minimalist demo would be ridiculous. Some markets, like the singer-songwriter genre, can break new artists and songs through frequent or at least significant synchronization placements. The country market, by contrast, rarely gets the opportunity to place its music in an advertisement, and is driven much more by radio than by television. By defining the nature of your catalog, you immediately begin to clarify the strategic options that can work for your business.

In the next chapter, we will discuss business strategies in more detail, as well as the benefits to developing a business plan for your company. But the planning cannot start until you focus your catalog in one well-defined area— because no single strategy will work across the board for every type of music. Focus is absolutely essential to establishing an identity for your company, becoming part of a musical community, and structuring an effective plan to achieve your goals. Attempting to do "everything" is likely to result in accomplishing nothing.

What to Do If You Won't or Can't Focus

I'm sure this little spiel on "focus" will not go down well with many readers. (After all, I saw Monica Lynch try it with considerably more finesse than I used here.) Musicians and creative souls will forever rail against the segmentation and specialization of the music industry—and certainly there are some negative aspects to the industry's increasing myopia. In the interests of all of you who absolutely refuse to give up the idea of pursuing several disparate musical directions at once, or even those who insist they can do "everything," I offer the following tips.

Keep It Your Dirty Little Secret

Some things are better left unsaid. Given the increasing fragmentation within the music industry, it is quite possible for the musical generalist to conduct business on a "don't ask, don't tell" basis. If you're meeting with a rock A&R person, simply play him or her your rock songs, and keep that experimental jazz demo to yourself. If you're asked about your current activity, mention only those cuts that would be relevant in the questioner's musical world. Do not think that someone in the pop world will be impressed by your work as a film composer. They will not. Decide instead that what they don't know won't hurt them or you. Let them think that whatever sort of music they're looking for is exactly the kind of thing you've dedicated your life to doing.

If this sounds like a bit like one of those guys that have four wives and spend their days secretly shuttling back and forth, it *is* like that. I never said it was an easy trick to pull off. But it is possible, and it is more a matter of respect than deception. The people who inhabit each musical subculture have built their businesses and in many cases, their lives, around one particular musical world. To imply to a jazz composer that you are able to dabble in his world, while simultaneously striking it rich as a rock star, may not go over very well. The jazz man is likely to view you as either a shallow dilettante or an arrogant profiteer. To play pop songs when you're pitching to a country producer is to waste not just your own time but the producer's time as well. A bit of reticence about your multiple musical ambitions is not dishonest. It is simply presenting yourself in a positive manner, as someone who respects the complexities, nuances, and demands of any specific musical environment.

You Oughta Be in Pictures

There is a special place in the industry where you can pitch a bluegrass song in the morning and write a power ballad in the afternoon, and follow it up with a future bass track to end the day. But it's not the record business. It's the magical world of film and television. Barbara Jordan, who I mentioned earlier, has built a very successful business writing and publishing songs for a vast array of movies and television spots. Her choice to center her business in this particular world allows her the freedom to indulge a wide-ranging love of music, and to experiment with the songwriting techniques of different historical periods.

> *"I have the opportunity to write in every style of songwriting under the sun—a song that could be sung by Billie Holiday for a movie set in the 1940s or a Seventies disco tune that belongs in* Saturday Night Fever. *It's very challenging, but well worth the effort. It's like being a time traveler, taking the best songwriting tools of every decade and transporting them back to your own."*

Increase the Brand-Width . . .

As I mentioned earlier, the advertising and branding business is another area in which versatility is a plus. With media agencies and advertisers drawing on every possible musical style to grab the ear of the listener, anyone working in this field must have the ability to cross into any genre and quickly assimilate the basic musical characteristics of the style. It is, in many ways, the ideal situation for a writer or publisher that resists categorization. Be forewarned, however. This business generally requires not just an interest in several types of music, but an openness to *every* kind of music, which is a different matter entirely. Yes, there will be days when you can indulge your secret love of Caribbean soca music, but there will be other days when you are trying to come up with something that sounds just like "Baby Shark." If you live by the sword of versatility, sometimes you die by it as well.

First, Get a Hundred Million Dollars . . .

. . .then start a really, really big publishing company. While I'm urging you to keep your catalog focused and specialized, the reality is that the most successful publishing companies in the music industry take exactly the opposite approach. Sony ATV, Warner Chappell, and Universal Music are all distinguished by the vast breadth of their catalogs, which include everything from jazz standards to classic rock to current hits. This is an extremely effective approach, as the catalog provides an almost bottomless source of income, allowing the companies to be extremely aggressive in courting new writers who then create the hit catalog of the future. Despite what I may have said earlier, I highly recommend this approach—if you have a lot of money.

These companies have been constructed largely through the acquisition of catalogs, which is usually a high-rollers game. (Recall that $132-million Jobete deal that I mentioned earlier.) If you happen to be independently wealthy or have access to significant funding for such a venture, this sort of acquisitive approach to developing a very broad catalog is a perfectly sensible strategy. In fact, the more broad the better, as a range of songs in different musical genres will protect you from the ups and downs of any one particular market. If there is an aspiring Merck Mercuriadis out there, I recommend you put this book down and pick up your checkbook.

Or Just Wait a While . . .

As your publishing company grows, your focus can widen along with it. That's not loss of focus; that is creative growth. Once you have established an identity for your company and you have become a part of a specific musical community, you can begin to expand your strategy into new areas—hopefully, without alienating your core market.

Prescription Music is a good example of this particular approach. Starting in the early 2000s with a catalog based primarily on the pop songs of producer Dr. Luke (Katy Perry, Pink), it is now a company that represents writers in a wide variety of styles from electronic dance music to hip-hop to country. But this was a gradual progression, undertaken as the company gained prominence, financial resources, and management structure.

If you are viewing your music business as a career, then it's not necessary that you tackle every market at once. Find the one in which you are best equipped to compete, focus, and create a success story. Then move on from there. The differences between the tortoise and the hare were largely those of discipline and patience. Ultimately, it is this focus that will allow you to compete with companies larger and more established than your own.

The primary weakness of the giant music corporations is that they are inherently incapable of focus, precisely because of their size. By directing all of your efforts and energy into one small segment of the music market, your small catalog can actually be competitive with the biggest guys on the block. This has been demonstrated throughout the history of the music business, in the development of virtually every important musical trend, from rock and roll to rhythm and blues, punk, hip-hop, electronic dance music, and trap. In each instance, the sound was developed by small, independent companies that were an integral part of that music community. Likewise, in almost every instance, the large corporations neglected what they believed was a niche market until that small business grew too big to ignore. It is by finding and focusing on these sorts of opportunities that the small independent company can gain a toehold in the industry.

You will never be able to compete with the corporate powerhouses by attempting to do everything that they do, only better. But if you choose one specific area of music (ideally, one that the large companies are neglecting) and direct all your efforts there, then you can compete—and also win. The large companies simply can't afford to focus with that degree of specificity. They have too many interests, too many writers, and operating costs that are too high for them to limit the scope of their company in that way. Monica Lynch knew this, because she had been a part of the development of Tommy Boy Records from its inception. Every musical entrepreneur from Sam Phillips to Ahmet Ertegun to Coach K has demonstrated the same lesson.

For the small independent company, *focus* is your secret weapon. Don't lose it.

5

The Business Plan: Do You Know Where You're Going To?

Okay, let's talk reality. While it's theoretically correct to say that anyone who's written a song is also a publisher, we don't live in a theoretical world. And in the real world, most people who own a catalog of songs are not publishers at all, because they haven't bothered to create a basic structure or any kind of plan for their enterprise. Just because you have a backyard filled with old stuff doesn't mean you're an antiques dealer. Theory only goes so far; to be in business, you need a plan. Before you hang your shingle outside your front door, there are a few important issues that you need to sort out.

I'll be honest: I'm not much of a planner. I'm more comfortable getting down to work, seizing opportunities when and where they come, than in devising grand strategies for world domination. Every year, I try to make a few New Year's resolutions, and inevitably by the next year, I've not only screwed most of them up, but half of them seem completely irrelevant. My life has changed so much in a year that I can't even remember why I made them. I'm not an X's and O's kind of guy. I prefer to run and gun.

That said, I *am* a believer in thinking strategically. Before I sign any new writer to a publishing agreement, I want to have some idea of who I can pitch the music to and what it will take to reach those people. There are some songwriters and publishers who see a demand in the market and then create music to fill that need. Others start with the music they have and try to figure out who might have an interest in it. Either way, you need to think about what strategies have worked for people in the past and what can work for you.

If you're looking for a thorough guide to business planning, this ain't it. Thankfully, there are a good number of those available. (For something specific to the music industry, I recommend Jonathan Feist's *Project Management for Musicians*.) My intent is simply to show you the thought process that can help take you from point A to B: setting reasonable goals, developing strategies to reach them, and recognizing when you are veering too far off course.

I'm not even going to insist that you write your plan down. I know that's an anathema to every accomplished business planner, but this book is for songwriters, and most of us can't even manage to correctly label our own music files. Besides, the music business is such a constantly shifting landscape, with trends emerging and receding faster than any company can respond, that it may be best to keep your business plan fluid, with general strategies and flexible goals. If you want to put it down on paper, that's great. But the important thing is to internalize your plan, so that you carry it in your head, constantly referring to it, reassessing and revising it as needed.

Goals: Before You Start Shooting, Aim

Goal setting is a personal process that very quickly leads to some hard, philosophical questions. What do you consider success? Is it measured monetarily? Is it measured artistically? Do you need the approval of your peers, your parents, or a stadium full of screaming fans? Is it a matter of quality of life, or is it found in a specific, measurable achievement? Most important of all, how bad do you want "it"—"it" being success, whatever that means to you. I'm not much for navel-gazing, but these are important questions that will influence every facet of your business planning. It's worth a few hours alone in a quiet place to think these questions through.

For most of us in the music industry, there is a constant tension between what you could call the artistic values (creative satisfaction, critical acclaim, and the like) and the business values (sales, profits, income). While I do not accept the premise that juxtaposes artistic and business success in an either/or framework, I am realistic enough to understand that one does not guarantee the other. You need to decide what balance you are comfortable with between these two core values. Is the fundamental goal of your business simply to sustain you, while providing a context for you to write music you love? Or is this a profit-driven venture aimed at meeting the needs of a specific market?

Don't say both. One of the most important elements in this planning process is to be clear and decisive, and "both" will not suffice. Something has to take first place, and whatever that is will determine the answers to all the questions that follow. I'm not saying that it's impossible to achieve both artistic and business success; that is certainly not the case. But it is important to know which is the core value of your company. Pick (a) love or (b) money, but there is no (c) all of the above. There is also no correct answer.

With the big-picture question out of the way, you can begin to think more specifically about what goals should be part of your business plan. Think of these goals as markers along a path. Each time you achieve one, you should move further down the path toward your ultimate destination. Anything that leads you off that path is not a worthy goal.

For example, if your ultimate aim is to strike it rich as a pop music publisher, then you should not set a goal of winning a Grammy award. I'm not saying that it wouldn't be nice to win a Grammy. But Grammy awards are given on a basis of peer voting, and are (supposedly) given for artistic achievement. They are also not given to publishers. Winning such an award is an honor, but it shouldn't be a goal, because it doesn't directly relate to your ultimate objective. If you want to make money as a pop music publisher, then set a goal of putting a song in the *Billboard* Hot 100, or on a platinum selling album. Leave the awards for someone else.

When you start setting goals, make sure that they are realistic, quantifiable, and of real business value. Goals are not the same as hopes or dreams; you should not cue the ethereal music and soft focus lens when you start talking about them. When you begin to think about your goals, you should begin by thinking of your ultimate objective, and then try to determine the benchmarks that will need to be achieved in order to accomplish your long-term goal. Avoid the warm and fuzzy stuff: "I just want to touch people with my music," "I want to publish songs that I'm proud of," "I want to help other songwriters realize their dreams." Lovely. Those are fine sentiments for your Song of the Year acceptance speech, but good luck trying to build a business around them.

Get Real

To say that your goals should be realistic is not to encourage you to aim low. It is merely to say that nothing in the business is as simple as it appears, and nothing happens as fast as you hope. There is enough discouragement in the everyday life of a music publisher without shouldering the burden of a business plan with goals that are impossible to achieve. What are reasonable expectations for a songwriter or entrepreneur starting their own publishing venture? Assuming this is your first foray into the music business and that you are not yet a well-established songwriter, I would say that a goal of having one song recorded and released by a major label artist would be a realistic target for your first year. This will not make you rich or even profitable. But it will let you know that you are moving in the right direction. Every year, try to raise the bar a little higher.

In a business as volatile as the music industry, I think long-term planning is little more than wishful thinking. I would suggest that your goals be set on a yearly basis. Certainly, your ultimate career objective should remain constant, at least for the first five years. But the goals that will lead you to your final destination will need to be reassessed and adjusted at least once a year. In that sense, a business plan for the music industry is less like a road map than a navigational chart, which has to take into account currents, winds, tides, and the occasional tidal wave. The constant shifting of musical trends and fashion, the evolution of technology, and changes within the corporate structures of the major record labels could all potentially impact the relevance of the goals you've set.

Pick a Number...

If there's a danger in setting your goals unrealistically high, there is an even greater danger in setting them somewhere in the "gray" zone—that vague area where numbers don't quite apply.

"My goal is:

. . . to get my songs covered."

. . . to increase my industry contacts."

. . . to make my business profitable."

All worthy aims. But lousy goals. These objectives are moving in the right direction, but they lack enough specifics to challenge you to reach them, or let you know when you've accomplished them. You need some numbers.

What if you said instead:

"My goal is:

. . . to get three songs covered this year."

. . . to make four new industry contacts each month."

. . . to make (x) amount in income this year, against expenses of (x) amount."

Now you've got a target. Even better, now that you have a number in front of you, you can begin to break that target down into manageable chunks. In order to get three songs covered in a year, you will need one song recorded every four months. To make four new industry contacts each month is really just one call to a new name every week. This is about as far as my math skills go—but the point is clear. Numbers give you a basis upon which to build a strategy. They also provide an early warning system if your strategy isn't working. If it's June and you still don't have one cover, you're falling behind. You'd probably better consider changing your tactics to get back in the game.

What's the Payoff?

Achievement of a goal that does not move you closer to your ultimate objective is time wasted. It might feel great, it may impress your friends and family, but all it really accomplishes is to distract you from those things that are necessary to reach the larger prize. A positive review in the local paper, an award from a local chapter of the Recording Academy, or a sold-out gig at the local club is not a goal—at least, not if your true focus is on generating income from your music publishing catalog. These are achievements that may come almost by accident as you pursue your goals, and if they do, by all means go out and celebrate. But they do not warrant being an objective within your business plan. On their own, they are simply not that productive. Your efforts should be directed toward those things that yield obvious, measurable benefits. It's like sitting through a movie: there's got to be a payoff at the end.

Strategy: Can't Get There from Here

Now it's time to play connect the dots. The dots are your goals, which, if chosen wisely, will eventually create a career picture of success. Strategy is what gets you from one dot to another. Needless to say, imagining where you'd like to end up is not all that tough. Getting there is a different story.

It would be nice to be able to simply provide you with a few foolproof strategies for developing your company—do this, then do that, avoid this, and before you know it, you're there. That would be nice, but I can't. Developing a strategy for your business is an in-depth, highly personal process that is entirely dependent on your own strengths and weaknesses and your ultimate objectives. Without knowing what you want your business to become, the style of music on which you're focused, or the quality of your catalog, any advice I offered would be of dubious value.

All I can do is play Socrates (probably the only time a weasel has attempted to put himself in those shoes), and try to ask questions that will get you thinking in a strategic way about your business. If you take the time to think about these questions, you will begin to see a path taking shape in front of you, and some of the barriers that lie in that path. It's up to you to draw, and follow, the map.

The Music Business Weasel's Pop Quiz

Your Market

1. To what musical genre do most of your songs belong?

2. Who is your competition in that market?

3. What are the strengths and weaknesses of the leading publishers in your particular genre?

4. How can you imitate those strengths?

5. How can you exploit the weaknesses?

6. What strategies have been used successfully in this market previously?

7. Is your genre growing or shrinking?

8. What are the demographics and characteristics of the audience for your genre?

9. What part of your market or segment of the audience is the most under-served?

10. In what city or cities are most of the publishing or record companies in this type of music based?

Your Resources and Challenges

11. What are the advantages and disadvantages of your current location?

12. How much money do you have to spend on your business?

13. What information do you need to compete in your market?

14. How can you get that information?

15. What relationships do you need in order to compete?

16. What relationships do you already have?

17. How can you meet the key people you need, or people that know the key people?

18. What are your strengths and weaknesses as a business?

19. How can you utilize those strengths?

20. How can you compensate for the weaknesses?

Your Music

21. What are the musical strengths and weaknesses of your catalog?

22. What are you doing now to establish your songs in the marketplace?

23. Is it working? If so, what part of the market is reacting most strongly? If not, why are you encountering resistance?

And finally, one multiple choice. This one counts double.

24. At present, what is the biggest obstacle to your success? Is it:

- Creative—Weakness in the catalog or demo presentation
- Financial—Lack of capital for business expenditures
- Social—Shortage of productive personal relationships and industry contacts
- Informational—Lack of knowledge regarding the industry or business in general
- Structural—Are you in a declining or nonexistent market?

Whew. Pretty exhausting, huh? But by now, you should be starting to see a general outline of what your overall business plan should encompass. Of course, there are a lot of specifics that will get filled in as we go.

Every publisher, whether an individual songwriter or a multinational corporation, has to address the five core functions of a music publisher. You will need to have a plan to acquire some songs, whether you're writing them or someone else is. There will need to be a system to administer those songs and to collect the income, and that means filling out registrations forms, issuing licenses, and putting together royalty statements. Of course, you'll have to protect your songs, as those "copyrights" are the primary assets of your business. This means more forms, this time for the Copyright Office, and vigilance in monitoring all types of media for unauthorized uses of your music. Depending on the financial resources you have and the earnings on your catalog, some of these jobs can be outsourced to other companies, who will help you with administration services or collection of income, for a fee.

Connecting the Dots: From Your Music to the Market

But most of all, every publisher must find ways to exploit their catalog, and this particular challenge cannot be so easily handed off to someone else. You should be the most committed and knowledgeable advocate for your own music. At least in the beginning, it will be up to you to get your songs heard and to find opportunities to place them on records, in television shows or advertisements, in video games or on the radio.

How you do that will vary greatly depending on the kind of music you publish, and we'll explore the specifics of exploitation in part II. But your business plan should reflect an in-depth understanding of your market: how things work in the segment of the music world where you are focused. In most cases, the music genre itself will determine what types of exploitation tactics will be effective. No one can break folk songs on Spotify or prog rock on television.

At the same time, you have to consider your own competitive advantages and disadvantages, as they will also determine what strategies will play to your strengths. Ultimately, your business will rise and fall on your audience's reaction to your music, both within the industry, among A&R people, music supervisors, and other artists, and from the general public itself. Ideas for collaborations, changes in the production of your demos, and a focus on particular types of songs are all strategies that will grow out of the answers to the last three questions of the Pop Quiz.

This process of matching an analysis of your market to an understanding of your own strengths and weaknesses, both on a business level and a creative one, is not a one-time activity. Your strategy should be something that you are constantly reviewing and revising in your head. Each time you learn something new about the business, make a new contact, have a success or a failure, there should be some small adjustment to your thinking.

Which leads to the final segment of the business planning process:

What to Do If Your Plan Doesn't Work

On this matter, I actually can offer you a good and simple answer that should work for one and all:

Change your plan.

One of the positive aspects of business planning is that establishing objectives allows you to measure your company's performance, and to recognize when the goals are getting further out of reach instead of closer. One of the greatest dangers of business planning is the tendency to cling to the original plan, even when it is readily apparent that things are not working out quite the way you expected. Dogged persistence in executing a flawed plan is like driving around in the dark for hours because you're too stubborn to stop and turn on Google Maps. Sort of like me finding my way around L.A.

The truth is, even the most successful companies are continually forced to alter aspects of their business plan in response to ineffective strategies, changes in the business environment, or shifts in musical styles and tastes. That's why every day someone gets fired and someone else gets hired. To find a flaw in your plan and react to it is not a sign of weakness; it is the ultimate sign of strength. The difference between the best companies and the weakest ones is not in the number of mistakes but rather in the reaction time.

A few final thoughts on business planning:

Listen to Your Phone

When I was a student at Berklee, one of my favorite instructors was Bob Freedman, a top arranger in the music industry. He was once questioned by a student who couldn't decide whether to focus his efforts on being a studio musician, a composer, or an arranger. How should the student make up his mind? Bob replied bluntly, "Your phone will tell you." He's right. And so is your phone.

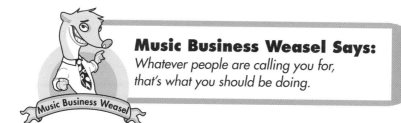

Music Business Weasel Says:
Whatever people are calling you for, that's what you should be doing.

Music Business Weasel

Regardless of your personal assessment of your catalog's strengths and weaknesses, the industry and the public will make up their own mind, and in the world of commerce, majority rules. If people are reacting positively to a certain sort of music, or a particular business approach, don't fight it. Do more of it. To do otherwise is to sail against the wind. When the public speaks, listen.

Hit 'em Where They Ain't

One of the best lessons I learned from working at Jive Records was the importance of targeting your efforts toward areas of the market that exist just under the radar of the mainstream music industry. When Jive had great success in the late nineties in the mainstream pop market, much of the label's success was built by focusing on the areas that everyone else was ignoring.

When Jive first signed the Backstreet Boys in 1994, teen-oriented pop music was all but invisible. Alternative rock and grunge were at their peak, New Kids on the Block were neither new nor kids, and MTV and radio had no interest whatsoever in a new group of singing and dancing teenage boys. If you were doing a business plan for the group at that time, you would have had to admit that the environment in the industry was a significant barrier to overcome.

What you would also have had to note however, is that such an environment provided a big, inviting void that was just waiting to be filled. For the screaming teenage girls that have gravitated toward boy groups since the days of the Jackson 5, there was nothing out there—no one was providing the music they wanted to hear. From the point of view of the record company, it was a market with little or no competition, relatively low costs, and an audience that, though small at the time, was intensely loyal and enthusiastic. A business landscape that originally looked like a black hole was in fact a big open field, just waiting for someone to throw seeds on the ground. A few years later, Jive did the same thing all over again, using outlets like Radio Disney and Nickelodeon to establish Aaron Carter as a "tween" superstar, before anyone else even knew there was such a market.

It's always best to avoid going head to head in competition with a bigger, stronger opponent. Better to stay out of sight, pick your spots, and exploit any weakness you can find. This has been the most consistently successful strategy for small independent companies in every industry. It is particularly effective in the record business, due in large part to the lemming-like nature of the Music Business Weasel. In a world in which the tendency is for everyone to copy the trend du jour, there are inevitably segments of the market that are abandoned. The trick is to get in early and avoid the crowds.

If You've Got Partners, Put the Plan on Paper

"But I thought you said we didn't have to write our business plan down." Did I say that? Are you sure? Perhaps you misunderstood? That was never what I meant....

Communication is a tricky thing. The goals or plans that seem so clear in your own head rarely translate to others with the same clarity. While a company controlled by one person can get away with a business plan that exists somewhere in the nether regions of his or her psyche, the business partnership requires something a whole lot more concrete.

For those of you creating a business that requires outside funding, there is no alternative to constructing a full, formal business plan. After all, you're asking people to invest their money and then let you run the show. A snappy spiel and a handshake are unlikely to seal the deal. You are required to provide a professional, formal business plan for the protection of your investors and yourself. I suggest that you speak to a lawyer or a business consultant to help you put your ideas into a proper format.

The typical music business partnership is a bit looser, and therefore probably even more dangerous. A shared philosophy, a few great lunch meetings, and suddenly you're opening a business checking account with your new partner—without much more to show for your planning sessions than a collection of million-dollar ideas scribbled on a napkin. I've seen this movie before, and you won't like the ending.

Almost inevitably, these marriages dissolve in recrimination, and it's not necessarily because either partner is dishonest, disloyal, or inept. It's a simple fact of human nature that none of us understand each other perfectly or perceive the world in exactly the same way. Thousands of years of human comedy and tragedy are built upon this fundamental truth. That's why businesses and other forms of human interaction are built on paper—lots of paper. Don't assume. Don't interpret. Get it in writing.

At the very least, you and your business partner(s) should proceed together through the process outlined in this chapter, including the Music Business Weasel's Pop Quiz. Formulate your answers together, and then put them on paper, making sure that you each have a copy of the plan when you're done. If you want to go through a more formal process, so much the better. The essential thing is that you and your partner have frank, honest, and concrete discussions about your goals for the business, how you expect to achieve them, and the role that each partner will play in the process.

Set a Deadline

You can plan forever. After all, it doesn't cost much, it's intellectually stimulating, and you can never be wrong—at least, not until you actually try to make it happen. The business plan is one step in the process of creating a business; it is not a business in itself.

The music industry is not conducted from an ivory tower. It does not diminish the importance of planning to acknowledge that much of a publisher's success depends on fortuitous timing, an aggressive response to any opportunity, and good instincts. Don't waste your time on endless theorizing, introspection, and the details of business structure. If your business plan has focused your thinking, provided a reasonable set of goals, and a game-plan for how to achieve them, then it has served its purpose.

The pre-game show only lasts but so long. At some point, it's time to take the field.

Setting Up Shop

With the possible exception of being a TikTok influencer, it's hard to think of a business with a lower barrier of entry than music publishing. Assuming you already have the songs, all you really need is a phone and a computer to get started. As your catalog of songs grows or you begin to represent writers other than yourself, you may need a software program to help with keeping track of the songs, splits, co-publishers, and licenses. Once royalties start rolling in, you will probably need some kind of program to generate royalty statements. Those are good problems, and we'll address the possible solutions later in this book.

For now, there are just a few things to consider before you hang out your shingle. As with any new venture, it's worth considering the appropriate business structure for your company. You should also give some thought to the setting you plan to work from. As with your business plan, these are not questions with right or wrong answers. The only wrong answer is one that has you spending a lot of money you don't have, doing a lot of paperwork you don't have time for, or taking on risks that are too high for the profit you can hope to earn.

Structure: What Am I?

If only to know what box to check on your tax form, you will need to ponder at least for a moment the best business structure for your publishing company. Choosing from a U.S. government-approved list of possible options, you could select: sole proprietorship, S corporation, limited partnership, partnership, and a corporation. Any and all of them can be effective structures for a music publishing venture. You'll just want to think about your own financial situation, need for investment, tolerance level for paperwork, and desire or willingness to work with others.

For example, one of the primary factors that influences the decision between a sole proprietorship and a corporation is the question of liability.

The *sole proprietorship* is the simplest of all business structures; it's what you are if you're not any of the others. As a sole proprietor, the owner (that's you my friend) is responsible for 100 percent of the business, keeps 100 percent of the income, is taxed on 100 percent of the profits, and assumes 100 percent of the liabilities. This means that you are personally on the hook for any debts or obligations incurred by the company, and your property, savings accounts, or other assets can be at risk if the company goes broke.

The degree of danger related to liability is directly proportional to how many other assets you already have. If you have a lot of personal assets like property, business interests outside of publishing, or a large amount in savings or investments, you don't want a problem with your music publishing company to put those things at risk. If your music business is your primary investment, then being a sole proprietor imposes no additional liability beyond what you already have. Unless your songs are dangerously bad, you're unlikely to do physical or mental damage to anyone with them. Even in a copyright infringement case, it's rare that you would be held liable for damages in excess of the amount the song earned (though you could be held liable for the other party's legal costs). Liability in the music publishing business is not nearly as significant as is something like aeronautics manu- facturing or pharmaceuticals. But do keep in mind that the music business is not exactly a sure bet for success. If you've got a significant nest egg, you might want to consider a structure better-suited to protect it: the corpora- tion.

The *corporation* is a bit more like Frankenstein's experiment. When you structure your business as a corporation, you are creating a new entity, sepa- rate from yourself. Your personal liability is limited to the amount of money you have invested in the corporation and your personal assets are never vulnerable. But while you limit your risk, you maximize your bookkeeping. The amount of financial reporting, form-filing, and record-keeping may soon have you feeling like you've indeed created a monster.

One preferred solution for many music entrepreneurs is the *Limited Liability Company* (LLC), a hybrid between the sole proprietorship and the corporation. The LLC has some of the simplicity of a sole proprietor- ship, particularly the potential for income to flow through directly from the company to the owner and to be treated as part of the owner's personal taxable income. But this structure also significantly limits the owner's personal liability, giving some of the same protections as a corporation, with considerably fewer accounting headaches.

If all of this sounds too daunting to face alone, then maybe a *partner-ship* structure is the best choice for you. Just as co-writing allows songwriters to find someone who can balance them creatively, a business partnership can provide support and a more diverse skill set for a startup company. Herb Alpert and Jerry Moss, LA Reid and Babyface, and Chris Wright and Terry Ellis are just some of the teams that have established hugely successful ventures together.

Or perhaps it's not active partners you're looking for, but rather some deep-pocketed investors. In that case, you could consider a *limited partner-ship*, with yourself as a general partner and one or more investors as limited partners. As a general partner, you own and operate the business and take on the same level of liability as a sole proprietor. But with limited partners, your investors do not have a right to make decisions regarding the business, and they do not have any liability for debts related to the business. I've seen these investor partnership structures used quite frequently, especially in Nashville.

A relatively new business structure that has recently become increasingly common for music publishers is that of the financial "hedge fund." Here, the company raises money from investors (in this case with the intention of acquiring music copyrights) and then charges those investors a fee for managing their investment. At the same time, the company takes a percentage of the income generated by the copyrights it acquires. It's nice work if you can get it. But don't get too used to it, as most of these companies are created specifically to be sold, ensuring that the investors get their money back, usually within ten to fifteen years.

In the end, the best business structure is the one that allows you to focus on the business itself. The goal is to find a structure that suits your personality, skill set, appetite for risk, and timeframe. Personally, I like the LLC. In my experience, a sole proprietor structure puts too much liability on the owner, and also tends to attract extreme scrutiny from the Internal Revenue Service if the earnings get too high. A corporation is too much work to set up and maintain. For most independent songwriters who will primarily publish their own music, I think the LLC occupies a safe and comfortable spot between the two. It can also accommodate business partners, investors or even hedge fund money if you're feeling that lucky.

In any case, be sure to check with a financial advisor or lawyer, to be sure that what you've chosen is appropriate for the state or country in which you live or the tax bracket you're in.

Location: Where Do I Belong?

The answer to the question of where to build your music publishing business geographically could be as simple as the room in which you're reading this book. If you've got an internet connection and a working electrical outlet, you're probably ready to launch.

At the same time, it might be worth giving the subject just a little more thought. After all, if you live in a studio apartment in Philadelphia, and you're hoping to start a country music publishing venture that will one day represent not only you but three or four other writers, your location is going to be a severe disadvantage. Likewise, if you specialize in English-language hip-hop and you're based in Belgium, you are always going to be a little out of the loop of the industry you're in.

In this age of easy worldwide communication and collaboration, the music centers like Los Angeles, Nashville, London, and Stockholm don't have the hegemony that they once did. Recently, I worked with two young hip-hop producers creating tracks from their basement in a small town in Germany, who still managed to have songs on four U.S. Top Ten albums in 2019. But the fact remains that any particular sector of the music industry is usually centered in one or two specific cities, and the people who live or have offices in those cities have a big advantage in becoming part of those communities. It's hard to be in the American pop music business and not be in Los Angeles. That's where artists are living, recording their albums, and collaborating with writers and producers every day. If you're in the country business, Nashville remains the power center of that particular universe. It's easier to be in the electronic music business in Amsterdam or Berlin than in South Dakota. There's a much better chance of lightening striking if you work in a place where it rains once in a while.

But if it's not possible to be where the action is, there's still a chance to put your office where you can build a local network of like-minded people. Maybe you or a friend run a commercial recording studio. Better to put your office there, where other musicians and songwriters are coming and going daily, than at your kitchen table. Could you share an office with a local booking agency, music journal, advertising agency, or festival organizer—ideally one that is supportive of the music genre in which you specialize?

In the past few years, one of the best examples of using location to a company's advantage is London's Tileyard Music. Taking over what was quite literally a collection of warehouses and tile factories in a scruffy industrial area in North London near Kings Cross, Tileyard built a campus of small recording studios, writing rooms, and office spaces, adding in a café and performing space to make the complex more of an artistic community. Mark Ronson constructed his studio there (and cut "Uptown Funk"), Lady Gaga came to record, companies like Ultra and Disney organized writing camps, and Liam Gallagher based his clothing brand Pretty Green there. Soon, music-related tech companies started moving in as well. Today, Tileyard is a hub of creative activity in London, with more than 80 studios and 142 creative companies working, interacting, and growing together.

With the savvy that you would expect of people who start such an enterprise, the creative team that developed Tileyard also started two different publishing entities, both of which are based onsite. Needless to say, the advantage of location is a major factor for those publishing ventures as they see a constant stream of the U.K.'s established and upcoming artists and producers every day, along with record label A&Rs, artist managers, and music-related tech developers. Unless you share an apartment with Mark Ronson or Kanye, you don't get that in your home office. Not surprisingly, similar shared studio-office work environments are now popping up in L.A., Amsterdam, Milan, and New York.

There's nothing wrong with a home office. It's cheap, convenient, and you can wear your pajamas if you feel like it. The only danger is isolation. Given that many songwriters lean toward the reclusive side anyway, there's a real benefit to a work space that forces you to mingle with other human beings, and especially ones who might be working in similar fields. If you opt for running your publishing company from home, you'll have to make a focused effort to remain connected to the outside world. All of which leads me to the last item you need to consider when setting up your office, the one tool of the trade that you can't survive without:

Information: Where Is the Loop, and How Do I Get in It?

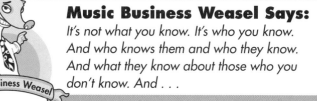

Music Business Weasel Says:
It's not what you know. It's who you know. And who knows them and who they know. And what they know about those who you don't know. And . . .

The real currency of the entertainment industry is information. Hot breaking news, inside tips, gossip, rumors, word on the street—this is what passes for knowledge in the world of show business. People are hired every day simply on the basis of the phone numbers in their iPhone. Indeed, the quest for inside information is so all-consuming that an entire industry exists to provide it, with a myriad of journals, magazines, and tip sheets devoted to keeping the Music Business Weasel always in the know. Part of setting up your office is getting yourself in the loop.

There are four basic types of information that you should be utilizing in your business: trade magazines or newsletters, directories or databases, tip sheets, and social media.

Trade Magazines or Journals

Other than social media, trade magazines and journals are the most comprehensive and easy-to-access of the various publications. Trade journals are a part of almost every industry. They chronicle day-to-day business developments, executive changes, political issues, and other news that affects those in that field. The key distinguishing characteristic of a trade magazine is that it is targeted toward those in the business, not the general consumer. *Rolling Stone* is a music magazine and informative reading for anyone interested in music. But it is not a trade magazine, as its orientation is toward the general music consumer, not the music executive.

The primary music business trade publications are: *Billboard, Music Business Worldwide, Music Week* (in the U.K.), and *Hits*. Beyond that, there are several entertainment business publications that have sections devoted to the music industry, such as *Variety* and *The Hollywood Reporter*. Then of course there are dozens of specialized newsletters, magazines, and websites for specific genres and segments of the industry: *Pollstar* covers the concert industry, *XXL* is focused on hip-hop, *Music Row* passes along all the news in the country music industry, and it goes on and on.

Don't worry. I'm not suggesting you read all of these. Better to sample a couple of different publications that seem relevant to your business, and then subscribe to one or two that give you the information you need.

Personally, I'm a *Billboard* guy. Despite changes in its editorial approach that in recent years have pushed it more in the direction of a general interest entertainment magazine ("What are the stars wearing to Coachella this year?"), it is still the most comprehensive trade magazine on the market. Its charts, which track the top singles and albums across all genres, remain the scorecard for the industry. It's also the one that covers almost every facet of the business, from live music events to radio to international business. I have a certain personal attachment to *Billboard*, because it helped lead me to my first gig in the music industry, which I'll tell you about a little later. Whether you get the print edition or just watch it online at *Billboard Business* a *Billboard* subscription remains an almost essential roadmap for navigating this business.

Of the other trades, my current favorite is *Music Business Worldwide (MBW)*. Free to anyone who visits the website or blog, it has grabbed some of the industry "insider" status that *Billboard* sacrificed in exchange for celebrity stories and fashion spreads. *MBW*'s investigative reporting is generally stronger than *Billboard*, particularly as it relates to stories in the world of streaming, and their interviews with major industry figures are insightful and engaging. This publication does not get into the chart-keeping business, nor does it spend much time on things like radio or the live industry. But for the modern music industry sectors of records, publishing, streaming, and artist management, it's a very useful publication.

Hits or its online version *Hits Daily Double* is also worth checking out. It's funny and irreverent, and a very entertaining read. For those in the mainstream pop, rock, country or urban sectors, it tends to have the most accurate inside scoop on what's really happening week to week at radio.

Film-industry publications like *Variety* and *The Hollywood Reporter* can be beneficial if your business is directed primarily at placing songs in television and movies.

Directories

While the industry trades can tell you what's going on and who's doing what to whom, they will not usually help you much with the next step, which is to get in touch with all those movers and shakers that you're reading about. This can present a problem when you're starting out in the industry, as most execs guard their contact information like the Holy Grail. Thankfully, there are a number of published sources that can help you track down companies and executives.

For my money, the most valuable directories are those put out by The Music Business Registry. There are a variety of different publications, such as *The Film & Television Music Monthly*, *Music Publishers Registry*, and a *Music Attorney* registry. But for music publishers, the most useful of all is the *A&R Registry*. This is a thorough listing of almost all of the major and independent record companies and the key A&R staff, which is updated every two months. Not surprisingly, *A&R Registry* is protective of the information that they supply, so the subscription is expensive. If you're serious about developing a music publishing business, I would suggest that you pay any price to get this particular publication. It is an essential investment.

Tip Sheets

Tip sheets are the real insider information—the music business equivalent to stock tips passed at cocktail parties, or a secret password whispered through a crack in the door. At least, that's the idea. Tip sheets are usually put out by small publishers, available by subscription only, and often require certain professional credentials in order to subscribe. For music publishers, there are two specific types of tip sheets: one tells you "Who's Looking" for songs land the other predicts the "Next Big Thing."

Who's Looking

Aimed primarily at pop-oriented publishers, the traditional "Who's Looking" tip sheet provides a periodic update on those labels, artists, producers, and managers currently seeking material. Although the business of pitching songs has actually grown over the past decade, for some reason tip sheets are harder to come by. Thankfully, some long-established publications, like Nashville's *RowFax* are still around, and *The Music Business Registry* has now launched one called *The Looking List*. Meanwhile, many music publishers and record labels prefer to create their own list, limiting access to those affiliated with the company or approved by the A&R staff.

In place of the old-fashioned "Who's Looking" list, this generation has created online platforms that function like mini-music communities, in which songwriters and publishers can see projects in development, share their material, and essentially put themselves in a position for managers, producers, and A&R executives to find them. Sites like Submit Hub, Music Gateway, MDIIO, and BeatStars offer songwriters an opportunity to see what A&R people and music supervisors are looking for, suggest songs from their catalog, and if one of those songs hits the mark, to build a direct relationship with others in the industry who like their work. To be honest, most of these communities do not attract the top songwriters, artists, label executives, or publishers. Those people rely on a personal network of contacts rather than a network based on a subscription price. But for those just entering the industry, these platforms offer an introduction to people who might actually give your songs a fair listen. When you are first starting out, that is no small thing.

The Next Big Thing

While the "Who's Looking" lists have dwindled, the last few years have brought an explosion in the prognostication business, with many of these services powered by the relentless flow of data from the streaming services and social media. These services consolidate the relevant data, spot the trends, mix it in with a little bit of old-fashioned ear-to-the-street A&R, and deliver to you a weekly list of new artists about to explode into stardom—most of whom, in the end, do nothing of the kind. Despite their spotty track record, these publications do serve to spread the buzz about new artists and bands to the A&R community. If you're an artist yourself, it might be a wise idea to try to get your name mentioned in one. Some of the most popular tip sheets or platforms of this nature include *Hype Machine* (driven primarily by music blogs), *Next Big Sound*, *A&R Worldwide* (which leans more toward the rock genre), *Instrumental,* and *Soundcharts* (for serious data-crunchers). For publishers, these are primarily of use to those interested in signing new artists or bands that write their own material. Another cheaper option might be to do some of the data-mining on your own, checking a few key blogs, watching the social media trends, and keeping an eye out for things gaining traction on Shazam or Spotify's Fresh Finds and Viral 50 playlists.

WARNING: If information is power, then you must be sure not to abuse it. Trade magazines, industry directories, and tip sheets are not mass mailing lists or sales-call fodder, and are not created for amateurs or hobbyists. The people listed in these magazines and newsletters are busy professionals trying to make a living in a very difficult business. *Do not bug them.*

In part II of this book, we will discuss at length the most professional and effective ways of pitching your material. This means using:

. . . **research** to find out what sort of music is appropriate for the person you are soliciting.

. . . **judgement** to determine what songs in your catalog are worth sending out.

. . . **etiquette** to approach people in a way that is positive, assertive, and respectful.

As you look into obtaining subscriptions for many of these publications, you will find that they can be expensive, and in many cases difficult to obtain without clear professional credentials. As you might guess, there's a reason. Particularly in the case of tip sheets, all subscribers rely on other subscribers not to inundate the A&R people and producers with substandard material. Remember, the publications I've mentioned in this chapter are the same ones that my colleagues and I use every day. Treat them with care.

Social Media

In many ways, the business of tip sheets, directories, and insider information has been challenged by the explosion of social media, which allows much more immediate access to artists, managers, record executives, and producers than any publication could provide. Someone hoping to pitch songs to Justin

Bieber doesn't have to employ an army of journalists to see whether or not he's in the studio this month, who he's working with, where he's recording, and his current musical direction. You could follow him, his manager, and his most frequent collaborators on Twitter or Instagram and probably figure it out. Artists and the creative team around them are more accessible than ever before, and in many instances, the best pitching strategy, particularly for producers and managers, can be a simple connection on social media or sites like SoundCloud.

But while the social media platforms are largely free, be aware that there is still an investment to be made. If your primary contact with people will be through social media, then your own social media presence needs to be impressive enough to give the appearance of an up-and-coming professional, not an Internet troll with a demo. Building up followers and friends is a job as well, and it will take time and ingenuity to grab the attention of a top producer or manager. In the meantime, you can focus on approaching developing artists, other young producers and writers just a rung or two above you on the music ladder. As with all networks, yours will gradually expand and start to open up opportunities for you.

So if all of these startup related decisions about business structures, office locations, and tip sheets feel like too many choices to make and too much money to spend, you can solve all that by just not doing it. You can simply call yourself a sole proprietor, make an office out of your kitchen table, and dig around the Internet to find the information you need. No harm done. In fact, if it's cheap, easy, and quick then it's not a bad place to start your enterprise. You are entering a high-risk business with many ups and downs and very slow cash flow. The last thing you need is additional paperwork or high overheads.

Humble Beginnings: Start Small, Grow Big

And now that story of my first music industry gig (courtesy of *Billboard* magazine)—and a concluding lesson. Just after I graduated from college, I happened to read an article in *Billboard* about an organization being formed by Tom Silverman, founder of the legendary Tommy Boy Records. Tom had the idea for an industry trade group, the Independent Label Coalition, that would represent the interests of the many independent record labels at the forefront of the budding hip-hop, alternative, and dance music industries. In the article, Tom mentioned with customary subtlety that he was looking for people to volunteer time to this venture and suggested that it would be a fine opportunity for young people looking to get a foot in the door.

A few weeks later, I went to New York to meet Tom and interview for the job (or whatever you call working for free). At that time, Tommy Boy was one of the leading indie labels in the country, riding on a string of hits that would eventually become hip-hop classics. Imagine then my surprise as I pulled up in a taxi to the address that I had carefully written down—91st Street and First Avenue (not exactly the heart of Manhattan)—and saw only a tenement building, its door covered with graffiti, and a sporting goods supply store specializing in soccer equipment. No sign. Nothing. I checked the address. The cab driver looked at me, shrugged. I got out. Rang the unmarked buzzer outside the tenement door and was let in. Walked up the dark, dingy stairwell, also covered with graffiti, to the second floor, above the soccer shop. And there was Tommy Boy Records. The office itself was professional and comfortable, but not lavish. Like good indie labels anywhere, it was full of boxes of press materials and promo merchandise and manned by a combination of eager kids working for backstage passes and over-caffeinated staffers working for just barely more than that. It was frenetic and noisy, and just hitting its stride at about 5:30 in the evening. In every respect, it looked, smelled, and felt like the record business—which is a compliment, in my book.

A few months later, having now relocated to New York, I went to another meeting, this one in the office of a successful songwriter, who was starting a production/publishing company of his own. He was certainly doing it with confidence—a midtown Manhattan address, reception lobby, a large office space that was spotless (and empty). It had the quiet, gleaming elegance of a financier's office. When I commented on the surroundings, the songwriter-turned-CEO informed me that having been involved with so many different small-time record labels and publishers during his career, he had resolved that his own business would be run in first-class style; he would do things, in his words, "the right way." It was an impressive, if not entirely persuasive, display.

The Moral

A few years after I worked there, Tom Silverman wound up selling his last shares of Tommy Boy to Warner Bros. Records for over $10 million; he had already sold a significant portion of the company several years earlier. By then of course, the company had relocated to a new space downtown, having long outgrown the old First Avenue address. Tom's career since has included being the head of NAIRD, the National Association of Independent Record Distributors, the founder of the New Music Seminar, and one of the most successful entrepreneurs to come out of the early days of hip-hop.

The other songwriter's business lasted less than a year. Not even enough time to fit any employees in those swanky new offices.

In the music business, the right way is whatever works. When it comes to setting up an office, cheap is right. Practical is right. Fast is right. Getting your hands dirty is right. One of my favorite songwriters, Billy Mann, has a publishing company called Tortoise Wins the Race. He's right about that. Your first office does not need to be a showplace. It's a starting point; it's not where you're planning to stay.

7

Setting Up Systems: It's All About the Paper

Recently, in a single day, I dealt with the following issues:

1. A song slated to appear in a major motion picture, with all licenses issued and all sync fees agreed upon, was suddenly found to have a third, previously unidentified writer, and correspondingly, a third publisher. As all publishers must grant licenses in order for a song to appear in a film (which is not the case with records), this meant that two days before locking the music to picture, the movie studio would have to negotiate a license and sync fee with a new publisher, who, being aware of the film company's position, would probably not be particularly easy to please.

2. It was discovered that a song already released as the single for a major artist was registered with BMI as belonging to an entirely different publisher altogether, and with an additional writer as well. This presented a sizable problem, as the artist intended to perform the song on five national television shows in the next week, all of which required licenses to be issued by the publishers on the song. To compound the problem, it appeared that BMI's information was incorrect. In fact, even the publisher listed by BMI denied owning the song. Still, someone had to issue a license to the television shows. Fast.

3. As part of a national promotion campaign, a selection of videos by up and coming artists were slated to play in a continual loop at thousands of franchises of a well-known fast food chain. All of the songs were licensed by the publishers on a "gratis" basis, which is

to say they were free—the theory being that this promotion would give exposure to these emerging artists and therefore ultimately help the writers and publishers as well. Days before the promotion was supposed to go live at restaurants around the country, it was discovered that a writer of one of the songs had contractual rights to approve the granting of a "gratis" license. The even bigger problem was that most of the "gratis" licenses issued by the other publishers included "favored nations" language, which meant that should the one writer demand and receive a synchronization fee, all of the other writers and publishers would have to get the same thing.

In each instance, the reaction was the same: Panic. Angry calls and emails flew, threats were exchanged, split letters and contracts were frantically dug up out of long-forgotten files, more phone calls were made, and after several hours of mayhem, someone finally fessed up. "Sorry, it was all a misunderstanding. Just a minor paperwork error. Not to worry." Conflict resolved. Life goes on.

Is there a point to these stories, other than to illustrate how quickly and often a day can go from good to bad, and when you're lucky, back to good again? Yes. The point is that in the publishing business, "paperwork errors" are not minor. That's because paperwork is what publishing is. It's like an accountant excusing something as just a "mistake in the math" or a surgeon shrugging off a "slip of the hand." As publishers, we don't have to write the songs, or record the songs, or sell the records. We just have to keep track of who wrote the songs, issue the licenses, protect the copyrights, and count the money. Accurately. The degree of accuracy is largely the difference between a good and bad publisher.

Off in the distance, the reader groans "Paperwork. Aargh."

I hear you. Trust me, I feel your pain. It's not why I got into this game either. In any major publishing company, there are people who have devoted their career to the proper administration of copyrights (which is to say, paperwork). It's honorable and important work, and I have nothing but respect for the people who do it. Nevertheless, I must admit, I fail to understand its appeal. But a day like the one I had last week brings home with painful clarity how essential the administrative process is to the proper operation of a publishing company. We've already touched on issues like split sheets and submission forms; now it's time to take this one step further and put systems in place. As you set up your office, you need to put in place administrative systems that will allow you to properly catalog your copyrights, recordings, and finances.

Systems? Isn't it a little early for that? Probably. The way to keep the paperwork requirements of publishing from consuming too much of your energy is to handle the paper before it handles you. Having a system will not entirely prevent situations like the ones I described earlier (all the publishers involved in those messes had plenty of administrative processes in place), but it will allow you to minimize them, and to resolve them quickly and accurately. In fact, that was another lesson learned during the day from hell. The systems actually worked in the end, and because they did, song number one stayed in the movie, song number two had its moment on the TV, and song number three showed up in your favorite fast food chain along with your burger and fries. If the systems had not existed, these issues could have taken months or even years to sort out.

The truth of paperwork is that you can pay now or pay later. If you start out correctly, investing the time to put systems in place and to stay on top of the work, you will be able to manage your business efficiently as it grows. If you choose not to spend the time now, you will likely find yourself unable to ever catch up, as the catalog keeps growing and issues keep appearing. This will force you to sort through the pile of paper on your desk to try to resolve the problems, which of course will put you even further behind, until you look up one day and realize that you have spent your entire week on administration issues.

One good example of the power of a good system is Kobalt Music. No company has invested more heavily in technology and administrative infrastructure than Kobalt, with its latest funding round estimated to be near $100 million, including backing from Google Ventures. Only in 2021 did the company finally report a profit, in part because so much is spent on continually improving the capacity of their systems. But the technology that Kobalt has developed has in many ways transformed the publishing industry and given the company immense competitive advantages: the capability of managing vast numbers of songs at a minimal cost, accounting with a level of transparency that was previously unheard of, and providing those accountings on a quarterly, rather than bi-annual schedule. Kobalt's systems are their selling point and the decision to invest in the infrastructure right from the start is what has made the growth of the company possible.

Of course, when it comes to setting up office systems, there are as many variations as there are publishing companies. Clearly, what works for you depends on the size of your catalog, your goals for the business, your access to capital, and your working style. The best I can do is attempt to give you a clear idea of the information you'll need to organize and a few suggestions as to how to tackle the task. It's up to you to customize the systems to your own liking.

There are three primary areas of your business you'll need to organize: administration, recordings, and finances. We'll take two different approaches to each—let's call it "old school" and "new school." You can decide which shoe fits.

Managing the Administration

Yep, back to those old split sheets. You should have a nice little stack of them by now, right?

Old School

Forms and Files. Every bureaucrat in the world swears by them. If it's good enough for the government, it ought to be good enough for your company. So take that pile of split sheets, and let's put together a system.

Begin by setting up a file on your computer or in your file cabinet (if you're seriously old school) for each copyright. Eventually, this file will contain all the information and paperwork relevant to that particular song. For the moment, the first thing we'll put in the file is the completed split sheet. To review, this letter should include the following:

- writers/publishers (including names, addresses, and IPI numbers)
- percentages
- date the song was completed
- signatures of writers

The next things that go into the file:

Lyrics. Every song should have a lyric sheet, stored either in the administration file or somewhere on the computer. Lyric sheets always seem like a bother—but sooner or later, you always need one. Most importantly, you only need one when there's an emergency at hand. The superstar is at the studio ready to cut the song, but no one knows the words. The song looks great in the movie, but some studio legal-eagle is sure she heard something objectionable in the third line of the verse. Inevitably, the call comes in while you're in the middle of a recording session, and you have to drop everything and try to decipher a lyric written two years ago that you can hardly remember anyway. Put a lyric sheet in the file.

Copyright Administration Checklist. The purpose of this piece of paper is to remind you of what you will eventually need to do to administer the copyright, though you don't need to do it right now. There's a sample of such a checklist on the next page.

Copyright Administration Checklist

Forms	Completed (x)	Date Completed
Split Sheet		
Lyrics		
Performance Society Registration		
Mechanical License Registration		
YouTube Claim		
Harry Fox Registration		
Music Reports Registration		
Sub-Publisher Registrations		
Copyright Registration		

NOTES:

    TERRITORIES EXCLUDED: _____

    REVERSIONS: _____

    LIMITATIONS: _____

    APPROVALS REQUIRED FOR:

        TELEVISION/FILMS _____

        ADVERTISING _____

        TRANSLATIONS _____

Translations

Language	% to Translator	Fee	Approved(x)	Territories

Sample Uses

Release	Artist	ISRC	Ownership %	Fee

For the moment, don't worry about the specifics of these procedures—we'll discuss them in detail in part III of this book. The important thing is to have something in place to be sure that you don't overlook a step in the process. The checklist should include reminders about the following:

- Split Sheets: But of course you don't need to be reminded about this, do you?
- BMI/ASCAP/SESAC Registration: When you register the song online with your performing rights organization, you should expect to see it appear in your catalog list within 8 to 12 weeks, with an ISWC #.
- Harry Fox Agency: Again, you can deposit the song online into your account. But be prepared to follow up and check that the song is in the system. Never assume that your work is done until you see it listed there.
- YouTube: Whether you do it through a direct affiliation with YouTube, an outside service like Audiam, or an administrative partner, it's important to be sure that your claims are submitted to YouTube promptly, as soon as possible after the release of the record.
- Music Reports: As we'll discuss later, Music Reports represents some major companies like Amazon and Pandora, and a lot of ground-breaking new media platforms.
- Copyright Registration: A handful of conscientious and perhaps slightly paranoid writers (and publishers) register their songs immediately upon completion. Given that there is a fee for registering, I suggest that you wait to register until the song has been placed in some sort of income-generating situation. The reality of most catalogs is that only a few of the copyrights ever really create any income. You can put your money to better use. We'll revisit this subject in more detail later.
- Notes: The Notes section of the form should include any information that may be pertinent to the copyright or its use. If you are the only writer for your publishing company, then there will likely be very few notes—and those will be the same for almost every song. But if you have several writers signed to your company or if there are outside co-writers that are part of the copyright, be sure that you have all the information you need. A few things to consider:

- o Reversions: For how long do you own the copyright? Do the rights to the song revert back to the writer at some point in time? Under what conditions?
- o Limited Rights: Do you have the right to exploit the copyright in any medium without restriction?
- o Approvals: Do you need the writer's approval to place the song in certain situations? This is the "gratis" license issue that popped up the other day. Writers often have approval over gratis uses, as well as advertising (particularly as connected to certain products), movies (anything rated R or X), or parodies.
- o Translations: Has there been a translation done of the song for a foreign market? If so, how was the translator compensated— did he or she receive a percentage of the song or a flat fee? Are there any other versions of the song in which the splits may be different than is outlined in the split sheet?
- o Samples: Has the song been sampled or interpolated in other compositions? If so, you'll need to know how much, if any, of the new composition you own, or if you received a flat fee in exchange for an ownership portion.
- These are just a few of the issues that can be addressed in the "Notes" section. Whatever you think you might need to know when shopping or collecting money on this song, put it in here.

New School

There are a number of different software systems that are well suited to managing your catalog's administration. For many years, the most popular publishing administration system has been Counterpoint Suite, which integrates the management of the administration, licensing, and royalty functions of music publishing into one set of software programs. But as many publishers have been investing heavily over the past decade in their own technology, those same companies are now competing with Counterpoint and selling their homegrown software systems directly to others. Companies like Songtrust and Sentric Music (RightsApp), both of which have a business model based on administering vast numbers of copyrights, market their systems to new companies looking to buy into the technological innovations that these high-volume businesses have inspired. At the same time, there is also a trend toward systems like Synchtank, DISCO, and Auddly that combine all or at least some of the Copyright Administration function with the second even bigger administrative challenge: keeping track of the songs.

Managing the Music

When I worked at Sony ATV, an organization with offices around the globe, I suddenly became aware of the never-ending challenge of assimilating songs from writers all over the world, cataloging them, and somehow disseminating them to A&R and sync departments at offices in each relevant territory. Clearly, one of the advantages of a large company like Sony is the prospect of a creative manager in Australia becoming a champion for a songwriter signed in the Dutch office or the sync department in L.A. landing an advertising placement for a writer signed in Japan. But how do you physically get the music into the hands and brains of those people in far-flung offices, giving them access without overwhelming them? The problem is compounded by the fact that the music just keeps coming: new songs are written, catalogs are acquired and the problems spread like weeds in a garden. Where do you start?

One good place is with one of the forms I mentioned back in chapter 3, the Song Submittal Form. This should be completed any time a new song demo is submitted. An example is provided in appendix B. This form contains all the necessary information to identify the demo recording, where and when it was recorded, and who was involved in the sessions. Again, this can be put with the rest of the documents relating to that song.

Now, the bigger question. What to do with the music itself? Here are two approaches to consider:

Old School

Thankfully, the era of the CD has passed, freeing up a couple square feet of additional space in every creative director's office where the tower used to be—that impenetrable yet precarious sky-high stack of CDs teetering behind the desk of every Music Business Weasel. Assuming that no one is so old school as to want to hang onto their shiny plastic discs, the attention then turns to our computers. I confess, my desktop screen often looks like my office used to, cluttered with sound files that I've grabbed from all different places, most of it labeled with indecipherable metadata (is it a demo? a master? a work in progress? and who sent this thing to me anyway?) Even in the brave new digital world, disorganization lives on.

If your catalog is largely limited to your own songwriting output, it's easy enough to just store everything in something like iTunes or a simple folder system on your desktop. Or you could also consider a cloud-based storage service like Box or Dropbox, which makes it easy to send or share files directly with others. These systems are particularly good if you have more than one person in your company on the creative side and you need all of them to be able to access everything in the catalog. Be forewarned, though: these storage systems can start to be become expensive as your catalog grows larger, especially if you have multiple versions of each song.

Many songwriters prefer services like SoundCloud, which again make it easy to share music with other writers and A&Rs, and also to track who listens. The caveat here is that if you pitch frequently to industry people, particularly music supervisors in the film, television, and advertising world, they will want to download the files they like in order to label and store the music in accordance with their own system. Nothing annoys me more than songwriters who send me SoundCloud files that are not downloadable, except maybe those who send links with expiration dates.

In this digital environment, storing your music is not the real challenge. The challenge is to organize it so that you can find what you want when you need it and then send it out quickly. And that's where you start to see the advantage of the....

New School

In part because of the consolidation that's taken place in the publishing industry over the past decade, with many small companies being acquired by larger ones and the catalogs of the surviving companies becoming ever larger, the challenge for creative directors to know and quickly access the songs has become daunting. Not surprisingly, a number of technology companies have stepped up with solutions to help publishers meet the challenge of understanding and managing their catalogs. Services like DISCO and Synchtank consolidate many of the administrative, music archiving and distribution functions into one all-encompassing system that helps creative directors find the songs in the catalog that could fit a specific project, get them out quickly to the A&R or music supervisors who need them, and track what has been sent and whether or not it's been streamed or downloaded by the recipient. Most of the music search aspect of this technology is based on the magic of metadata.

Managing the Metadata

I remember back in the pre-digital era, when my desk was overflowing with CDs, it was always a source of fascination to me how many songwriters would show up at a meeting with unmarked, unlabeled discs, or discs with a sharpie-scrawled designation like "Sampler #2," and then happily leave this utterly unidentifiable record of their life's work in a stack of similarly unmarked CDs in my office. "Call me when you've had a chance to check it out," they would say. Sure.

What really fascinated me was that I knew that when I was a songwriter, I had done the exact same thing. There's something about the songwriter brain and labeling things that don't fit together. Now that we've moved into the digital age, I can verify this little psychological insight by noting that the labeling of MP3s is no better than it was with CDs.

Metadata is the non-musical information embedded in the MP3 or WAV file. It's the labeling that pops up on iTunes (for instance) when you play the file. If your song reads:

TRACK 001-RUFF- FEMVOX_8-12 BY UNKNOWN ARTIST

...then you have metadata problems. No music supervisor or A&R person wants a track like that sitting on their iTunes, begging the question of "what is this and where did it come from?" At its most basic, metadata needs to include title, artist, composer, contact details, and rights owners (labels and publishers). That information can be entered as necessary in the iTunes "Get Information" and "Comments" section.

But that's just the beginning of what metadata can do. The value of most music archiving systems is they allow you to tag your files with information that will make it easier for yourself or those to whom you send the music to search for specific types of songs. You can tag songs to indicate key lyrics, tempos, genres, or moods. Particularly for those who pitch frequently for placements in the synchronization world, these systems can be big timesavers.

Of course, many of these music management systems are expensive and only make sense for companies with catalogs of hundreds, or even thousands of songs. The good news is that metadata and tags are available to everyone and can be used in your own iTunes or other storage system. The key is to take the time to enter all the necessary information each time you add a new song or even a new mix to your catalog.

While you're listening to a song for the first time, you should be making notes about where the song will fit in the catalog. Does it go in the top drawer, the middle drawer, or the bottom? Why? Are there any particular artists or projects for which the song seems particularly well suited? Does it need an edit or a new demo?

Clearly, if the song belongs in the bottom drawer or needs more work before it's marketable, then there's no need to add tags. You're not going to be sending it out in its current form. But if the song is finished and ready to pitch, that's when you want to add the tags that will ensure that it pops up when you search your system. What are the key lyrical themes? Tempo? Mood? What sorts of films, television shows, or advertisements could it work for? Does it sound like something from the '60s, the '90s, or today's Top 40? Whatever you think are the defining characteristics, try to incorporate them into tags, so that when the hunt is on for something specific, you can find the proverbial needle in the haystack.

Warning: Safety First!

One other warning when it comes to archiving your music—and this one applies to both the old school and the new. No system is infallible, no computer is indestructible and no publisher is beyond hitting the delete button by accident every now and then. Always keep a backup! Whether it's keeping your files backed up in the Cloud, on an external hard drive, or even a flash drive, make sure that you're covered in the case of disaster. There is nothing more depressing to a writer than having a publisher lose one of his or her songs. Even when it's an accident, it always seems to register as an insult.

And now, on to happier subjects. Counting your money. This is paperwork that you've got to get right . . .

8

Financial Accounting: Show Me the Money!

Depending on the nature of your business, your financial record keeping can be relatively simple or extremely complex. The primary determinant of the type of accounting system you need is whether you will be the sole writer represented by your company or will have several writers signed to you.

If you are the sole writer, then it's probably not necessary to break down your expenses or income, as there's only one writer to whom they can be assigned. If you wish, you can go through the process of paying royalties to yourself (and charging yourself for recoupable costs). An accountant can probably advise you as to whether this is necessary; it will depend largely on the structure you've selected for your company.

If you have several writers on your roster, your life just got a lot more complex. Not only will you need to set up a system to assign income and expenses to each writer, you will also have to keep track of each writer's account balance, determine whether or not royalties are due, and charge the writer back for any recoupable expenses. Before we get into the details of setting up an accounting system, let's take a second to understand the basic economic structure of music publishing and the path that a song's income stream will take from record company to publisher to writer.

This gets more than a little confusing. Consider the following running scoreboards.

The Income Distribution Game

FIRST QUARTER: The Kick-Off (Advances)

	Writer	Publisher
INCOME		
Advance	$10,000	
EXPENSES		
Writer Advance		($10,000)
Demo Costs		(7,500)
Travel Costs		(2,500)
SCOREBOARD	**$10,000**	**($20,000)**

The game kicks off in the first quarter when Publisher gives money to Writer, giving Writer a significant head start. Publisher pays advance to sign Writer: $10,000. Pays for $7,500 worth of demo expenses. Forks up another $2,500 in travel costs for a writing trip to L.A.

- Income to Writer: $10,000
- Total expenses to Publisher: ($20,000)

SECOND QUARTER: The Return (Gross Income)

	Writer	Publisher
(Balance from Q1)	$10,000	
INCOME (Gross)		
Performance Royalties	10,000	
Mechanical Royalties		$15,000
Performance Royalties		10,000
Sync Fee		5,000
SCOREBOARD	**$20,000**	**$30,000**

In the second quarter of the game, the money begins to roll in. Publisher receives $15,000 in mechanical royalties for copyrights belonging to Writer. Receives $10,000 in performance royalties generated by those same copyrights. Pulls in another $5,000 in sync payments for having put one of the songs in a movie. And keep in mind, if the publisher received $10,000 in performance royalties, the Writer also received his or her own check from the performing rights organization for the same amount. As we discussed earlier, performance payments are made directly to writers and publishers, with each receiving an equal amount from BMI, ASCAP, or SESAC.

- Total Income to Writer: $10,000
- Total Gross Income to Publisher: $30,000

But wait. There's a reason that this income is called "gross," and it's not because it's ugly. In fact, it looks pretty good. But it's just a representation of what's come into Publisher's account, before anyone looks at the debts that need to be paid, or divvies it up according to the contract between Writer and Publisher. Now, we have to determine how this "income stream" is actually assigned. This is the third quarter of the game.

THIRD QUARTER: The Hand-Off (Distribution)

	Writer	Publisher
(Balance from Q2)	$20,000	$30,000
INCOME		
Mechanical Royalties	7,500	
Sync Fee	2,500	
Mechanical Royalties (co-pub share)	3,750	
Performance Royalties (co-pub share)	5,000	
Sync Fee (co-pub share)	1,250	
(Total Income)	**40,000**	**30,000**
EXPENSES		
(Debt from Q1 Investment)		(20,000
Mechanical Royalties (advance/distribution to writer)		(7,500)
Sync Fee (advance/distribution to writer)		(2,500)
Mechanical Royalties (advance/distribution to writer)		(3,750)
Performance Royalties (advance/distribution to writer)		(5,000)
Sync Fee (advance/distribution to writer)		(1,250)
(Total Expenses, including $20,000 in new outstanding debt/unrecouped advances)		**(40,000)**
SCOREBOARD	**$40,000**	**($10,000)**

When we last tallied the score at the end of the second quarter, Writer had $20,000 in his or her pocket from the advance and the check from our friends at the PROs. Publisher was sitting on $30,000 of gross income. But let's assume that Publisher's contract with Writer is a somewhat typical co-publishing agreement, which means that Publisher controls half of the publishing share and Writer controls the other half. This means the income stream for the song needs to be apportioned as follows:

- **50 Percent to Writer:** Remember, the writer continues to own his or her "writer's" share; this share always represents half of the entire pie. The publisher collects all the income for the song, but the writer never (or almost never) has less than 50 percent of the "income stream." Publisher should pay Writer $7,500 (half of mechanical income) and $2,500 (half of sync income). Writer is credited $10,000 total.

- **25 Percent to Writer from Publisher Share:** This is the nature of a co-publishing agreement. The writer keeps the entire writer's portion, and takes a split of the publisher's share. Publisher now is committed to pay Writer half of the remaining mechanical income, which is $3,750, half of the performance monies totaling $5,000, and half of the remaining sync income equal to $1,250. Writer goes up an additional $10,000.

- **25 Percent to Publisher:** After all those payouts to Writer, there's not much left from that $30,000 in gross income: Publisher holds onto the remaining mechanical income of $3,750, the other half of the performance income for $5,000, and the remains of the sync fee which is $1,250. Total take: $10,000.

Seems pretty equitable, right? Three entities—Writer, Writer's Publishing Entity, and Publisher—all running neck and neck. Or are they?

Let's tally up the score.

Writer has already received a $10,000 advance, a $10,000 check from ASCAP or BMI, and is now credited another $10,000 in income. Writer moves up to $30,000. Then, add in the Writer's take of the Publisher share: $10,000. Writer just keeps rising—total score: $40,000.

Publisher, on the other hand, is still digging out of a hole. Remember that Publisher paid $10,000 in an advance, and another $10,000 in expenses, starting the game $20,000 down. Now, having played three quarters of the game, Publisher has only $10,000 in net income, against that $20,000 debt, to show for all his or her efforts.

Uh oh. Things may look rosy for Writer, but they look decidedly dire for Publisher, who is $10,000 poorer than prior to getting into the game. But wait. It ain't over 'til the fat lady sings—and in the final quarter of the game, a new rule is introduced.

Music Business Weasel Says:
Everything is recoupable.

Recoupable. Say the word again. How does it feel? You will learn to love it. Every weasel does. This is what it means:

Every expense incurred by Publisher on behalf of Writer—this includes advances, demo costs, travel expenses, mailing costs, equipment rental charges, and almost anything else Publisher can think of—can be recouped by the Publisher. This is to say that Publisher can charge back, or deduct, all recoupable expenses against Writer's account. Recoupable expenses are deducted from the amount due to Writer, not from the total income received by Publisher.

The concept of recoupable expenses is at the core of almost every music business contract, whether it's a recording agreement or a music publishing agreement. It is also at the center of most accounting disputes, and plenty of flat out chicanery as well.

The general principle, outlined in most contracts, is that any expense paid by the publisher specifically on behalf of the writer is recoupable, but general business expenses incurred by the publisher (office costs, salaries to employees, T&E expenses) are not recoupable. Personally, I think that recouping mailing costs and the like is somewhat tacky, but that's easy to say when you work for a relatively large, well-established company. When starting a small independent publishing company, you will probably need to be as aggressive about recouping costs as is legally acceptable. Just remember, any recoupable expenses will need to be identified specifically on the writer's accounting statement, so at some point, you may have to defend them directly to the writer. Be aggressive, but honest.

Given that this book is directed primarily at songwriters, and probably a fair number of artists, you will likely experience the concept of recoupable expenses from the opposite side of the ledger book as well. My advice here is fundamental: if anyone in this business "gives" you anything, you can be sure that it's recoupable. This includes stuff that seems sort of necessary, like $20,000 video budgets and Studio One at Abbey Road, and some stuff that's just plain cool, like that BMW rental car, or the first-class flight to Australia. It's never a gift. Read your contract, make sure you know what your rights are to approve expenses, and then read your statements carefully. And try to live humbly. Don't take candy from strangers or Music Business Weasels.

Now back to the game. Let's go back to the end of the third quarter and tally the score all over again, playing by the new rules.

FOURTH QUARTER: The Final Charge (Recoupment)

	Writer	Publisher
Balance from Q3	$40,000	($10,000)
INCOME		
Recoupment from Writer		20,000
EXPENSES		
Recoupable Q3 advances	(10,000)	
Recoupable Demo Costs	(7,500)	
Recoupable Writing Trip	(2,500)	
(Total Recoupable Expenses)	(20,000)	
SCOREBOARD (Final)	**$20,000**	**$10,000**

It's true that Writer earned $40,000 dollars in income by the end of that very exciting Third Quarter. But Writer is also carrying a $20,000 debt to Publisher in the form of recoupable expenses. In reality, the Writer still has the $10,000 advance, the expense paid trip to Los Angeles ($2,500), and his or her demo costs have been paid ($7,500). This advance money and the reimbursement for expenses (which are considered "additional advances") are non-returnable. Even if Writer fails to generate $20,000 in income, Writer will never be obligated to actually write a check to the Publisher to pay it back. But it is *recoupable,* meaning that it will be paid back from Writer's earnings.

Luckily for Writer, the other money that Publisher can't take away is the $10,000 in performance income that Writer received back in the second quarter. Because the writer's share of performance income is paid directly by ASCAP or BMI to the writer, there's no way for the publisher to use it toward recoupment. But that means that all $20,000 worth of income credited to Writer's account in the third quarter is instead staying in the account of Publisher to pay off those recoupable advances. Writer finishes the game with $20,000 more than he or she started, along with some well-recorded demos and a few good Insta photos of a week in Hollywood.

But look at the comeback by Publisher. Publisher now erases the $20,000 debt, still hangs onto the $10,000 that represents Publisher's share of the gross income, and finishes the game $10,000 ahead. The two sides just got a whole lot closer. Which is the whole point of recoupable expenses.

So here's the challenge: How to devise an accounting system that will allow you to keep track of all income and expenses (recoupable or not), properly credit the writer's account, and properly deduct the recoupable expenses from those accounts. And remember, you'll need to be able to generate coherent account statements for each writer twice a year.

Managing the Money

Old School

A spreadsheet always works. Whether you keep it in a book (does anyone still have a ledger book?) or on a simple Excel file, you can set up a page for each copyright, then list in columns each credit for income received or debit for each recoupable expense. Then in the adjacent columns note the nature of the payment or expense, a description, and the amount assigned to the writer.

Remember, in a standard publishing agreement, the total income stream of mechanical and sync income is divided 50 percent to the writer, 50 percent to the publisher. Performance payments for the writer go directly to the writer, while the "publisher's share" goes directly to the publisher. In a co-publishing agreement (in which the writer retains a portion of the publisher's share), the mechanical and sync income will be split 75 percent to the writer, and performance payment will be split 50 percent to writer and 50 percent to the publisher.

At the end of each accounting period (June and December), you will add up the accounts for each song, then total the amount due to the writer. The writer should receive an accounting statement (due in March and September) that lists the total income for each song, and the percentage due to him or her. It will also list all recoupable expenses being charged to the writer's account. Here's a sample income/debit statement.

The Income Distribution Game

Accounting (period ending December 31, 2020)

Souce	Income Received	Writer Share	Debits/ Expenses	Net Writer Income	Description
Harry Fox Agency	15,000	11,250		11,250	Mechanical Royalties
Big Film Productions	5000	3750		3750	Synchronization
			-10000	-10000	Writer Advance
			-7500	-7500	Demo Expenses
			-2500	-2500	Travel Costs (LA Trip)
Unrecouped Balance				-5000	
Total Due Writer				NO PAYMENT DUE AT THIS TIME	

Of course, all statements received from ASCAP, BMI, SESAC, Harry Fox, and sync licensees that detail income should be copied and filed, as they will be needed for your own accounting purposes and any possible audits by writers.

You will probably need a separate ledger or spreadsheet for your company's general expenses, like phone, utilities, and travel. While these costs are not recoupable to the writers, they are nevertheless legitimate business expenses that can be deducted from your taxes. This part of the record-keeping process is integral to the operation of any sort of business. If you need more information about how to set up this sort of accounting system, consult a good general-business book oriented toward setting up and operating your own company.

New School

There's a myriad of software options to manage this information, whether you need something specifically aimed at music publishing such as Counterpoint Suite or Music Maestro, or would prefer a basic accounting system for small businesses, like Quicken and Oracle that could be adapted to meet the needs of your company. Or you could consider a "white-label" option, like those software systems developed by larger publishers like Songtrust and Sentric Music.

If this chapter has left you feeling more like an accountant than a creative executive in the music industry, I sympathize. Music industry accounting is not exactly straightforward, and never seems to entirely please either the corporate bean counters or the creative community. But there are two important points that should be gleaned from the preceding discussion.

The first thing that becomes apparent is that the complexities of the accounting process increase greatly when you begin to take on writers other than yourself. The more complex the deals are that you make with additional writers, the more headaches you will have. If you structure similar deals for all of your writers, either on a co-publishing basis (you keep half of the publisher's share) or, even better, on a full publishing basis (you keep all of the publisher's share), you can set up administration and accounting systems that continue to be effective as you acquire more and more catalogs. If each writer's deal is completely different, it will be difficult to construct an accounting system to accommodate all the variables. In your eagerness to sign a particular writer, it can be very tempting to negotiate agreements that are unworkable in practice:

> *"We'll do a full-pub deal, but only on new copyrights. Any of the old catalog will be done on a co-pub basis, unless we get the song cut, at which time our share will go to 40 percent of the income stream, or if we put it in a movie, at which time we'll take a full-pub share, but only on the resulting sync fee . . . "*

I see these sorts of deals all the time. Sometimes, it's the only way to get a writer to sign the contract. But it's an administration and accounting nightmare that usually leaves everyone in the Copyright and Royalties departments scratching their heads for months after the deal is in place. For a small company, I recommend that you keep your deals simple and standard, and make sure you factor in the accounting work when you negotiate exceptions to the rule.

The other point that should be glaringly obvious is that without the principle of recoupable expenses, it is easy for a publisher to watch a writer grow wealthy while the publisher goes broke. Though creative people forever complain about the insatiable greed and general shadiness of the Music Business Weasel, the truth is that many entrepreneurs in this industry started as idealistic fans who just wanted to help foster the music they loved. It was only when they realized how difficult it actually is to keep a company solvent while retaining just 25 percent of the income that they became the hardnosed skinflints that we know today.

Our quick study of the income stream makes it clear: If the publisher fails to charge back the expenses incurred on behalf of the writer, the writer is likely to find himself or herself without a publisher to complain about. This is a high-risk business. If you intend to survive, generosity is not a quality that will serve you well. Your first priority must be the fiscal health of your company. Every deal you make and every deduction you take should reflect that ultimate objective. "Dishonest" is not a compliment in this business or any other—but "tough" is.

Welcome to the jungle, baby.

Finding Your People:
The A Team

Even when you're in business by yourself, you should not be in business alone. When you're entering the jungle, it's good to have friends out there—particularly among the natives. The first step is to find those people and organizations already established in the industry that can help steer you down the right path. In addition to becoming part of a musical community, you should also be in the process of building a team that can support and promote your company to the larger industry.

The Lawyer

For better or for worse, the music business is now dominated by lawyers. They are in top positions in many of the largest corporations. They have expanded into artist and producer management roles. They are wedged in the middle of every music business interaction. More new songwriters and artists are introduced to me through lawyers than through managers or even other songwriters. This is my way of saying, "Go get a lawyer." There's certainly no shortage of them out there. But how do you choose? Here are the basic criteria:

Knowledge
Yes, of course. You need someone with a solid understanding of entertainment law, which is a relatively specialized field. It is not sufficient to try to get by with a family lawyer, a friend with some general legal knowledge, or a business lawyer with an interest in expanding into show biz. You need someone whose entire practice is devoted to entertainment law.

But let's be real. Most of the issues handled daily by music business attorneys hardly require intricate legal knowledge. Very few music business lawyers achieve prominence because of their vast command of contract law. It just ain't that kind of gig. Like everyone else in show business, lawyers are prized for the contacts they bring, the people they know, the doors they can open, and the deals they can command. You need someone with . . .

Contacts

Keep in mind that lawyers are well aware that their value is measured in part by their ability to open doors. That means they work hard to develop relationships and contacts and will not treat them cavalierly. A good music lawyer will want to become familiar with the sort of music you do, make some judgments regarding the quality of it, and probably see some positive activity before he or she starts placing calls or setting up meetings. This will not happen right away. But the key is to find an attorney that has access to the people you need. A couple of things to consider:

Location

Generally speaking, it makes sense to have your lawyer in the same city in which you reside—but there are exceptions. If your business is based outside of one of the music industry centers (New York, Los Angeles, Nashville, Atlanta, Chicago), then it is even more important that you find an attorney who is based in one of those cities. Likewise, if you are based in a city that is not the center of the sort of music that you do, consider finding an attorney who can give you an industry presence in the heart of your particular business. If you're living in New York, but pitching songs primarily in the film and television world, find an attorney in LA. If you're a musical theater writer in Nashville, find a lawyer in New York. Or at the very least, make sure that the law firm has offices in one of the other music capitals.

Specialization

While music industry lawyers do not limit themselves by genre in the way that a writer or producer would, it is only natural that most of them find themselves focusing predominantly on two or three types of music. As we discussed earlier, it's a very big industry and it's impossible to know everybody. Consequently, most people concentrate on finding their niche. There are distinct differences in the way business is done in each segment of the industry—you don't want a New York lawyer from the hip-hop world negotiating a country publishing deal in Nashville. Trust me, you just don't. Try to find an attorney who is experienced in the genre in which you'll be working.

Availability

It's easy to get caught up in big-name hunting when you're looking for a lawyer. You can contact the prestigious firms, the people you see written up in Billboard's annual Top Music Lawyers list or that represent your favorite artist. If your story is compelling enough, they may be willing to represent you. This is great news—with one caveat: Make sure that they will be reasonably accessible to you when you need them.

If you are new to the industry, you need a lawyer who is willing to invest a small amount of time on spec (that is, without an hourly charge). Many of the issues with which you'll need help are not things that generate significant income for a law firm. The problem with high profile, big-name lawyers is that they naturally gravitate toward the high profile, big-number deals. You need to be confident that your lawyer, or at least an associate within the firm, will be available to you when needed and able to complete deals in a reasonable amount of time. If you need a little help with a sync license, you don't want to wait six months while your attorney wraps up the Travis Scott contract renegotiation.

A bit of corresponding advice: Never take more of your lawyer's time than you absolutely require. Remember, lawyers are used to working on the clock. Their time is, quite literally, money. Don't call to chat, don't ask questions that you could figure out yourself, and don't expect negotiations or contracts to be completed overnight. (It will never happen—and it won't happen any faster if you call every day to see if it's happening). If your lawyer likes you so much that he or she calls you to chat, make sure you're not being charged for it.

Affordability

This can be a hard thing to determine. Begin by understanding that if you judge a lawyer's hourly rate on the scale of a musician or a songwriter, or even a producer, no decent lawyer will ever appear to be affordable. The hourly rates of top attorneys in New York and LA make the presidents of many mid-size publishers look underpaid. The good news is that most lawyers don't work solely on an hourly basis. In most cases, they will structure their charges to be a percentage of whatever amount the prospective deal is ultimately worth. Obviously, this encourages the lawyer to be as aggressive as possible in negotiating on your behalf. Likewise, it gives incentive for the lawyer to be reasonable as to how much time he or she puts into the process relative to the potential pay-off. One of the things that I admire most in an attorney is an ability to read the terrain in advance, decide how much money is potentially at stake, and structure negotiations accordingly. You don't want a lawyer spending three months on a $5,000 single-song deal.

Here's a quick word to the wise for the dangerously naïve. If your lawyer is willing to invest time on a speculative basis or for a fraction of his or her regular fee, by all means take advantage of it. But be aware, if and when you hit the big money, your lawyer will expect you to pay the full hourly rate and then some (charges for faxes, long distance calls, you name it). This is not unfair. I believe the legal term is "quid pro quo." It's life.

Trust

This is even harder to determine, not because lawyers are inherently diffi-cult to trust (of course not), but because there are competing forces at work. While your lawyer is working for you, he or she is also working for the law firm that pays them and, ultimately, for themselves. It is impossible to deter-mine exactly what someone else's priority might be, but a cursory knowledge of human nature would suggest that in this instance, it's probably not you. It is conceivable that there may be times when your lawyer's interests, rela-tionships, or the law firm's relationships could compromise his or her negoti-ations on your behalf. Some big law firms will even ask you to sign a Waiver and Consent letter, acknowledging that you understand the firm may be representing a major music company in certain matters unrelated to you at the same time they're negotiating with that company on your behalf. Because it's a relatively small, relationship-based industry, clear conflicts of interest that would set off alarm bells in more traditional businesses are accepted by most people in show business as the price of working with the well-con-nected. In the end, all you can do is try to find someone with whom you feel comfortable and who you believe will make your welfare his or her primary concern.

But what if you're wrong? If you can't trust your lawyer, then who can you trust? You. Read your contracts, learn as much as possible about music business law, and when in doubt, ask questions. If you have misgivings, voice them. If you still have misgivings, don't sign the deal. Never sign something you don't understand. When it comes to lawyers or anyone else in this busi-ness—trust, but verify.

The most common method for finding a lawyer is good old-fashioned word of mouth. You can get recommendations from other writers, publishers, or industry execs—the most useful information will come from those who've had success in the same market in which you'll be working. Another alterna-tive is to study the industry trade magazines and keep tabs on the attorneys who are at the center of the action. I think *Hits* and *Billboard,* are the best sources for this information, particularly when *Billboard* runs annual lists like Top Music Lawyers, Thirty Under Thirty, or Power 100. You can also dig around a bit on social media and the internet to uncover who's representing your favorite artists. It's not always easy to source this information, but with enough permutations on Google search, you can often find a name that will pop up in relation to the signing of a new record deal or involvement in a copyright lawsuit. Do keep in mind that lawyers who handle litigation (such as copyright cases or other lawsuits) are often specialists and not necessarily the attorney who handles an artist's day to day business. Don't buy a pit bull when what you want is a guide dog.

The Trade Association

One advantage to joining a trade group is that you're not just adding one helper to your team; you're adding a whole network of them, spread across the industry. Trade associations—organizations funded and operated by businesses in a specific industry—exist in every sector of the economy, and the music world has quite a number to choose from. These include the Recording Academy (for those in the record business), A2IM (for those in the indie sector), and Songwriters of North America or the Nashville Song-writers Association International (for songwriters). For publishers, the most useful of these sorts of industry-wide support groups are the Association of Independent Music Publishers (AIMP) and, on a larger scale, the National Music Publishers Association (NMPA).

With branches in L.A., New York, and Nashville, the AIMP is reasonably priced and offers a wide variety of services and resources to its members. The greatest value to being an AIMP member is having access to information about current legal and business issues affecting publishers, new technology available to help on the administration side, and the good advice of others who have confronted the same challenges that you are. Even if you don't live near a local chapter, most of the educational information that the organization provides is available on their website.

The National Music Publishers Association is a much larger and more powerful organization, as its membership includes the companies known as the "majors"— Sony, Universal, and Warner. Like its closest counterpart in the business, the Recording Academy, the NMPA is primarily a lobbying organization, using its muscle to push lawmakers and the Copyright Board for better protection of copyrights and higher royalty rates, to advocate in the media for the rights of songwriters and publishers, and also to take collective action against companies who are infringing copyrights, whether it's Spotify, Peloton, or TikTok.

Especially in the current music business environment in which new platforms are constantly disrupting the marketplace, organizations like the AIMP and NMPA are a vital source of information and knowledge. They will help you to be the first, rather than the last, to know how publishers are navigating their way through all the problems and conflicts that keeping popping up like zombies in a videogame. While the work of NMPA is essential and important, I think the organization is too large to be a comfortable spot for most small publishers or songwriters who publish only their own catalog. I would recommend the AIMP as a better fit and a more cost-effective solution for those just starting out in the publishing business.

The Performing Rights Organization

We've already talked about the primary role of BMI, ASCAP, and SESAC, which is to collect the performance income from radio, television, live shows, restaurants, and any other venue where recorded or live music is used, and distribute this income to the songwriters. These companies have other roles in the music community as well. One of the most important functions of the performing rights organizations (PROs) is to act as support networks within the songwriting and publishing community. This is a role that is not necessarily central to the organizations' objectives, but it's something that most of the PROs have embraced.

ASCAP offers a variety of songwriter-oriented programs, including the ASCAP Experience, the ASCAP Foundation's Pop Songwriting Workshop and Musical Theater Workshop, and an extensive scholarship program, with awards in the name of Abe Olman, Lieber and Stoller, Harry Chapin and others. Not to be outdone, BMI also provides a wide spectrum of showcases and workshops, including BMI's Jazz Workshop, Lehman Engel Musical Theater Workshop, and an introduction to how PROs work with BMI 101. SESAC and the new kid on the block, Global Music Rights (GMR), are less active in regards to educational programs. GMR in particular focuses its efforts on attracting top tier writers who are already having big success, and presumably are less in need of instructional workshops or networking opportunities.

In addition to the myriad of programs, panels, and other events provided by ASCAP and BMI, both of them also have a staff of writer/publisher relations representatives, whose primary responsibility it is to keep the writer and publisher members happy, and to encourage new writers and publishers to affiliate with their organization. These people are the great unsung heroes of the songwriting community. They go to endless shows, buy hundreds of meals, listen to thousands of demos, and meet with countless writers every year. They do it not only because it's their job, but because they genuinely care about songs and writers, and they enjoy seeing new writers and companies develop into success stories. In an industry where you do not necessarily have a large number of genuine advocates, these people are the real deal.

"Great!" you say. "Someone wants to help. Where do I join? Who do I join?" Hold up. Not so fast. Unless you have a song that is commercially released, garnering a significant number of streams on Spotify, actively being played on the radio or television, or being performed in some other major venue, you don't have any performance income to collect. This means you don't need to join a performing rights organization yet. This is not a bad thing.

We will talk about the process of choosing a PRO and the process of affiliation in chapter 21. Right now, you're in the dating stage—which means that you try to meet as many people from each of the organizations as you can, develop relationships with anyone who takes an interest in what you do, learn as much as possible about the differences between the groups, and see where it all leads. The object is to see what organization takes an interest in your company, what writer relations reps are willing to offer help or advice, and what programs are of benefit to you. The fact that you are unaffiliated is a plus in this respect, as it allows you to get the best of all three worlds. At this stage, you're free to "play the field."

As a publisher, this freedom will not necessarily disappear once you have a song that's generating income. As a writer, it is necessary to join one specific organization. While you can move from one to the other, you do need to choose one PRO to license your material. On the other hand, a publisher is not only permitted but often required to have an affiliation with each of the three organizations: ASCAP, BMI and SESAC. (GMR does not currently have publisher members).

If you are the only writer represented by your publishing company, then your publishing company will need to be affiliated only with the organization that represents you as a writer. For example, if you join ASCAP as a writer, your publishing company will need to be affiliated with ASCAP. But if you represent several writers, you will likely need to have publishing entities at each PRO. To elaborate on our initial example, if your company were to add a second writer who was already signed with BMI, your publishing firm would need to create a second publishing entity (just a name really) that would be your BMI affiliate. Any major publisher will have an ASCAP, BMI, and usually a SESAC affiliate—this allows the company to publish any writer, regardless of the organization to which the writer belongs. For instance, the company where I work has Shapiro Bernstein & Co. Inc. (the ASCAP entity), Painted Desert Music Corp. (BMI), and Swimming Upstream Music (SESAC). As a publisher then, you will want to maintain relationships at all the performing rights organizations in a way that you might not as a writer.

And again, the warning:

If you handle yourself correctly, the folks at BMI, ASCAP and SESAC will be your friends (not all of them, but at least a few). But remember that they do not work for you. They are not your manager, lawyer, or PR agent. This is to say, be grateful, not greedy. A call to your contact at the PRO once every four or six weeks with a question, update, or invite to a show is reasonable. A call once a week is annoying. A call every day is abuse. These people are the best advocates that songwriters and publishers have. Don't disillusion them. Treat them with the respect that they deserve.

Interns

The same goes for interns. The entertainment business is fortunate enough to have a healthy supply of bright young people willing to work for college credit, a foot in the door, and some record industry swag. The smart companies learn to use interns wisely, and smart interns use the opportunity to make an impression and find a way into a difficult and exclusive industry.

I'm not sure that anyone's done a survey, but I'm guessing that at least two-thirds of the people in the music business found their first opportunity in the industry through some sort of intern position. Before the days of million dollar, CIROC-popping videos, even Sean "P. Diddy" Combs was an intern for Uptown Records CEO Andre Harrell. We've all been there.

The position that first brought me to New York, at the Independent Label Coalition, was an internship of sorts—which is simply to say that I brought very little experience to the job and was paid (or more precisely, not paid) accordingly. Nevertheless, it was an invaluable opportunity, allowing me to work with a variety of record labels, helping to develop contacts that led directly to my first publishing deal, and providing a crash course in the music business, taught by some great independent music entrepreneurs, including Morris and Adam Levy, Eddie O'Loughlin, Sergio Cossa, Joel Webber, and Tom Silverman.

For a small company with little room for payroll costs, the effective use of interns can be crucial. Much of a publisher's day-to-day workload requires minimal expertise, and can easily be done by someone other than you. Archiving new material, answering phone calls, checking for unlicensed uses on YouTube or researching contact information for a prospective writer is not the best use of your time, especially if you are already trying to balance the dual role of writer and publisher. It only makes sense to tap into the supply of people eager to break into the business, for whom this work can provide experience and a means of making those first contacts in the industry. Contact your local colleges and trade schools, or try putting an ad in a local music paper. Then hire with care. The fact that you are not paying much of a salary doesn't mean that any set of hands will do. A good intern is invaluable, but a bad one exacts a sizable cost. Find someone that you believe can develop into a real partner in the business.

Then it is up to you to make that development happen. If you have something at stake, so does the intern, who is expecting this opportunity to be productive, enjoyable, and educational. Just because the intern is working for a pittance does not make them your servant. Don't bark orders—explain what you need and why. Don't guard your contacts jealously—introduce your intern to them, and let them know that you view the intern as part of your team. Don't leave your intern sitting idle until you think of something you need—think strategically every day about what your intern can be doing to contribute, and have tasks set up when he or she arrives. Better yet, empower the intern with enough information, knowledge, and autonomy to decide what to work on. The more you invest in your employees, the more you get back. This is likely your intern's first foray into the music business. It should be an education, not a hazing.

The ability to effectively build, nurture, and maintain an effective team is often underestimated, particularly by the independent types that gravitate toward the music business. I've heard it said derisively about executives, business owners, producers, and even writers: "They don't really do much, it's their _____ (fill in the blank: co-writer, engineer, business advisor, assistant) that really made the success happen . . . " as if the only legitimate claim to success was to single-handedly control every aspect of your business. The real leaders in any industry are those who can spot talent (whether it's business or creative), develop a team, inspire the troops, build allies, and preserve relationships. I'm not impressed by soloists. Give me the guy who can lead the band.

Because now it's time to strike it up . . .

PART II
EXPLOITATION:
THE REAL WORK
OF PUBLISHING

10

Mapping the Musical Landscape: Where Opportunity Lies

And so the fun begins. Now that your office is set up, all systems are go, your catalog is a model of organization, and your team is in place, it's time to get down to the real work of music publishing. I'm not sure if exploitation is really the most important aspect of the music publishing business, but it is the function that starts it all. Without it, nothing happens. So what is our first goal as music publishers?

Make Stuff Happen

Make what happen? Well, at this stage, anything. Stuff. Pitching songs is not an exact science; it's not really a science at all. It's more like the chaos theory of the universe: everything is in motion all the time, setting off reactions that trigger further reactions without any predictable pattern or logic to govern it all. (Didn't think I'd get that sophisticated on you, did you?) The point is, action is always better than inaction, and any small opportunity that allows your song to be heard has the potential to lead to better opportunities somewhere else. Of course, you want to find the best and most lucrative placement for your song, and I'm not suggesting that you sell your catalog short. If you have a real reason to think that Camila Cabello is going to record your song, don't be too quick to give it away to a new artist on a tiny indie label. Duh.

What I am suggesting is that many opportunities arise simply from putting your songs in play, and when first starting, there is almost no opportunity not worth pursuing. It's easier to pick up speed when you're already moving than when you're standing still. So what kind of stuff are we talking about?

Recordings

This is the big one. While there are other placement opportunities that are becoming increasingly lucrative, recordings are still the primary money-maker for music publishers—in part because having a song on a record opens up other doors as well. If your song is recorded by an artist (hopefully supported by a record label), the song then has a chance at getting on the radio (generating performance income), and from there, becoming a hit. If your song becomes a hit, it has a better chance of being placed in a movie or advertisement. Although the balance of power in the industry is changing, the record business is still more often than not the driver that puts the process in motion. Whatever style of music is represented in your catalog, it is always beneficial to get your songs on commercially released records.

Now of course, the definition of what constitutes a "record" keeps changing, and undoubtedly the term will continue to be redefined in the future. Is an MP3 you put up yourself on SoundCloud a commercially released "record"? What about a demo that's not available on any platform but is used in the key scene of a major TV show? Or a song that you've never "released" but shows up in a TikTok video?

As far as publishers are concerned, there is certainly a hierarchy of "records," with some recordings being much more valuable than others. Generally speaking, commercial releases on a major label are at the top of the desirability list, indie labels are a close second, self-releases are a distant third, and self-releases to platforms like SoundCloud are at the bottom. On what basis do publishers make the judgment about the value of various types of "records"? That's easy. The answer is always money.

It doesn't take much experience in music publishing to deduce that having a song recorded by a well-known artist on a major record label is likely (though by no means guaranteed) to generate more revenue than a release by a little-known artist on a small, indie label. Although, both those options will probably exceed what you can earn by putting the song out on your own (unless of course you already have a well-established fanbase). Even if you put something out on your own, there is a considerable difference in the publishing income generated by a release that goes to Spotify, Apple, Amazon, YouTube, and Pandora (i.e., services which pay meaningful streaming royalties) and a release that goes only to SoundCloud and TikTok (which pay only a very minimal rate).

Of course, this hierarchy is upset all the time. That indie artist no one knew turns into Anderson Paak, the superstar artist flops, or the YouTube video of you playing your song in a classroom for Pharrell Williams goes viral and leads to a major label record deal. But if you have a choice between an established artist on Columbia Records recording your song or doing it yourself and putting it up on SoundCloud, you have to play the odds of success. Whatever decision you make, any recording of your song that's of good quality and available for public consumption is a strong first step toward generating some business as a publisher.

Artist or Band Demos

Artist or band demos are not nearly as lucrative as having a song on a record, but you gotta start somewhere. If an artist, band, or producer wants to record your song as part of a demo package to shop for a record deal, it may be an opportunity to get in early on a project that everyone will be clamoring to work on a year from now. Beyond some good old-fashioned A&R research, scouring YouTube, Spotify, social media, and the trade magazines to find an artist or band that interests you and fits your music, there are also sites like BeatStars, MDIIO, SoundBetter, and Vocalizr that can help you get your music out to new artists who are looking for a songwriter or producer to work with.

One of the biggest hits I had as a writer was a song called "Nothing My Love Can't Fix," which was written with the artist Joey Lawrence and my songwriting partner Alexandra Forbes. The song was one of the first that Joey wrote, several months before he obtained a record deal. The song managed to stick on the project all the way through the making of the album, and eventually became the first single. Sometimes, the early bird really does get the worm.

Radio

Every successful writer remembers hearing his or her song on the radio for the first time. Of course, the obvious way to make this happen is to place the song on a record, and let the label worry about getting it on a playlist. For the more independent-minded, you could also release it yourself, hire a radio promoter, or hope that some momentum on Spotify eventually propels it onto satellite radio and then into rotation on your local Top 40 station. This is a very difficult road, but there are a reasonable number of artists who have followed that route to success.

In fact, that's not even all of the potential opportunities to pick up some airplay. Listen to the radio, and pay attention to *all* the music you hear;

there's a lot more music out there than you think. Jingles, background music in commercials and promo spots, parodies for the morning show audience, underground, DJ-only "white label" tracks for the Saturday night mix shows, and local-band feature spots are all opportunities to get your music on the radio.

Several years ago, I had a situation in which a song was licensed to a music library, which is a business that provides "background" music for use in local advertising, television, and other venues. The song was plucked out of the library by a radio station in Amsterdam, who used the song in an on-air promo for an upcoming concert festival. Strangely enough, the song became quite identified with both the festival and the station, to the point that we received a request to commercially release the song in Amsterdam, as it had become something of a local summer anthem. Like I said, it's chaos theory, not rocket science.

Television

As I mentioned before, television has become as much a part of the music industry as radio. If video hasn't killed the radio star, it's certainly wrestled him to a draw. In the past several decades, there has been a real role-reversal between television and radio, with cable and streaming services allowing television to drastically increase the diversity and range of its programming, while radio—with the possible exception of some satellite radio—finds itself increasingly at the mercy of vast conglomerates, who systematically enforce ever-more-restrictive formats on their programmers. When we're talking about television today, we're talking about everything from Netflix to ESPN to community access programming, not just the major networks. If your music isn't appropriate to any single show on any one of those hundred channels, you may be a bit too unique for your own good.

Movies

Regarding movie placement, again, don't set your focus too narrowly (think wide-screen). The movie business is not just about the features at a local cineplex near you, but also independent features, foreign films, direct-to-video movies, documentaries, short subjects, and student films. Even if you're issuing a gratis license to a small-budget production, you're building relationships and getting your copyright some exposure. There's no telling where that can lead. *Once* was an independent Irish film with a budget of roughly 112,000 GBP; it starred Glen Hansard and Markéta Irglová who also composed and performed the original songs featured in the film. It became a surprise success, with Hansard and Irglová's song "Falling Slowly" winning the 2008 Academy Award for Best Original Song and being nominated for a Grammy Award. Four years later, a stage adaptation opened on Broadway, and won eight Tony Awards. All of this from a set of songs that the two song-writers created for their indie band. If you put that story in a film, the critics would say the plot was too far-fetched.

Advertising

Talk about a growth market. When I first started in the music industry, there was a very clear distinction between what were known as "jingles," which is to say, music written for an advertising campaign, and pop songs. Most "jingles" were written by "jingle houses," which were companies made up of composers and producers whose primary career focus was to provide advertising firms with catchy theme songs. The money was great, the work was plentiful, and the writers and musicians that did the work usually found that jingle writing provided a much more comfortable lifestyle than the weasel-run record business. Seldom did the two worlds meet.

I had lunch last week with an old friend who owned one of the leading jingle houses in New York back in the day. In our conversation, he bluntly confirmed what I had been suspecting for some time. The jingle business has almost vanished. Turn on your television, and you'll wait a long time before you hear one of those catchy "sing it with a smile" sort of theme songs—those attention-grabbing Charmin ditties being one of the few contemporary examples. Instead, what do you hear? The Beatles' classic "Revolution," "Good as Hell" by Lizzo, or "The Final Countdown" by Europe. Pop songs of all ages and styles have become the primary source for music in advertising, and this is good news for publishers. Rather than paying a jingle house to write and produce a thirty-second piece of music, usually on a work-for-hire basis, advertising companies are now licensing songs—and at times, master recordings—to give their product a more contemporary identity. The best part is that in many cases, the songs selected are not necessarily huge, recognizable hits. Songs like "Festival" by Eagles of Death Metal or "Naeem" by Bon Iver are selected in part for their "cool quotient," which rates higher than that of a Top Forty radio record. The stigma that was once attached to lending your song to an ad campaign has largely been erased as well. After all, the Beatles probably need the money less than you do.

Live Performance

Live performance is not necessarily a big money maker, in terms of music publishing, but remember: the idea is to get your music in front of people.

If you are a singer/songwriter or part of a band, you are probably performing your songs already, as often as possible, in whatever venue you can find. Whether it's in a club, bar, festival, coffeehouse, open mic night, street corner, or someone's living room, performers need to perform and songs need to be heard.

Beyond the obvious venues, think about other events that can incorporate a musical performance. One writer I worked with toured the country for a year performing his song at WNBA half-time shows. Sports events, corporate meetings, political gatherings, and church and school activities can all offer opportunities for songs to get the exposure they need. Even if you're not a performer yourself, you can seek out local artists, bands, or theater groups that can give your songs a voice.

Interestingly, the economics of having a song performed live differs drastically between the United States and many other parts of the world. While all performing rights organizations around the world license the live performance of music, the rates charged by ASCAP and BMI to concert venues, clubs, and festivals in America are far lower than the rates in most other major territories. I work with a publishing company that represents a number of popular heavy-metal bands who tour actively around the world. The discrepancy in income generated in America and Europe is stark. While the performing rights income in the United States is minimal (ASCAP and BMI income is generated primarily through radio and television, rather than live shows), in Europe, the performing rights royalties from concerts and especially festivals are actually the primary source of publishing income for this catalog. If your song is being performed live, it's better that it happen in Europe than in the United States. We'll talk later about what you need to do as a publisher to be sure you're collecting the money generated when your songs are being performed outside of America in front of a paying audience.

Stores, Restaurants, Clubs, Gyms

Okay, so it's not exactly an audience. It's more like a group of bystanders. But bystanders are people, and if they aren't exactly listening, they are at least aware of the music playing as they shop, eat, drink, dance, whatever. While many businesses use music programs provided by companies like PlayNetwork, Mood Media, and Soundreef (these are also places you can pitch your songs to), there are always small stores and boutiques that may be willing to work your music into their programming. Likewise, restaurants, bars, clubs, and hotels are all about vibe, and if your music fits their market, they may be more than happy to put your tracks in the mix. I know one prominent music producer who changed course more than ten years ago and established a company specializing in music "curation," helping hospitality companies to identify the right musical soundtrack to enhance their brand. In some instances, it's as simple as curating a playlist from existing music. In other cases, the job involves creating original music to fit the image of the hotel, bar, or restaurant. Pitching music "curators" of this sort is a smart strategy, especially for publishers with a catalog focused on things like lounge music, ambient, EDM, or instrumental tracks. An equally smart strategy might be to create a music curation service yourself, and plug your music into the playlists you create for your clients.

Streaming

If all of this talk of records, radio, movies, and concert halls sounds like your grandfather's music business, it kind of is. And it kind of isn't. The reason that the myriad of digital streaming platforms, from Spotify to Apple to SoundCloud and YouTube, are at the end of this chapter is that sadly, that's often where they stack up in terms of their earning power for publishers. In many cases, you could earn more from one small synchronization placement on a modestly popular television show than from one million streams on Spotify. Records, radio, television, film, and even live concerts (on a world-wide basis) are still the more important sources of income for people who earn their money from songs, rather than master recordings.

Then again, the point of a stream is not where it starts but where it leads. The power of the digital streaming services to break new artists and songs is obvious, and it's the possibility of launching a viral hit that makes them valuable far beyond their royalty rates. These services are where labels go to find new talent, where radio goes to find songs that are ready to be the next "White Iverson" by Post Malone, where music supervisors go to find a song that is familiar and cool but not yet mainstream, and where booking agents go to find new acts whose following can translate into ticket sales. There's no question that your songs need to be on as many social media and streaming platforms as now exist or have yet to be discovered. But it's worth asking where you should focus your efforts, which depends largely on the kind of music you work with. Here's a quick analysis.

Spotify

Spotify is the big Kahuna, with the highest visibility and the most influential playlists. But at the moment, it is increasingly algorithm driven, which puts artists with no track record, or a weak track record, at a decided disadvantage. If you don't have the support of a label, distributor, or outside service that can help promote the artist to playlists, it might be better to think about launching the song on a format like YouTube or SoundCloud, and building some momentum before pushing it to Spotify. Then again, Spotify changes its playlisting philosophy all the time, so it's hard to say if the current direction to make playlisting decisions less about the tastes of an individual curator and more about data will endure. When you're going to a platform as big and powerful as Spotify, it pays to read up a bit in the trades and see what strategies labels and managers are using at the moment you're releasing your song.

YouTube

Needless to say, if the artist releasing your song is an amazing visual performer, YouTube offers a big advantage over Spotify and other audio-only sites. Also, its algorithmic system rewards artists for posting more content and penalizes them less for releases that don't perform well. Consequently, it may make sense to release songs on YouTube first, and then only move them to Spotify if they react with the audience. It's also useful to keep in mind that certain genres, like Latin, world music, reggae, and dancehall, are often much stronger on YouTube than Spotify.

Amazon

Amazon is a harder format in which to break new artists, but it also has some advantages in reaching certain types of audiences. Older, more mainstream listeners that gravitate toward genres like country, classic rock, jazz, or adult contemporary are much more prevalent on Amazon than something like SoundCloud.

Apple

The big advantage with Apple is that you might actually get paid a fair royalty. Apple has been one of the only digital services to avoid an openly contentious relationship with the record labels and publishers, in part because they have been considerably more willing to meet the industry's asking price as far as royalties. While it's difficult to calculate the exact difference, as streaming rates continually vary, Apple pays considerably more than Spotify or most other digital services. They're also one of the only services not fighting the increased royalty rates for music publishers that were approved by the U.S. Copyright Royalty Board back in 2018.

SoundCloud

SoundCloud is no place to make money; the system provides for little or no compensation to songwriters and artists posting material on the site.

What they do offer, however, is exposure to a highly engaged audience, especially for new, unknown electronic, dance, hip-hop, and trap artists. Just ask Kygo or any one of a whole genre of SoundCloud rappers; this is a place to generate that first spark that starts the fire.

TikTok

Until a licensing agreement with the NMPA was reached in 2020, TikTok was a free-for-all, in every sense of the term. Record companies paid influencers to do videos of their songs, while publishers were threatening lawsuits. As you could guess, the publisher's objections were centered on the lack of any real licensing process and royalty rates that are, well, free for all. While the royalty rate for publishers from TikTok remains minimal, at least there is now an infrastructure for the licensing of the music. Whether with music publishers or the U.S. government, the one thing not in contention over the past few years in regards to TikTok is the platform's almost cult-like hold on its young audience. When it comes to songs that appeal to teenage girls or lend themselves to silly dance moves, this format can turn artists like Lil Nas X or Roddy Rich into pop stars literally overnight.

Needless to say, what we've been discussing so far is a scattershot approach to exploitation—a sort of jumpstart in the song pitching process. It will be impossible to pursue every possible opportunity, particularly if you are running this publishing company on your own. But it makes sense to explore as many outlets for your material as possible and to use the reactions of each market to develop your overall strategy.

In the end, much of that strategy will be determined by the song catalog itself. Depending on the nature of the music, some markets will be viable, others less so, and some not at all. If your catalog is all death metal, you probably don't need to sink much time into sending music out to advertising agencies. Follow the path of least resistance, and go where the music leads you.

11

Understanding the Music Marketplace

While it's impossible to discuss every type of music that may be represented in your catalog, here's a quick overview of some of the largest genres, and the strategies that are most effective within those particular worlds:

Pop

The hardest part of talking about "pop" music is trying to define what "pop" is. Is it just a shortening of the term "popular" music, referring to anything that enjoys mass appeal? Or is it an actual style of music, something not quite rock, and not really R&B, and not genuine country, but "pop"?

The answer: both. Certainly, there is an actual style of music that can be defined as pop, which encompasses artists like Ariana Grande and Nick Jonas, R&B-influenced singers like Justin Bieber and Charlie Puth, singer-songwriters with a mass appeal like Shawn Mendes or Ed Sheeran, as well as international acts like BTS or Dua Lipa. There's no other way to describe the music of those artists, except to call it "pop." At the same time, "pop" music also includes a large number of artists or bands that did not start off pop, but simply became so popular that they now enjoy an appeal that stretches beyond the genre from which they came. Drake is hip-hop, but he's also pop. Lizzo or Khalid appeal to fans far outside the R&B music audience. Imagine Dragons is a rock band, but also a pop act. Get popular enough, and there you are. You're pop.

Because mass appeal tends to mean massive royalties, the pop market is always one of the most competitive and difficult markets to break into, whether you're an artist, a label, a songwriter, or a music publisher. When you're out there pitching pop songs, you are up against Max Martin, Benny

Blanco, Sia, Julia Michaels, and Steve Mac—writers with long discographies and plenty of platinum records on their walls, most of whom are represented by large, well-established publishers. Almost all of the artists in the pop world are on major record labels, are represented by large management firms, and are very difficult to get songs to. If you do manage to get a song in the mix, there are usually forty or fifty other songs on "hold" for the project. When you're playing in the pop game, you are in the big leagues. Be prepared for the challenges you will face.

So am I telling you to avoid the pop market? No. Despite all the drawbacks, the pop world remains one of the most viable markets for songwriters, for two obvious reasons. First, many of the artists in the pop genre are not self-contained; they don't write all their material. Even those stars who are involved in the writing will often co-write with other songwriters or producers. The pop market then is a good fit for either pure songwriters, topliners (people who write mainly melody and lyrics), or writer/producers. It's less suited to singer/songwriters who write very personal, intimate songs about their own experience. Which leads us to the second reason that the pop genre remains a viable publisher's market....

Pop music is all about *hits*! While a successful rock act may be able to make an interesting album that sells despite a lack of radio singles, or a country artist like George Strait may remain viable long after his hit-making days have disappeared, even a superstar pop artist is dependent on a hit single to reach a mass audience through exposure on New Music Friday, Pop Rising, and radio stations around the country. Especially in this streaming era, in which the release cycle for every artist has changed from three singles off an album to an endless stream of content—EPs, albums, singles, and features—every pop artist needs yet another hit, and hits are what songwriters and publishers are supposed to provide. One of the most frustrating aspects of developing a pop act is this constant need for that elusive, all-important song that will break your artist, or keep your artist at the top of the heap. You'll hear it every day from every weasel in town. "We're still looking for that next single." "Single" is just a less intimidating way of saying "hit."

So now you see why you keep your hits in the top drawer of your desk. Because that's what everyone's looking for. To be more precise, what they're really looking for most of the time is:

- something up-tempo (most radio singles are up-tempo). Keep in mind, though, that this is more a question of feel (aggressiveness, rhythmic energy, overall attitude) than an actual beats per minute target.

- something with an interesting, perhaps provocative, but certainly attention-grabbing lyric

- a big, dramatic chorus that jumps out melodically and repeats at least three times in the song
- an aggressive, dynamic track with a lot of energy and some sort of instrumental part that functions as a secondary hook

If that sounds like a formula, it is. The greatest "pop" songwriters tend to be formulaic writers. They have a recipe that they follow again and again, using their creativity to infuse each song with something fresh, but sticking with a tried-and-true structure that works consistently. Holland-Dozier-Holland, the Brill Building writers, Diane Warren, DJ Snake—they all have a very precise idea of what it takes to make a hit, and they make sure that every song they write has the required elements. Pop writing is a discipline, and to succeed at it, you have to embrace, rather than resist, the formula.

If pop music is one-half formula, the other half of the equation is fashion. Pop music, more so than almost any genre other than hip-hop, is a slave of fashion. Rhythms, sounds, production elements, and lyrical subjects all reflect the times that we live in, and consequently, are constantly going in and out of style. Part of the art of pop songwriting is learning to understand music as fashion—to know what things are about to be cool, which ones are still cool, which things are no longer cool, and which things are so old they're almost cool again. Songs that are dated or out of step with popular culture are missing one of the essential qualities of pop music. It must be timely and relevant. Sure, it's often trendy, but it's the soundtrack to our lives, and it's inevitably of the moment. The trick is to always be ahead, rather than behind, the trends.

If you are going to focus your publishing company on the pop market, you've got to have hits in your catalog. A collection of interesting, personal, introspective ballads will not work. It takes a certain killer instinct to be a pop writer. At Jive Records, where pop songwriting was something of a religion, we used to call it "going for the jugular." The pop market is not a place for quiet, unassuming subtlety. Remember, you're writing songs for artists who want to reach millions of people all over the world. You need songs that make big statements, in a big way, no holds barred. I remember Jay Landers, a renowned producer and A&R executive, asking me a question after I pitched him a song for his big Disney artist: "Can you really hear 50,000 people in a stadium singing along with that chorus?"

It's a good question to ask yourself if you're pitching pop songs.

Of course, the upside to the pop market is the payoff. A big pop hit is the musical lottery jackpot. It doesn't get any better in this business. In addition to generating huge mechanical and performance payments, a pop hit can easily be placed in movies, television shows, advertisements, and just about anywhere else. Someone might even do a parody of it. Nobody parodies an obscure track on an unknown album.

Hip-Hop/R&B

We're casting a pretty wide net with this terminology. What is sometimes referred to as "urban" music encompasses hip-hop and trap and all the sub-genres within that world, as well as R&B and all the varieties of that genre as well. Everyone from Chris Brown to Travis Scott to Ella Mai to Khalid can fit under this umbrella. Not always comfortably, but they'll fit. Of all the genres that feed into the Hot 100, hip-hop and R&B are the ones that just keep growing. Artists like Post Malone, Bruno Mars, and Cardi B are mainstream superstars that transcend any racial or cultural barriers. Certainly at the present moment, you'll hear a lot more hip-hop and R&B music on a pop radio format than you will hear "pop" music.

Not surprisingly then, this is a good area in which to be a publisher at present. That's because the music is enjoying increasing commercial success, and also because it's one of the most vital, fast-changing, entrepreneurial areas of the music industry. The accessibility of platforms like YouTube, Spotify, and SoundCloud; the growth of indie distribution companies like DistroKid and Tunecore; and the influence of powerful regional labels like Quality Control in Atlanta or South Coast Music Group in the Carolinas have allowed a multitude of young writers, producers, artists, and executives to feel that mass success is only one viral hit away.

The hip-hop and R&B business relies heavily on writer/producers who find talent, develop it, write the songs (or at least co-write them), and produce the records. The work of DJ Mustard or Mike WiLL Made-It and the producers associated with them are good examples of the sort of writing and production camps that are the primary breeding ground for songs in the urban world. There are also writers that specialize in lyrics and melodies. These writers may be associated directly with a production house, but more often they move between a variety of producers. And of course, there are the artists themselves, who, at least in the hip-hop world, usually write their own raps or "toplines." Except for certain exceptions, hip-hop and R&B music is largely a team sport, and it's important to be part of a specific musical community. Many of the top production squads have several writers associated with them. These writers work their way up the ranks, learn the craft, and then, once they find success, break off and form their own companies.

For all its dynamism, urban music does pose some unique challenges. Particularly on hip-hop tracks, the prevalence of sampling can cut the ownership of a copyright down to an amount hardly worth administering. At the same time, the slang-influenced language of most raps limits the international reach of the music. Only the superstars of the hip-hop world command an audience in Europe or other non-English speaking territories. The lyric subject matter of many R&B hits can also limit exploitation opportunities, especially if you don't have a "clean" version on hand. While film and even cable television opportunities can work, network television and advertising is trickier. It's hard to put "Twerk" by City Girls on a prime time television spot. Finally, there's not much comfort zone in this market. Fashions change in the hip-hop and R&B market faster than anywhere else. You can go from cold to red hot to cold again very, very quickly. Sustaining a long-term career in this world requires at least nine lives.

Country

Seems like it's always the best of times and the worst of times down on Music Row. Spend a few days in Nashville, and you'll be amazed at the scope of the country music industry there, with more and more New Yorkers and Californians (including pop stars like Justin Bieber and Marshmello) jumping into the marketplace, international interest building quickly, and the genre itself expanding to include everything from the neo-traditionalism of Chris Stapleton to the pop sounds of Dan & Shay.

At the same time, have lunch with any group of Nashville song pluggers and you'll get more gloom and doom than one of those old-time country songs: tightening playlists, too much reliance on the "hit" single, overly cautious A&R, and too much power in the hands of radio. "If it weren't for bad luck I'd have no luck at all...."

The bottom line is this: there are still more successful independent publishers in the country market than anywhere else, primarily for one important reason. For the most part, country music artists don't write their own songs. There are many exceptions to this, of course. But unlike the pop and urban markets, where the artist is often at least a co-writer in the process and usually takes outside material only for potential singles, there are still some country artists who will have eight or nine outside songs on an album. You don't have to crunch those numbers very hard to see the amount of opportunity that this opens up for writers and publishers. This is why Nashville has always been a song town. Unlike New York and L.A., there is a real appreciation for songs and the craft of songwriting and music publishing. You can find more songwriters in the Fido coffee shop near Music Row than in all of New York.

And these guys are good. Real good. Nashville songwriters are the consummate professionals—disciplined and extremely well-versed in the craft of writing a song. This means everyone writes music, lyrics, and melodies, and most are pretty good guitar players as well. Such competition makes this a very tough town to break into. When someone refers to "overnight success" in Nashville, they're usually talking more like five years.

On the publisher's side, despite all the complaining of the creative directors, the country market is the last bastion of true, old-fashioned music publishing. Unlike their New York counterparts, who tend to focus on the banking aspect of the gig, Nashville publishers still develop writers, critique songs, suggest rewrites, and then run the songs around town until they get them cut. I called the head of a major Nashville publisher recently and was told he was "out playin' some songs for people." That doesn't happen much in New York. If you want to truly learn music publishing from the ground up, Nashville is the place to do it.

And if you're gonna take on the country music market, Nashville is where you need to be. While the town has expanded well beyond country music, with thriving Americana, rock, hip-hop, Christian, and gospel communities as well, the country music business is still very much centered in Nashville. Ultimately, you will benefit by the constant exposure to other writers and publishers that Nashville provides. The toughest part of the country genre is breaking into the close-knit, and yes, sometimes closed-minded Music Row establishment, made up of longtime label execs, a relatively small number of record producers, and the prominent artist managers. The sooner you acquaint yourself with the beast and begin to understand it, the sooner you can take it on.

In many respects, Nashville is the direct opposite of the hip-hop and R&B market. While urban music is dominated by writers who are also producers, country music tends to draw a very distinct line between those two functions. Most country writers do not produce the songs they write. Instead, they pitch their songs to a handful of well-established producers who control the majority of projects in town.

While they're often slow to acknowledge it, country music publishers do have some advantages over their colleagues in the pop and R&B world. First of all, Nashville is still a place where a relatively simple demo can grab attention, provided it highlights the best aspects of the song. And while the hip-hop market is a wild ocean of constant change, the country market by comparison is a slow-moving stream. In Nashville, everything lasts for a good while: singles stay on the charts for months, artists can stay popular for a decade or more, trends last for four or five years, and writers can keep churning out hits for several decades. Memories last a long time down there, as do grudges, feuds, and burnt bridges. It takes a lot of patience to break into the country club, and a great deal of care and feeding of your relationships to stay in it.

While getting songs on records, preferably by big name artists, remains the primary focus of most song pluggers in Nashville, the real value of having a song recorded in the country market is not mechanical royalties, but the possibility of radio airplay, should your song be selected as a single. Top country albums these days often sell less than a million records, with streaming numbers considerably below those for R&B or pop music, so there is not a huge return in mechanical royalties. However, a country radio single can be extraordinarily lucrative, as there are more country music stations than any other format in the U.S. Country singles often spend as long as a year in regular radio rotation. That makes for a mighty big ASCAP or BMI check.

The live market is also an important one for breaking new country artists and songs. Unlike the pop business, where you need a pretty big hit in order to be able to tour, even a relatively unknown country artist can often piece together enough opening slots, festivals, and club gigs to stay out on the road and even make a little money doing it. The live business of country doesn't do much for publishers, but it does help break artists and puts new songs out where they can be heard. So do the famous songwriter circles in Nashville, where groups of songwriters gather together to share songs and stories, with each writer in the circle performing one of their songs and the others joining to accompany them on it. A slot in a songwriter circle at the famed Bluebird Cafe won't make anyone much in performance income. But it puts your writer in front of a potentially powerful mix of other, more established songwriters, industry execs, and hard-core country music fans. It's an important part of "moving your writer up" the industry ladder which is something we'll discuss in chapter 18.

On the downside, country music never gets a fair shake in the sync world, getting far fewer placements than would seem fair, given its popularity. There's the occasional truck commercial or a film spot (usually for something more on the traditional or Americana side), but overall, country publishers have learned to live without a steady stream of synchronization income. It should change, and there are some signs of progress, especially as country music takes on more and more pop elements. But radio, records, and live performances remain the primary income sources for the country business.

In my experience with country music, the two most helpful things you can have in your publishing business is at least one artist on your roster, and lots of time (or money, which is kind of the same thing). While Nashville publishers are traditionally built around pitching songs, most publishers also strive to be in the artist development business. They want at least one or two writers on their roster who they can develop into viable artists, while also pitching those writers' songs to the superstar acts. If a song gets cut by a big artist, it only builds the buzz and moves the writer that much closer to getting their own record deal. At the same time, if an artist/writer starts to gain traction as an artist, he or she will have an obvious outlet for his or her songs. In the same way, producer/writers in Nashville need to be developing new artists, not just hoping to land the big Blake Shelton cut. There just aren't enough slots for outside songs on big, established artists for that to be the sole basis of your business. You need a couple different paths all leading to the same destination: a song on the radio.

Then you need to settle in for a long journey. If you're not willing to put in three to five years in building your business before you see any real success, then Nashville may not be the spot for you. Most publishers in the country music business fail because they give up (or run out of money) a year too soon, just before that song that's been on hold for months finally gets cut and becomes the hit single. It's an ironic twist that only a country writer could love. You're usually shutting down the office and pawning your guitar at just the moment you hear your song come on the radio.

Rock

Because the rock market revolves primarily around self-contained bands and singer-songwriters, most rock publishers focus primarily on trying to sign bands or artists that either already have an established audience or that look like they're building one. Yet even this strategy, which sounds about like betting on a sure thing, carries plenty of risk. Unfortunately, it's not enough that the band has a devoted live following or shows up on all the right Spotify playlists. Live shows and streaming simply don't generate much in the way of income for publishers. A rock publisher needs an artist or band that gets on the radio or pulls in the sync placements.

Clearly, this gives genres like modern rock, alternative rock, singer-songwriters, or classic rock a big advantage over death metal, punk and post-punk, or jam bands. Rock radio is a narrow format, with a big chunk devoted to classic rock stations, which primarily play songs from the '60s through the early 2000s. In fact, the catalogs of the immortal rock artists (the Who, Springsteen, Foo Fighters, Red Hot Chili Peppers) are generally the most valuable in all of publishing, primarily because they show up year after year on the carved-in-stone playlists of those classic rock stations. Good news for those rock stars, of course. Not so good for anyone in the business of signing new bands.

I'm guessing that most readers working in this genre are not as interested in acquiring other new artists as they are in representing their own work. If you are a singer-songwriter or an active writer within a band, the challenge you face as a publisher is not unlike the challenge you face as an artist. First and foremost, you need to establish an audience base. Few new bands can jump into rotation at modern rock radio or attract the attention of a music supervisor for an advertising agency without a big streaming story or a strong touring presence. In that sense then, all the hard work you and your management are doing to move forward as an artist, firing up the tour bus, trying to get some press, or looking for a record label to support your next release will also help build your publishing business. In the early days of a band or artist's development, the tasks in a rock publisher's job description are not much different from those of a good artist manager. But there is one thing, and it's a big one: synchronization.

The primary place in which a publisher can play a transformative role in the life of young band or singer-songwriter is in the world of synchronization, both by generating income and increasing exposure. By placing a song in an advertising campaign, a video game, a high-profile television spot or a major movie moment, a publisher can sometimes ignite interest in an artist or song in a way that circumvents the obstacles of breaking into radio rotation or the wear and tear of a relentless tour schedule. It doesn't happen often but it's possible—just ask artists like Ingrid Michaelson, the Dandy Warhols, or Cage the Elephant. The only thing that most developing bands want from a publisher is synchronization—as much and as high-profile as possible. That's not an easy job, as every other publisher is trying to do the same thing. But it does mean that when you're publishing a rock band or artist, your focus as a publisher is crystal clear.

But what if you're a rock writer, but not a performer? Wow. That one almost stumps the panel. Pitching songs to largely self-contained bands or singer-songwriters is just about the toughest proposition in the music business. Still, it can be done. Most of the writers that have been successful in this endeavor are also producers. The expectation is usually that the producer will write with the band, produce the record, and hopefully provide the hit single that the band was unable to come up with on their own. People like Jake Sinclair (Panic at the Disco), Jeff Bhasker (Rolling Stones, Harry Styles), and Alex Da Kidd (Imagine Dragons) are known as collaborators who can help to shape an artist or an album, contribute to the songwriting and also add their sonic polish on the production side.

This is a different business than pitching a finished song. You're really pitching the writer's ability to work with the artist to come up with the right song. In order to sell yourself or the writer you represent in that way, you are going to need some sort of track record of success. It's not an accident that many of the most sought-after collaborators are people like Jack Antonoff or Dan Auerbach who are also members of well-known bands.

If you're not already a rock star, then this means starting small and slowly moving up the musical food chain. Find an unsigned, developing artist to work with, try to write some songs together, see if you can produce the demo, and help them to land a record deal. Next, go out and find a signed band that's struggling. Maybe their first album didn't do as well as expected, or they're an older group in need of reinvention, or a new act that the label just can't get a handle on. Again, if you can give the project shape, and provide a hit song in the process, you can take the next step up. It's a long climb to the top. But hey, that's rock and roll.

You might also want to consider diversifying. I know I said all that stuff about focus and now here I am telling you to widen your horizons. But it's tough to survive as a songwriter or publisher focused solely on the rock market. Even Alex Da Kid and Jack Antonoff do more pop records than rock ones. Sometimes, a producer with more of a rock sensibility is just what a pop artist wants to add a little edge to the project. You might also consider taking a more global approach. Outside the U.S., rock artists are not nearly so self-contained, particularly if they are making an English-language album. Don't be afraid to try something a little outside of your own frame of reference. You may find a secondary market that can sustain you until that big record deal comes your way.

Other Genres

There you have it. Pop, hip-hop, R&B, rock, and country. Which leaves only about 36,785 genres and sub-genres in the contemporary music world that I've failed to mention. Let me guess: what you do falls into one of those neglected categories. Okay, fine. Let's take a look at a few more markets, but we'll keep it short and sweet. Here's a thumbnail summary.

Electronic and Dance. This world breaks down cleanly into two camps: *producers*, who are often DJs, and *topliners*, the songwriters responsible for writing the melody and lyrics. Your job as a publisher is to match one with another. In the end, a producer/DJ desperately needs a great topline to make it into the upper echelon of the DJ Mag Top 100, and the topliners need their lyric and melody on tracks by people who can get them on the top playlists and in front of the biggest club audiences. The publisher's job here is all about collaborations—and figuring out song splits.

Latin. Another booming market in which artists are constantly featuring on one another's releases, creating a constant product flow of new songs, remix versions, and side projects. Miami is where much of the action is, and like the urban market, this game is all about developing your new artist through the right features and collaborations, and working your hot young producer into one of the production camps of the genre's biggest stars.

Instrumental Music. Many of the opportunities here tend to be in the film, television, and advertising worlds. Consider contributing to music libraries as well. There may be some income in print music; you may want to work with a sheet music publisher to exploit those markets.

Enough already. The point here is that the rules of the game change drastically depending on whose field you're playing on. You must adapt your approach to fit the market you're in.

In the following chapters, we'll discuss at length the role of a creative director within a publishing enterprise, and the various strategies that can be employed to exploit copyrights for fun and profit. Depending on the genre in which your catalog is based, some of these strategies will be more useful than others. Don't get caught up in specifics, and don't be too quick to decide that a particular approach won't work in your market. Remember, until *Hamilton* came along, no one thought hip-hop could be viable for musical theater. Try to understand the general concepts and then adapt them to your company's specific needs. It's always easy to see what doesn't work. Only experimentation will show you what does.

GENRE	STRATEGIES
Pop	Pitch to major artists, labels, and management; collaborations; development of new artists.
Hip-Hop	Collaborations with top producers; development of new artists, independent releases. Utilize SoundCloud, TikTok.
R&B	Collaborations with top producers, artist development, independent releases.
Country	Pitch to major artists, labels, and management; collaborations; development of new artists; live performance.
Modern Rock	Advertising and television placements, independent releases, live performance. Spotify and touring numbers are key.
Singer-Songwriter	Television and film placements, independent releases, live performance. Also collaborations/features/remixes with electronic producers/artists.
Electronic/EDM	Collaborations with topliners and DJs, independent releases. Spotify and SoundCloud are crucial.
Traditional Rock	Some advertising and film placements; video games; live performance. Target Europe, Central America, and South America.
Heavy Metal/Punk	Some film placements, video games, live performance. Target festivals, especially outside the U.S.
Latin Pop/Urban	Pitch to major artists, collaborations with top artists or producers, some synchronization at Spanish-language media. YouTube is key.
Traditional R&B	Pitch to major artists and their management; specialty and satellite radio. U.K. and Europe are key markets.
Gospel/Christian	Pitch to major artists and labels; development of new artists; build relationships with large church-affiliated production companies.
Jazz	Pitch to established artists; collaboration with other artists (especially in hip-hop or R&B), live performance. Europe/Asia/South America are important.
Folk	Independent releases, some TV and film placements, collaborations with other artists (especially in electronic or country), live performance.

Theater	Find backers, develop productions, some opportunities for print income and cast albums. Grand rights are primary source of income.
Nu Classical	Film, television and advertising placements, live performance; independent releases. Target Spotify playlists, production music libraries.
Film Score	Production music libraries; film, TV, and advertising placement; sound design. Target indie directors; theater, dance, and corporate productions.
Reggae/Dancehall	Independent releases, YouTube videos, collaborations with top artists. The underground network of clubs, artists, and fans is crucial.

FIG. 11.1. Song Pitching Strategies by Genre

12

The Creative Director: "Say My Name"

Now that you've got your very own publishing enterprise, have you given yourself a title? It's a little weird right? Especially if you're the only person in the company. But what did you go for? President? Impressive. CEO? Very corporate. Manager? A little bland.

I've got one for you: creative director. Because whatever else you are—accountant, office manager, receptionist—this is what you really need to be. This job gets a couple of different titles in publishing companies. Sometimes, it's professional manager (which is probably the vaguest title in the entire corporate realm), or creative manager (which is okay), or my first title, creative services (which is just plain weird). But whatever you want to call it, this is the job that you signed up for when you became a publisher. A good creative director is a music critic, producer, song-plugger, publicist, coach, and cheerleader, all rolled into one. Being all of those things is what part II of this book is about.

When I first started in the publishing business, I had very little actual job experience and not much knowledge of the complexities of the industry. Thankfully, the one thing I did have was songwriting experience. Having been signed to several different publishers, I had the opportunity to work with a variety of top-notch creative directors, all of whom approached the job in slightly different ways, but all of whom provided invaluable guidance and direction to this wayward songwriter. I just wish I had listened to them more closely at the time. I did know this much about the gig: I was supposed to *make stuff happen*. Since then, I've learned how and what.

There are three primary functions that should occupy the creative director's day:

- getting the music right
- getting the music out
- moving the writer up

In that order. Put a note on your bulletin board, or tear this page out of the book and frame it on the wall (just kidding). Keep these three things in mind at all times.

Now that you have recognized their importance, it is a fundamental law of the universe that all forces will conspire to continually divert your focus from these three things. Paperwork, business affairs, accounting questions, and copyright problems will always be there lurking, ready to devour the hours of your day. You can't ignore these other issues, but you can control them and keep them in their place. Remember your job title. First and foremost, you are a creative director. Get the music right. Get it out. Move the writer up.

Getting the Music Right

First things first . . . and in the music business, getting the music right *should* always come first. Before strategies are in place, before calls are made, before schmoozing is done, and before you start emailing music to all those names in the *A&R Registry*, the music must be right. As a creative director, you simply cannot put yourself in the position of pushing songs that you don't believe in. You may not always have a smash hit to pitch for every project, but every song that you send out must meet your professional standards. When an A&R person or a music supervisor listens to the song you've sent them, it's not just the song being judged. It's also you, the sender. These professionals are judging your taste level, your musical standards, and your ability to understand what they are looking for and to provide it. If they think that you are trying to sell them material that you know is substandard, they will be insulted and rightly so. If they think that you don't even know the material is substandard, they will write you off entirely.

Your first role then is that of music critic. As I mentioned earlier, one of the chief benefits to acting as your own publisher is to afford you a certain distance from your own songs so that you can critique them with objectivity. Songwriters often work in a rush of creativity that makes it easy to overlook inherent problems within a song or musical shortcomings in the demo. The creative director's role is to step in after that initial burst of energy, recognize a song's strengths and weaknesses, and make suggestions as to how to fix the elements that aren't working. The creative director must have the discipline to send the writer back to the studio (even if the writer is you) as many times as it takes to get it right. You are your publishing company's Quality Control Department. Nothing goes out until it receives your stamp of approval.

Here's a test for you. Pull up your most recent demo and hit play. Now close your eyes, and imagine that you're sitting across from the most important power broker in your sector of the industry, pitching your song. Are there things you want to make excuses for? Then those need to be fixed. Is there a lyric line that makes you wince? Change it. Any notes in the vocal that make you cringe? Tune 'em up. Is it getting boring halfway through the second verse? Add something to the arrangement. As the song ends, try to imagine the boss weasel's reaction. Is he or she bouncing out of the desk chair, arms waving with enthusiasm? (Note: this is rare). Is he nodding half-heartedly? Is she checking her phone?

The point is simple. When you play a song for anyone in the industry, you should be able to do so with confidence. No excuses, no explanations, no imagination required. Ultimately, a song is going to have to do a lot more than pass your quality test in order to get cut. It's going to have to blow people away. Quality control is the minimum standard.

Of course, the difficulty is that songs can be maddeningly hard to judge. Anyone that's been in the business for long has been fooled at least once, and either rejected a song that became a hit, or recorded a song that was a sure smash, only to see it flop. And of course, everybody who hears a song has an opinion, for whatever that's worth. But if you listen to enough music every day, you start to develop a pretty clear picture of what's important in a song and where most songs tend to go wrong. With allowances then for a certain subjectivity and gut instinct that is part of the process, I offer you: The Song Quality Checklist. (This should be fun, huh?)

1. Does the title sound like a "hit"?

I can almost invariably tell whether a song is any good simply by looking at the title. Real "hit" songs have "hit" titles—interesting, provocative, funny, and unique. "Break Up With Your Girlfriend, I'm Bored," "Can't Feel My Face," "Sweet But Psycho," "10,000 Hours"—these titles stand out. Most of the time, it's obvious which songs have single potential just by looking at the titles on an album. Bland, dime-a-dozen titles like "With You" or "You Are the One" can and have turned into hit songs, but the titles are a hurdle to get over, rather than a hook. My first reaction to those titles is that I've heard that song too many times already.

Fixing a title is tricky. It's a little like fixing the framework of your house after it's already been built. But sometimes, it's just a matter of adding or subtracting a word or two, or even changing the punctuation. Britney Spears' " . . . Baby One More Time" is more interesting than "Baby One More Time." Try to picture how the title of your song would look on the *Billboard* chart. Would it stand out?

2. Is there a concept for the song?

A weak title is usually an indicator of a more serious problem. Songs called "With You" are often not really about anything, or at least not anything very interesting. There's not an original idea at the core of the song. Take a look at the hit titles. You can see that there's an idea, a concept behind every song. The song "10,000 Hours" draws upon the popular idea that any skill can be mastered with an investment of 10,000 hours, and applies it to a romantic relationship. That's an idea worth writing a song about. Most songs miss the top drawer because the core idea of the song is simply not compelling. If the concept is weak, it's very hard to rescue the song, no matter what you do with it musically or lyrically.

3. Is the lyric effective? Appropriate? Convincing? Singable? Appealing? Cliché free?

It's the eternal debate between composers and lyricists: do lyrics matter? I'll settle it for you here and now. Yes. Of course, it's possible to come up with examples of songs in which a banal lyric is redeemed by a great track, just as it's possible to come up with a lyric that has made something special of a relatively standard melody. There are an awful lot of songs out there; you can find an example to prove almost anything. But as someone who listens to songs every day, I will tell you plainly, lyrics matter. A lot.

This is not to say that there's anything wrong with a simple, direct lyric. In many cases, particularly in dance music or R&B music, that's the only kind of lyric that will be effective and appropriate. "Music Sounds Better with You" is a great lyric—one interesting line, repeated over and over. It's exactly what the song needs. Conversely, a lyric that sounds false or forced can kill a song on the spot.

The words have to sing. If there's a line in a song that makes you cringe, it's usually because the lyrics feel awkward; the melody and words are out of sync with one another. This is a job for the creative director. Find those clinkers and get 'em out of there. Also, the singer has to want to sing the words. Lyrics function not only within the song but also within the context of the artist's image. Songs that put the singer in a poor light are tough to get covered. Most artists prefer to present themselves as strong and independent, rather than needy and whiny. (They save the needy and whiny stuff for offstage).

Finally, one quick word about clichés. Stock rhymes, like "fire" and "desire," or trite, predictable metaphors drive A&R people nuts. When you're writing a song, it's easy to pass these clichés off. After all, the line sings well and it's only one line. But when you listen to hundreds of songs a day, it's not just one line. It's the same stupid, clichéd line that you've heard on ten other songs already today. I once listened to twenty songs in a catalog, and found that eighteen had references to birds flying, and nineteen mentioned rivers running. You start to notice that sort of stuff. Spare me. Spare us all.

4. Is the song structured correctly? Is there a natural build and release within the song structure?

For many years, song structure changed very little. From the mid '60s through the first decade of the 2000s, the old verse/prechorus/chorus progression was the framework of almost everything on the Hot 100, the country charts, and the R&B charts.

The last ten years have brought more change to song form than the previous three decades combined. One reason for this is the influence of hip-hop, which often eliminates B-sections and utilizes much more repetition on the musical side (usually four-bar loops that just repeat throughout the song) but far less repetition on the lyrical and melodic side. At the same time, the impact of EDM, with its focus on "drop" sections, has forced songwriters to rethink what a "chorus" can be.

The other major factor accelerating the evolution of song form has been the advent of streaming, with its emphasis on algorithms and playlisting. Contemporary songwriters and producers are acutely aware that they have very little time to grab the interest of a listener and that the longer they can hold it, the better their algorithms will look and the more likely they will be to move up to better playlists. In a sense, Spotify and other streaming services have taken the audience research that was pioneered by radio, refined it, elevated its importance, and then made the whole process relatively transparent, so that songwriters can see how audiences are reacting. The result has been the virtual elimination of intros and bridges, the overall shortening of song lengths (from an average of 3:50 to something more like 2:30), and second verses that diverge melodically from the first verse. Songs like "Sicko Mode" virtually ignore traditional song form entirely, proving only that there are no rules left.

There are however some basic principles to guide your thinking: use the best parts more than once, don't take too long to get to the best parts, and have at least one section that comes as a bit of a surprise. If in doubt, ask yourself at what point in your song might the listener skip to the next song on New Music Friday. You just found the weak part of your structure. So cut out that boring part, move the chorus sooner, or go straight into the chorus after the bridge. As the creative director, you should feel free to experiment with any options you feel move the song along more effectively.

5. Does the arrangement serve the song? Does it enhance the song?

People often speak about arrangement and production as if the two were synonymous. I prefer to distinguish between them. Arrangements are concerned primarily with musical parts and structure, while production is centered around sonic and performance considerations. A drum pattern is an arranging issue; a snare sound is a production one. A background string line is an arranging element; the fact that the strings are out of tune is a production problem.

The first rule of arranging is that nothing should detract from the listener's focus on the melody and lyric. Background parts should not clash with the vocal, and the instrumentation and tempo should fit the mood of the lyric. Most songwriters are protective enough of their songs that this is usually not a problem. Lyricists particularly tend to be ever-vigilant about anything that might obscure their favorite line. (Every line is a lyricist's favorite line.)

More often, the problem is that songwriters fail to use the arrangement to enhance the song. In an effort to keep it simple, the demo is just a generic, personality-free vocal over a dull, predictable arrangement and a groove that doesn't really groove. This dreaded middle ground is the No Man's Land of songwriting. When A&R people hear these demos, they just say: "No, man."

On any classic record of almost any style, there is some sort of instrumental hook built into the arrangement of the song: the bass line in "Billie Jean," the string lines in "Yesterday," the banjo sample on "Old Town Road," or the orchestra hits in "Happier"—these elements support the song and give it a unique identity. They can also add a sense of dramatic development, providing a jolt of surprise when they first appear, a sense of change when they disappear, and emphasis when they reappear.

Listen to your demo and identify the instrumental hooks. If you're not sure your song has any hooks, then the song isn't done. Go back to the drawing board.

6. Is the tempo right? Does the song drag?

You never really understand the importance of getting the tempo right until you play your song at a pitch meeting. Suddenly, the up-tempo track that felt so in-the-pocket when you heard it in the studio seems to plod, and the slow songs seem to run out of gas entirely, stalling to a dead stop somewhere around the second verse. Something must be wrong with the computer. Take it from a veteran of this syndrome: the only thing that's gone wrong is the song's tempo.

In my experience, you want to push the tempo up to the breaking point and then pull back just slightly from that. You'll hate me for it until you get to the pitch meeting. You can thank me later.

7. Does the production of the demo have the right presence and impact?

A "demo" recording is short for "demonstration record" (not "demolition," although sometimes it seems more like that). It's the recording of the song that will be used to "demonstrate" (and hopefully sell) the song to A&R people, artists, producers, and anyone else that might be buying.

It's also the culmination of all the work you've put into getting the music right. Only you hear the song as it exists in your head. Everybody else hears the song as it's recorded on the demo. And that's what they're judging. If it's wrong on the demo, it's wrong. End of story.

"Production" is a term that can encompass almost every element of a recording, from the instrumentation to the vocal performance to the mix. My primary concern here is sonic quality and musical performance. Keeping in mind that some productions are deliberately lo-fi, others strive to sound as "live" as possible, and some go for over-the-top bombast, does the production elicit the emotional response it's looking for? Are the sounds fashionable, fresh, and interesting? Are the reverbs, delays, distortions, and other effects used judiciously? Is the mix properly balanced (keeping in mind that what constitutes a proper balance differs radically from genre to genre)? Are the instruments and vocals in tune and in time? Does the recording have momentum and energy?

Songwriters are always complaining that A&R people lack imagination ("Why can't they envision what the song would be like with strings and horns?"). The truth is, imagination is unpredictable and you may not want A&R people using theirs. Sure, they might imagine the song better than it sounds on the demo. They might also imagine it worse. Better to remove the variables and give it to them exactly the way you want them to hear it.

8. Does the song fit clearly into a specific genre? Is the demo appropriate for that genre?

For many songwriters, the creative process is one of complete freedom—an impulsive act of imagination unrestricted by commercial considerations. But it's not like that for the creative director. It's your job to figure out where this particular piece could possibly fit in the giant puzzle of the music industry—and then make sure that it fits there. Often, this requires more creativity than was used in writing the song.

Sometimes, the only way to discover where a song belongs is to narrow it down, step by step. What type of artist would sing this lyric? How young or old would the artist need to be? What rhythmic feel and tempo works best for this particular melody? I try not to get too caught up at first in chord progressions and the instrumentation on the demo, as those elements can sometimes deceive you. If a song's melody, lyric, and rhythmic feel really fit better into a genre different than the one in which the song was originally conceived, it's always possible for a writer to restructure the chord progression and redo the demo.

For example, if a ballad needs to be sung by an older male artist, it's in 3/4 time, and it's a lyric about the tragic loss of a loved one, it's a country song, no matter what the writer thinks. That's about the only genre where you'll find an older male artist or in which radio will play a ballad in waltz time, particularly one with a tear-jerking lyric.

This means that the song needs a country demo. Don't try to sell a song in one market with a demo that is suited for another. Nashville has a very specific demo approach, which usually involves recording with a live band; the other option is sometimes a simple "unplugged" type demo, with just guitar, vocal, and maybe a fiddle or mandolin. Pop and hip-hop demos on the other hand generally need a full production that sounds like a record. Many electronic producers like to receive demos that are just piano/vocals; they'll keep the vocal and replace the track.

There's no one right answer to what the demo should be, but it has to fit the market to which you're selling. If you're truly not sure about the market for your song, then save your money and do a simple work-tape. You can wait until you have a clear picture of where you're pitching the song before you do a full demo.

Often it's up to the creative director to figure out what a song truly wants to be, then to imagine where it could fit in the market, and then somehow reconcile those two realities. That's why you get to have "creative" in your title.

9. Does the song have the potential for mass appeal? Is it the right size?

No, I'm not talking about the length of the song—that stays under four minutes, no matter what. I'm talking about something much more conceptual, something . . . big.

This is something I was never much aware of as a writer, but it's become increasingly apparent to me as a publisher. Most writers write small, rather than big. So many songs are like lovely little miniature paintings: a melancholy little lyric, with a little hook buried at the end of each little chorus, with a lot of little chords and a melody that never really strays too far from a little six- or seven-note range. In the end, the listener is touched by a little emotion and reacts with a little smile, a nod, and then, in very little time, forgets about the song entirely.

Contrast that with something like "Something Just Like This" by the Chainsmokers and Coldplay. That's what I mean by BIG. One of the great things about both artists, despite being in very different genres, is that they write BIG—BIG ANTHEMS WITH BIG UNIVERSAL LYRIC IDEAS AND BIG MELODIES MADE TO BE PLAYED IN BIG PLACES FOR BIG CROWDS.

Of course, not every song needs to sound BIG. Billie Eilish's "Bad Guy" is small, almost eerily so, in its production. But the lyric is brash, confrontational, and at least for the teenage girls it's aimed at, about as universal as they come. It's a BIG song done is a small way and its impact is just as strong, like a shout in a library.

There's nothing inherently wrong with a small song. It can be intimate and touching, and quite satisfying to a coffeehouse full of friends and family. But if you want to reach a large audience and create a song that has the potential of becoming a classic, you're going to have to think bigger. I read an interview once with Eminem, who talked about his primary challenge as a young performer being that of learning to come out of his shell, to lose his self-consciousness, and project the larger-than-life persona that he has today.

This is where the cheerleader aspect of the creative director comes in. One of the most important roles a creative director can play is to encourage his or her writer to paint on an increasingly large canvas, to move from miniatures, to portraits, to murals. Or the main stage at Coachella.

Obviously, this is tougher to do if you are not only the creative director but also the writer. Still, the truth is that most of us talk to ourselves all the time—writers more so than most everyone else, except for the crazy guys on the subway. Your work as a creative director should be reflected in your interior dialogue, and the conversation should be one of a tough, but supportive coach—not tolerating any attempt to take the easy, safe way out but rather demanding that you set your sights higher and aim for greatness rather than mediocrity. Most songwriters fail to leave an impression simply because they think too small and aim too low. Go for the BIG hit.

Wow. A checklist for songs. That felt very creative didn't it? Sort of like checking a car for defects when it comes off the assembly line. Wouldn't it be easier to just go by gut instinct and decide whether you like the song or not?

Maybe. There's no question that many songs succeed better when listened to than when analyzed. "I Want It That Way" by the Backstreet Boys was probably one of the best pure pop songs of that generation, despite the fact that it starts out by rhyming "fire" and "desire," and has a lyric that I still haven't been able to make any sense of. But it also has a can't-miss melody and a brilliant arrangement and production. It just works. Of course, it's easy to follow your first impression and give a song the old "make it or break it" test. No need to dissect the thing. You either like it or you don't.

The problem is that as a creative director, your job is not to decide whether you like or dislike the song. It's to figure out how to fix it. Or improve it. Or improve the writer. A quick gut reaction is not going to accomplish that. A writer needs to understand what works and what doesn't, and be offered some constructive suggestions as to what can be done to make the song viable. In order to provide that, a creative director has to learn to look at songs in an organized and thorough fashion. "Nah, I'm not really feeling it," is just about the most depressing thing you can say to a songwriter—not because it's negative, but because it implies that the song is hopeless.

As you practice listening to songs in a more precise way, you will also start to find that things are often better than they first appear to be. A few lyric changes, a new drum pattern, or a new demo singer can reveal that there was more potential to a song than you might have initially thought. A careful consideration as to where a song fits in the market may reveal that it has potential in more than one genre. If nothing else, a consistent approach to looking at songs in this analytical way will help you, as creative director, to better understand your writer and his or her strengths and weaknesses—even if you and the writer are one and the same person. By maintaining an unrelenting determination to get the music right, you will begin to figure out what it will take to move your writer up.

13

The Art of Collaboration: We'd Be So Good Together

Analysis is easy.

In case you haven't noticed, there are plenty of people in this world who are happy to tell you what's wrong with something. There are far fewer who are interested in trying to help you fix it. What if you figure out which elements in a song need to improve, and you send your writer (that is, you) back to the drawing board . . . and the song comes back no better than before? What if you simply hit a creative wall and every idea starts to fall into the same old rut? What then?

First of all, don't panic. This is not unusual. It's never easy to rewrite, and everyone has those moments when everything they do starts to sound the same. Secondly, don't give up on trying to get the music right. The standards of the industry don't change just because you're having trouble reaching them. Step three: pick up your phone and call someone who cares:

A co-writer.

When I was a songwriter, it always seemed that creative directors spent most of their time setting up collaborations between writers. I suspected that this was because it's a lot easier than going out and trying to get songs cut. I was right.

For a good creative director, setting up co-writes is an easy, low-risk proposition—a couple of phone calls to another creative director. ("Why don't we have your guy write with my guy? How's Tuesday?"). In no time, you've made something happen. If the collaboration goes poorly, who can blame you for trying? It's like your mom setting you up for a date with her best friend's son or daughter.

The strange thing is, often enough, it actually works, which is probably more than you can say for Mom's attempts at matchmaking. Done strategically by a competent creative director, co-writes can be productive—both musically and from a business standpoint. Co-writes can help shore up a writer's weaknesses, increase his or her presence in the community, provide an entrance into new markets, and often, just keep a writer from growing stagnant or frustrated. Sometimes, a new face in the studio and a different perspective is enough to break a dry spell.

Shortly after I signed my first publishing deal as a songwriter, I ran into what was the most difficult case of writer's block I've ever experienced. Even now, twenty years later, I can recall the terrible mix of emotions: the pressure of wanting to prove myself to my new business partner, the desperation as deadlines for projects grew ever closer, and the absolute inability to generate one simple idea, either musically or lyrically. I was completely dry.

What finally brought me out of this ordeal was a trip I made to the U.K. to record the one song that I'd managed to eke out. While I was over there, my publisher set me up with several U.K. writers to work on material for various projects that the company was developing. At that time, I wrote primarily on my own. I had written with one or two people in New York, but I was hardly an experienced collaborator. (I was hardly even an experienced songwriter.) Suddenly, I was in someone else's studio, in a different country, with a co-writer staring back at me, expecting me to do something creative. And almost immediately, I could feel the clouds in my head begin to clear.

I have never forgotten the experience and think of it often in my work now, when I see one of my writers sliding into a funk. Writing can be a tremendously lonely experience. Sometimes, a writer just needs some company. It's amazing how easily another writer can walk in and solve a problem that has been perplexing you for days. "Why don't you just go to this chord, and then have the chorus come in like this?" Eureka. Sometimes getting the music right means getting the right people in the room together.

Finding Collaborators

Alas, getting the right people in the room is sometimes easier said than done. For readers located in a music center like New York, L.A., Nashville, Miami, or Atlanta, finding other songwriters should not require much sleuthing. If you can't find someone to write with in Nashville, you'd better take the boards off your windows and doors and start getting out a little more. In all of these cities, there is a full calendar of events sponsored by the performing rights organizations, the Recording Academy, and other groups like the

Nashville Songwriters Association International (NSAI) or the Association of Independent Music Publishers (AIMP). These events are intended to provide information and professional advice to songwriters, as well as to offer them a chance to get together and develop relationships. A more obvious approach is to simply immerse yourself in the local music scene and begin to approach those writers who interest you. Don't forget to also check out universities and music schools in the area who may have active songwriting programs, like New York University's Clive Davis school (which has launched songwriters and artists like Emily Warren and Maggie Rogers) as well as NYU's Steinhardt program, UCLA, Belmont University in Nashville, and of course Berklee College of Music in Boston.

Once you find someone with whom you click, the number of other interested parties will likely grow. Every songwriter knows at least one other writer, and writers have been known to gossip every now and then. You can also begin to utilize your A&R contacts to find collaborators. Within the conversation at a pitch meeting, try to get a sense of which writers the A&R person is working with right now or which developing writers he or she is excited about.

Or, you can always ask another creative director. As I said before, they usually like to set up co-writes. Be prepared to offer some sort of description of what you do, who you have worked with or who recommended you, and, if possible, what projects you or your writer are currently working on. You should also expect to be asked for a compilation of some of your work. You can request the same for any writers suggested to you. Writers and publishers work in a variety of ways. Some creative directors take a hands-on approach to managing their writers' calendars and will book every appointment, while others may just give you a phone number for a writer and suggest that you get in touch directly.

It's important to remember that the collaboration is between not just the writers, but the creative directors as well. Follow up with the other creative director after the writing session to let them know how it went, thank them, and tell them when to expect the demo. Once the demo is in, you can follow up again to get his or her reaction and brainstorm as to where the song could be shopped.

If you are far outside of any music business center, then all this gets a little more challenging. If you are in a city that at least offers a vibrant local music scene, you can simply focus on trying to develop relationships in that community, using local writers groups, songwriting associations, music festivals, and other events as an opportunity to get to know the active songwriters in your area. But if you are in a more remote place, without any local music scene to speak of—well then, I'm afraid you'd better pack your bags.

No, not to relocate. But you are going to have to hit the road every now and then. Find the location best suited to your particular style of music and plan a trip. Ideally, plan to divide your time between writing sessions and A&R meetings. You may want to consider scheduling around an industry event or conference: the ASCAP, BMI, or Grammy Awards in L.A., Tin Pan South in Nashville, the Indie Music Publishing Summit in New York, or the Latin Songwriters Hall of Fame in Miami. This gives you a reason for being in town and an event to fill your day if you're not able to book a full calendar of writing sessions. It also helps to ensure that most people will be in town when you are.

Unless you have a significant track record, it can be challenging to break into a new music community in this way. Plan your trip a reasonable time in advance, and don't set your hopes too high. You will build contacts here the same way as anywhere else: one co-write at a time. You need to emphasize to the writers and creative directors with whom you're working that you will be making regular trips. Then, try to find ways to keep the writing relationships active even when you're back at home, sending lyrics or tracks back and forth to write to.

That capability of sharing files online, the necessity for isolation and social distancing that came to us all courtesy of Covid-19, the potential of Zoom to connect us all even in pandemic lockdown, as well as the advent of collaborative platforms like BeatStars, Vocalizr, Vocal Kitchen, and MDIIO, has pushed many songwriters to adopt long-distance songwriting as their primary working method, seeking out collaborations with people who they've never actually met. It's effective enough that it yielded "Old Town Road, which grew out of a BeatStars transaction between Lil Nas X and Dutch producer Young Kio. The rapper simply purchased the track in what is essentially a vast online music marketplace, then wrote and recorded the rap and hook. Months later, the song exploded onto the charts. For those who are limited in their collaboration opportunities by economic realities or geography, this new way of accessing co-writing partners is a game-changer.

Admittedly, there are limits to the interaction that can happen between people in such a format, and often the topliner/producer collaboration can amount to not much more than "you doing your thing" over "me doing my thing," rather than an actual exchange of ideas. It can also be an isolating way of working, especially for topline writers who wake up with an inbox full of faceless tracks to which they need to write melody and lyric and record a vocal. All too often, the topliner then sends that melody and lyric idea back to the producers, only to hear nothing but silence in reply. If merely to preserve your sanity and the joy of making music, it's best to find a balance between long-distance collaborations and some face-to-face interactions with other creative spirits.

For that much needed human contact, writing camps have become a popular solution. Whether it's highly exclusive, record label-sponsored camps that pull in top-level writers to create the next single for a superstar act, exotic junkets to a Greek island, a beach in Thailand, or a castle in Transylvania (yes, these really happen), or activities organized by or around major music conferences like South By Southwest, Amsterdam Dance Event, or MIDEM, many up-and-coming writers keep their bags packed at all times, bouncing from one songwriting gathering to the next. Most of these camps are by invitation only, pulling together between ten to thirty songwriters who then pair off in various combinations for several days of intensive writing and even more intensive networking. As the ability to travel has disappeared during the pandemic, Zoom writing camps have begun popping up, bringing writers from all over the world into a virtual collaborative environment that can be technically challenging, but still creatively productive. A writing camp will certainly bring you out of your shell—some writers love them and others can't wait to get home. From the standpoint of a Creative Director, a writing camp brings both good (lots of new songs, renewed energy for your writers), bad (lots of half-finished songs, travel issues, and the cost of the camp itself) and the ugly (split issues with dozens of different collaborators who scatter across the globe as soon as the camp ends). Follow-through, on the part of both writer and creative director makes all the difference between whether a writing camp experience is a productive burst of creative energy or a bacchanalian spring break interrupted by a bit of songwriting.

Indeed, it's vital that you do your homework thoroughly before scheduling any writing trip. This means identifying the key writers that you want to make contact with, finding out who books their writing sessions, securing a place to work (hotel room, studio, writing room), understanding how the co-writers like to work and what they consider their strengths and weaknesses, and managing the calendar so that there is enough time with each collaborator to be productive.

Working styles are very different from one city or one genre to another. Nashville tends to be very businesslike, with writers keeping something approximating banker's hours and booking writing sessions four to six weeks in advance. Most writing sessions in Nashville are done either at someone's home or in a publisher's writing room (which usually includes some sort of crude recording equipment for making a quick work tape). Conversely, New York and LA writers think a noon start is early and are constantly rescheduling to take advantage of whatever opportunity might have popped up a day before your session. You'll need to be more flexible in these situations and have backup plans in case of a last-minute cancellation. When I send writers to LA, I almost always try to book one writing appointment during the day and one in the evening, just to be safe. While country and pop writers tend to book sessions with different writers every day, artists or producers in the rock or singer-songwriter world often need two or three days together to work effectively.

And then of course there's that old wild card, "chemistry"—a lack or a surplus of which can throw even the best-laid plans askew. It is one of the great mysteries of human existence: Why can two people meet and within minutes be finishing each other's sentences, while another two are in a screaming match in the next room? Why do some people write well with people they can barely tolerate, while others find it impossible to work with their best friend? Why is Jagger so much better with Richards than anyone else? Or McCartney with Lennon?

Matchmaker, Matchmaker . . .

You've now entered the realm of the great human experiment—the artificial union of human beings based on abstract and possibly random criteria. Matchmaking. I'd love to be able to offer you the Ten Steps to Setting Up Successful Collaborations, but I have no idea what they are. All I know is that the formula for good co-writing chemistry is based on some strange combination of personalities, artistic temperaments, musical tastes, and complementing strengths and weaknesses. And a lot of it depends on what mood the writers are in on that particular day.

Nevertheless, after setting up hundreds of collaborations, and having been a writer/guinea pig in dozens of others, you do start to develop some instincts as to what sorts of things will work and what won't. I think there are three primary considerations for a creative director in assessing whether a match-up makes sense.

Musical Compatibility
First of all, note that music, as always, comes first. It would be nice if all great musical teams got along happily on a personal level as well, but they don't. And they don't need to. After all, this is a job for everyone concerned, and it's reasonable to expect a writer to deal with a little personal frustration if it yields good work. If the music is great, it's worth all the pain and suffering.

Likewise, you should never be in a position of setting up co-writes solely for business purposes. Too many creative directors treat their writers like pawns who can be placed here, there, and everywhere in the interests of a larger strategy. They set up co-writes to develop relationships between companies, or as paybacks for favors rendered on other projects, or with the hope of finding an in-road into an otherwise inaccessible project. Certainly, these strategies are all part of the game, but they cannot be the driving force behind a collaboration. If you don't think two writers belong together musically, then do everyone a favor and don't put them in the same room.

So what else makes a musical collaboration work?

Complementary Strengths and Weaknesses

Composers need lyricists, and lyricists need composers. Melody and lyric writers go with track-oriented producers. Two composers together give you an instrumental track and two lyricists give you a poem. This may sound obvious, but I have seen many co-writes where the two writers arrived to find that no one in the room played an instrument. Or three writers arrived only to find that there were two track guys and a melody writer, and no one brought a pen and paper because no one wrote lyrics. First and foremost, a creative director must understand what each writer in the collaboration does and what their limitations are. And you better be sure that those add up to a finished song.

That's the easy part. The greater challenge is to use the collaborative process to compensate for weaknesses a writer might not even be aware he or she has. Not everyone who writes both music and lyrics is equally adept at both. Not everyone who can write music knows how to put a track together. Just as you have taken a cold, hard, objective view of your own catalog's strengths and weaknesses, you must do the same with others' catalogs—and then figure out if you can provide the missing elements. Lennon added an edge, and a bit of salt, to McCartney's sweetness. I still haven't figured out the Jagger/Richards thing.

Shared Tastes and Differing Influences

I once arrived at a writing session while my soon-to-be collaborator was finishing up a phone call. The writer asked me to make myself comfortable in the living room and assured me that she'd be off the phone shortly. While I waited, I began to look at my co-writer's music collection. Of course, I already knew what sort of music she wrote, but I was curious as to what she listened to (which is often very different). As I looked through her collection of vintage vinyl, I began to get a sinking feeling in my stomach. Her entire music library was the sort of music I hated.

When she finished her phone call, she came into the living room, and we commenced with the customary small talk that usually takes up more of a writing session than the writing. As we talked, she asked me what sort of music I was listening to. I listed off a few current favorites, and now it was her turn. Her face grew worried. She hated every record I'd mentioned. I think we both knew at that moment (although we spent the next few hours proving it) that this particular collaboration would never work. Today, we both remain good friends and admire each other's work. And we laugh about the impossibility of writing with someone whose musical tastes are antithetical to your own.

Conversely, some of the most successful co-writes that I have set up have been those between two writers from two very different genres. When Eugene Wilde, one of our R&B writers, went to Nashville to write with Jason Blume and George Teren, whose backgrounds are in the country market, they came up with two songs for Britney Spears. Go figure.

I think the key to musical compatibility is the right combination of shared musical tastes and different musical influences. As I mentioned earlier, most writers have a knowledge of music that extends far beyond the type of music they happen to write, and almost every writer has strains of several musical influences running through his or her work. If you compared the record collections of two collaborators, you'd like to think that there would be a least a few commonalities between them.

At the same time, too much agreement isn't always positive either. Part of the value of co-writing is to draw each writer out of his or her own comfort zone into a world where each is creatively challenged. This is why it works to put Rob Thomas with Santana, Taylor Swift with Brendon Urie, or Maren Morris with Marshmello. Of course there is common musical ground, but each writer comes from a very different place and brings with them a distinct musical point of view. These collaborations present a challenge to the writers involved. They are probably a bit awkward at first, requiring both writers to stretch outside their own world. That's often when co-writing yields the most exciting results. Vive la différence.

Personal Compatibility

I like songwriters. Having met with hundreds over the years, I can comfortably say that most songwriters are pretty nice people. If nothing else, they're a good hang. So when I'm talking about personal compatibility, I'm not just talking about avoiding writers who are arrogant, rude, disorganized, or suffering from drug and alcohol problems or the like. Although that's probably not a bad rule.

Like the question of musical compatibility, the real challenge of personal compatibility is not only to find two people who can sit in the same cramped writing room for four hours without killing each other. The challenge is to understand how each personality will add something to the equation. For example, I like to combine older, more experienced writers with younger ones. I think the older writers bring discipline and a larger perspective, while young writers bring fresh energy and a cutting-edge sensibility. Two young writers together can sometimes (not always) be a bit too unfocused and experimental. Two veteran writers together can sometimes be too comfortable and safe. I like to combine experience and energy. Even if the song doesn't turn out well, the younger writer will have learned something about life and the business from his or her exposure to the older writer. And the old pro will have gotten a jolt of excitement and youthful perspective from the up-and-comer.

It's also wise to consider the work habits of the writers you are putting together. Some writers are flighty, undisciplined, and easily distracted—they need co-writers who are patient but forceful, and who can offer them clear, firm direction. Other writers are highly insecure—they need partners who are supportive and confident. And some writers have a tendency toward laziness and complacency—they need someone who's going to light the room up with ambition and push them beyond what they're used to. Just as you assess a writer's musical qualities, a creative director must also understand a writer's personal qualities and take into account how they will affect the collaborative process.

Keep in mind, though, music first. Not every co-write has to be a love match. Frustrations, arguments, screaming matches, even fistfights are not necessarily a sign of a bad collaboration. In fact, those situations are probably preferable to two writers sitting in dead silence or happily having a three-hour lunch together when they're supposed to be writing. A little tension can be productive. At least it's a sign that each writer's comfort zone has been breached. A creative director is part matchmaker and part agent provocateur.

Business Compatibility

This is when a creative director has to think strategically. To the novice, collaborations are simply about two writers writing a song together—a pure, unfettered expression of a shared musical experience. Sure. But to the savvy creative director, collaboration is also a networking opportunity, a résumé item, and a thinly veiled song plugging opportunity.

Each time you set up a co-write, you increase your network of contacts substantially. You now have a relationship with another writer, his or her publisher, manager, or record label, and potentially, anyone to whom the other writer and his office shop the song. Your writer is exposed both to the co-writer and, more often than not, to the co-writer's circle of other collaborators, singers, musicians, engineers, and friends. It's like the old "Six Degrees of Separation" game. The more collaboration you do, the wider your reach in the industry becomes.

You can also begin to climb up the ranks of the musical food chain simply by association with a more established co-writer. While you don't get into the pantheon of A-level writers without being directly involved in a hit song, you can sometimes make it into the B-level just by working with an A-level writer. When an A&R person inquires about what a writer has done, the mention of a few well-known collaborators can confer immediate credibility.

Finally, a smart creative director can use a co-write as an entree into an otherwise closed shop. There is no better song plugging opportunity than collaborating with an artist or producer for a specific project. Rather than casting around in the dark, you can now tailor-make something from scratch with someone who knows exactly what is needed and now has a vested interest in using the material. If the artist or producer thinks they were part of writing the song, it can only help. Often artists and producers intent on controlling a project will be more open to co-writing than listening to your finished songs. Fine. Do whatever it takes to get in the door.

The key to using collaborations for business purposes is to make sure that in most instances your writer is writing "up" rather than "down." Pair your writers with people who are more experienced, more successful, or more connected. If that sounds cold and opportunistic, it is. I never said the weasel was an attractive beast. Nevertheless, it is important that the creative director seek to use the collaborative process to a writer's advantage by connecting with already successful writers (whose work is presumably in demand), with writers who are affiliated with strong publishers (giving you another active partner in pitching the song), or with producers or artists that are involved in specific projects (giving you the inside track in developing songs for the album).

And now, a word to the songwriter in you. For many writers accustomed to writing on their own, the suggestion of a co-write can be almost insulting. "Are you saying I can't write lyrics?" "What's wrong with my tracks?" Toughen up. The ability to examine your own talent and identify the strengths and weaknesses is a sign of maturity. The inability to do so borders on self-delusion. Richard Rodgers and George Gershwin collaborated with other writers; you probably can too. If nothing else, co-writing offers an on-site education in Songwriting 101, affording you the opportunity to watch and learn from another writer's approach to the craft.

Ultimately, every writer has to determine what his or her temperament can bear. Some writers are downright promiscuous, writing with any and all takers; others are married for life to one or two partners. When first starting out, be open to as many opportunities as you can find, at least until you've found a few partners with whom you consistently work well. Don't overthink the process. If it sounds like a somewhat interesting matchup, give it a shot. Even a disastrous co-write is rarely life threatening. Check out the "Rules of Collaboration" at the end of this chapter to increase your co-writer appeal.

And finally, a touching personal tale to show you that not every collaboration I did was a disaster.

When I was a career songwriter, I was set up by my publisher to write with Steve Lunt, a writer with a number of hits to his credit (including "She Bop" for Cyndi Lauper). The day before the session, I called Steve to introduce myself and to see what time he wanted to start working. As we talked, we began to realize that neither of us had been given the right information about what the other did. He thought I played piano (I play guitar) and programmed tracks (I can arrange them, but I'm not much of a programmer). We were both on the verge of canceling the session but finally decided to persevere and see what happened. As it turned out, we ended up working together as a writing/production team for two or three years and then became colleagues at Zomba Music. In fact, it was Steve who led me to the job, while he was the VP of A&R at Jive Records. We've been friends for almost three decades since that first awkward phone call.

At worst, a co-write means staring at someone you barely know for a few hours wondering how you ever got into this sorry situation. If moderately successful it means writing a good song, possibly learning a little about a different way of working, adding to your network of contacts, and probably having a few laughs in the bargain. At best, collaboration can mean the creation of a hit song, along with an opportunity to make a good friend and ally in the industry. All in all, a chance worth taking.

The Rules of Collaboration

1. Talk. Mark D. Sanders who wrote the classic "I Hope You Dance" says, "If I can talk with someone and learn what is interesting or important to them, we can usually write a song together." Don't be afraid to open up.

2. Listen. The reason Mark can write a song from a conversation is that he listens to what's being said and draws an idea from that. The song is out there; you just have to hear it.

3. Follow through. Nothing is more frustrating to a co-writer than a demo that never gets recorded or a lyric that never gets written. Whatever your responsibility is, get it done.

4. Experiment. The whole point of a co-write is to try something new. Don't insist on doing what you've done before.

5. Be humble. Don't rub your credits, accomplishments, or current success in your co-writer's face. You will both have your ups and downs. Keep them to yourself.

6. Be confident. No matter how new to the game you are, you've somehow made it into the co-write session—so your opinion is worth something. Present it with confidence.

7. Be honest. If you don't like something, say so. If you don't want to finish the song, offer to let the co-writer take his or her part back or bring in a third writer to finish it.

8. Be prepared. If you're a lyricist, come to the session with some titles or concepts in mind. If you're a composer, have a musical progression started. At least it gets a conversation going.

9. Be open. If your co-writer doesn't like your idea, or has a different one, then try something else. The things you stumble on are usually the most interesting.

10. Have fun. Songs written in misery usually sound, well, miserable. If you're stuck on something, take five, go have a slice, tell a few stories, and come back to it. This ain't life or death.

Oh yeah. I almost forgot. One more:

11. Get a signed split sheet at the end of your session!

14

Understanding the Ancient Art of Song Plugging

For creative directors in publishing companies with even a handful of writers on the roster, it's easy to be so caught up in getting the music right that you never quite get around to the second phase of the job. You're hanging out in the studio checking out the new demos, putting together collaborations, listening to work tapes . . . it's all very . . . well, creative. Who has time to be cold-calling artist managers? If you are a songwriter representing your own catalog, the dilemma is even more severe. When you devote a good portion of the day to figuring out which chord to go to in the B section or the best rhyme with "perfect," it's hard to be inspired by the idea of following up with the A&R you met with last month. That sort of thing just feels like being a salesman or something.

The Facts of Life as a Creative Director

- You will not be successful if you spend your time sitting around listening to your catalog. You'll be successful by getting other people to sit around and listen to your catalog.
- Those who send out the most songs win.
- Every element in your day will conspire to prevent you from sending out songs.

News flash: You are a salesman. Get used to it. If there is one frustration that most writers have with their creative directors, and quite frankly, that most *companies* have with their creative directors, it is that nobody seems to want to sell songs. I suspect it's also the greatest unspoken frustration that most songwriters have with themselves. Everyone likes to create music, listen to music, sign new music, or critique music, but no one seems to want to be bothered with actually sending the stuff out. The truth is that selling songs is the only part of music publishing that actually generates income. The whole enterprise, whether it's Warner Chappell or Walt's Next Big Hit Publishing is reliant on someone going out and getting a song on a recording, in a movie, or in an advertisement—-and no one wants to do it. This is a jumbo-sized problem.

And you, creative director, are the solution. Getting the music right may be your first task, but getting the music out is your primary one. You must have the discipline to set aside a portion of your time every day to devote to this particular part of your job. If you do it well, you will build a profitable enterprise and bring your writer fame and fortune in the bargain. If you don't, your publishing venture is kaput. How's that for a pep talk?

Beyond survival, there's one more important benefit to mastering the art of song plugging. If you succeed in building a track record of placing songs, you will likely find yourself well positioned for an executive position in the larger publishing industry, if at some point that's of interest to you. As I mentioned, there is a severe shortage of dedicated song pluggers in the music publishing industry. Every company needs them, and no one can find enough of them. Contact any major music publisher, tell them you are willing to focus solely on pitching songs, and offer a résumé that gives some indication that you are effective at that task. I can almost assure you, someone will be interested in meeting with you. There's a certain job security in understanding the ancient art.

Of course, the first step in getting the music out is deciding just who to get it out to. Finding opportunities for songs is a bit like detective work. You check your sources, follow the leads, do your homework, round up the suspects, and try to figure out who's really running the game "behind the scenes."

The following three basic questions should give you a pretty substantial list of names to investigate.

Who's Looking?

It's always easier to sell something if you can find someone who needs it. The point of determining "who's looking" is to focus your efforts on a buyer at the right moment.

Tip Sheets

We've already mentioned the tip sheets, so if you've got the *RowFax* or *The Looking List* laying around the office, that's a good place to start. But it's really just the tip of the iceberg. Most of the projects currently in development are never listed on a tip sheet, for any number of reasons. Many A&R types are skeptical of the quality of the material that a tip sheet listing brings in. Others are hesitant to acknowledge publicly that an artist is having trouble writing the songs for a project. The dedicated creative director must dig deeper. Underneath that pile of tip sheets in your office, there should be some industry trade magazines. Let's move on to those.

Trade Magazines

While the major trade magazines will not necessarily publish precise information about who's looking for songs, they will provide you with a comprehensive overview of what's happening in the industry. Here's what you're looking for:

1. Any mention of new signings, new projects in development, or artists switching record labels.

2. Information about newly created labels, production companies, or management firms.

3. Notices of executives moving into new positions or new companies.

4. Chart listings of artists who have a first single currently released, but no album out. If the single is doing well, you can be sure that the label is working on more releases.

5. References to movies or television shows currently in development.

6. Information about new trends or upcoming companies in music-related businesses such as video games, advertising, or social media.

Depending on the particular market that you are targeting, certain trade magazines will be more useful than others. If your primary focus is the record industry, *Billboard* should give you a good comprehensive overview. *The Hollywood Reporter* offers good coverage of the current movies and television shows in production. Or if you are particularly focused on placing your songs in advertising, you may want to check out *Ad Age* or *Adweek*, which can provide the inside track on that complex world. Sites like Music Gateway can also sometimes give you information as to what projects a company has in development. Leave no stone unturned.

Direct Inquiries

If you want to know something, it's never a bad strategy to simply ask. Most major music publishers make up their own "tip sheet" or "who's looking list" several times a year. There's really not much to it. Each creative director reaches out to the various record labels, producers, and management companies, and asks what they're working on. Like I said before, this business isn't exactly rocket science.

Dig into that pile of paper on your desk. Under the tip sheets and next to the trade magazines, find your industry directories. You'll need to narrow down which companies are relevant for the sort of music you do, and try to identify one or two A&R contacts within the correct department. Then start sending out some emails.

These days, I prefer using email or even texts for this kind of cold contact outreach, as opposed to calling the office. A phone call to someone you don't know feels much more intrusive than it did even a decade ago. In most offices, any cold call solicitation never makes it past the receptionist. Besides, in this information-gathering stage, it's not essential to have a one-on-one discussion with the name in the directory. When most major publishers put together their tip sheets, much of the information is gathered from A&R coordinators, assistants, and receptionists who have been briefed by their bosses as to what projects are in development. If the A&R staff or their assistants can send you out a list of what the various acts on the roster are looking for, that should be enough to get you started.

Here's how the email should go:

1. Identify yourself as the creative director of the publishing company. There's no need to indicate in any way that you are also a songwriter. The nice thing about email is that you are in complete control of the information you put out there. No one's on the other end asking questions. You are from a publishing company, nothing more.

2. If you have a sufficient story, offer a one- or two-sentence description of your company, mentioning any noteworthy activity, success, or business partners. This is the time to drop that name, if you've got one on you.

3. Explain that your company is in the process of updating their list of projects currently seeking material. Ask if there is a list (it's usually called a "pitch sheet" or a "who's looking list") of acts on the roster currently seeking songs and if there are specific projects that are current priorities. If there are projects at the company that you've

learned about in your previous research, inquire about those. You'll earn extra points for having done your homework.

4. Ideally, you'd like to know not only the name of the artist, but also some information about the project itself:

- What type of material is being sought
- Who is the appropriate A&R contact person
- What's the current status of the project, and any deadline information
- What producers or other writers are involved in the project?
- If the artist is involved in the writing, is he or she open to collaborations?
- Is the company looking for finished songs or just tracks for others to write to?

Most companies or executives who reply to your email will give you as much of the above information as they think is relevant in the list they send back to you. If there are details that are missing, you can do some research yourself to fill in the blanks.

Otherwise, the best approach is to save the follow-up questions until after you've sent over a couple of songs for the project. If what you've sent has at least kept the door open for future submissions, that's the time to inquire about any additional information you might need to fine-tune your pitch.

Word of Mouth

And now, I'm going to shock you with a startlingly generous suggestion, coming from a weasel like myself. Once you've begun to compile a useful list of projects seeking songs, call a few of the other songwriters and publishers in your musical community (you are part of a community, right?), and share some of the information you've gathered.

Huh? Share? After all your hard work finding out who needs songs, I'm telling you to give it away to other people? Your competitors?

Well, I'm not telling you to share *all* of it. But throwing a little inside information into a conversation never hurts. Because it gets people talking. Before you know it, your creative cronies, not to be outdone, are offering up a few of the projects they've heard about. Suddenly, you are part of the proverbial grapevine, through which all essential information flows. Having a spot on that grapevine is far more valuable than any inside scoop you're giving away.

One final tip regarding the "who's looking?" method of song plugging: This particular approach relies more than anything else on a quick response. Get the tip, enter it into a list on your computer, or write it on a whiteboard on your wall, then immediately start looking at your catalog for an appropriate pitch. If you don't have anything that works, see if your writers can come up with something that same week. As soon as you've got something to send, get it out of your office and into the hands of the A&R person. Correction to my Facts of Life item: those who get the most songs out *fastest* are the ones who win.

Who Is the Song Right For?

This is the flip side to the first approach. The problem with the "who's looking" list is that inevitably there are many artists who are looking for something that you don't have. Likewise, there are a lot of songs gathering dust on your shelf, waiting for the right artist to show up one day on the tip sheet. You need a secondary plan of attack. By asking "Who is the song right for?" you can take a more proactive approach to exploiting all, or at least the best, songs in your catalog.

So here we go: three easy steps to finding Mr. or Ms. Right for your song.

Know Your Audience

You must start with an understanding of the market in which your song will be pitched. I don't mean just having a general impression. I'm talking about having a real, in-depth knowledge of that particular world of music—who the top artists are, who the up-and-coming artists are, which artists are struggling, and why. You need to know what differentiates each artist from the other, in terms of production, lyrics, melody, rhythmic approach, and chord progression.

If you send songs out blindly, the problem is not so much that you fail; it's that you usually embarrass yourself in the process. You cannot pitch the same "pop" ballad to Ariana Grande and Olivia Rodrigo. They are two completely different types of singers. A country song is unlikely to be perfect for both Jason Aldean and Blake Shelton. You must take into account the age of the artist, the image, the vocal range, and the musical history. Only after you've fully considered all of these factors, should you ever venture to suggest to a manager, artist, or A&R person that a song is "perfect" for their project. Remember, your credibility as a creative director hangs in the balance. You must do your homework before you make that call.

Keep It Real

You must also occasionally douse yourself with a quick splash of cold, bracing realism. There's nothing wrong with identifying one or two multi-platinum artists for whom the song would be a fit. But that's a wish list. It's not a strategy. In order to determine who the song is really right for, you've got to set your sights at a realistic level.

If you are just starting to build a name for yourself in this business, then you should be targeting artists that are accessible and open to new material, producers who customarily work with outside writers, and lower-level A&R people, who may not have a budget sufficient to hire the top-call writing teams for their new act. If you're sure your song is a hit for Bruno Mars, you're kidding yourself. Bruno Mars writes his own songs with his production crew. That project is closed. If Panic at the Disco is the only band that can sing your song, those "High Hopes" will probably not be realized. Direct your efforts to developing artists, those in need of a hit to revitalize their career, or those trying to cross over from a small market to a larger one. The idea is to avoid wasting your time and energy reaching for the stars. Instead, get in at the ground level and ride the elevator up.

Put On Your A&R Hat

The greatest difficulty that most creative directors have in figuring out who could perform their song is that they are thinking like creative directors. The mindset is that of a publisher, whose primary focus is finding high-quality, commercial songs and then sending them out to people who have done similar sorts of songs in the past. The problem is, this is not how most artists or their various handlers put together an album.

In order to pitch songs (or write them) effectively, it is sometimes important to slide over to the other side of your desk and put on your A&R hat. When you do, you begin to see that for most managers, record execs, and producers, a new record is all about artist development. Most major record companies do not consider the making of hit records to be their ultimate goal. The ultimate goal is the creation of hit *artists*, because that's where the real money is. If you're going to wear the A&R hat, you have to understand Artist Development.

Reinforcing the Artist's Persona

If the artist is your priority, it's not enough for a song to be catchy. It must also be appropriate to the artistic direction of the project.

- *If the artist is to establish a public image, the lyrics the artist sings must reinforce that persona.*

- *If an artist wants credibility, he or she will have to show artistic growth. It's not enough to record songs that reconstruct past hits.*

- *If an artist wants to be perceived as a leader in the genre, it won't work to record songs that sound just like what's on the radio. That sound will be old by the time the album comes out.*

Often a creative director will argue with an A&R person who's passing on a song, " . . . but it's a smash." The A&R person will respond, "Yeah, I know. But not for this artist on this album." When you go through the process of identifying the right artists for your song, you must see things through the artist development prism. Think of each artist on your list, and put yourself in the position of his or her manager or A&R person. What new sounds should the act embrace? What aspects of their old sound should they avoid? What sort of image should they project? What markets do they need to capture to increase their sales? It's not enough to pitch songs that sound just like an artist's past work. You've got to anticipate where an artist is headed and try to provide songs that will lead the way.

Remember, music publishers are all about the song. Everyone else in the record business is all about the artist.

Who's Listening?

If songwriting is often a lonely, isolated business, the rest of the modern entertainment business is the polar opposite. Most entertainment projects—whether they are records, movies, or television productions—are raging tempests of divergent opinions, political power plays, competing interests, and shifting alliances, out of which, somehow, an actual piece of product eventually emerges. Usually, it's not a particularly good product, but by that point, everyone's just happy the thing got made at all.

Music Business Weasel Says:
There is always more than one chef in the
kitchen. And more than one hand in the pie.

Music Business Weasel

As a creative director, this committee approach to decision making is both
boon and bane. It's a boon because it allows you an endless array of ways to
work a song into a particular project. If the producer doesn't like it, you can
try getting it to the manager. If they say no, you can call the A&R person.
Hope springs eternal. The bane is the endless list of people who need to give a
thumbs-up just to get your song recorded. Every approval is issued condition-
ally: "I like it, *but* I'll have to send it to so and so, and get their feedback...."
There's always one more hoop to jump through.

The key to success is to learn to take advantage of the chaos that surrounds
most show business endeavors. This means understanding who the players
in any particular project are and deducing who has the power of the final
decision. Of course, both the players and the power are constantly shifting,
which is what makes the game so darn exasperating. Here's a quick breakdown of the usual suspects that show up on most projects:

- **Artist:** If you can get your song directly to an artist, you've entered
  the inner circle. But don't assume that the artist calls all the shots.
  Superstars usually have the last word about what they're going to
  sing, but many new artists do not. Still, any time you can develop
  a relationship with the face on the Spotify profile, you're in a good
  position.

- **Manager:** Most creative directors don't spend enough time pitching
  the artist's manager. This is usually the most trusted figure in
  the artist's world—the one person with 24/7 access. Best of all,
  managers are the least likely to be inundated with a constant stream
  of demos. Their ears are somewhat fresh.

- **Label:** It's important to try to decipher how the A&R process works
  at each different label. Some companies will assign a specific A&R
  person to each project; that person will generally be the only one
  listening to material for that album. Other companies use more of
  a team approach, with the whole A&R staff gathering songs and
  making a collective judgment as to what gets recorded. You can

usually figure out each label's way of doing business by the size of the A&R staff. A label with four or five different VPs of A&R probably gives ample autonomy to each of them. A company with an A&R staff of three people, or one senior person and several junior people, is more likely to work together on all of the acts on the roster.

- **Producer:** The role that a producer plays can vary widely from project to project. Producers that are active writers are unlikely to be open to songs from the outside, although many such producers also employ teams of writers (some credited, some not) who may be available for collaborations. Producers that are not writers are generally always on the hunt for "hits." In many cases, their ability to land the production gig is dependent on them finding a song that everyone likes. Because most producers have a background as musicians, writers, or engineers, they are often more accessible than many of the executives in the business.

Film and television projects bring their own cast of characters. In the case of soundtrack projects, these Hollywood people are added to the list of players we've already discussed.

- **Director:** Some directors have very distinct ideas about the music for their film; others, less so. On smaller films, the director may be relatively accessible. On blockbusters, the director is usually far too busy trying to figure out how to blow up the car in mid-air or how to coax the stars out of their trailers to be bothered listening to your song.

- **Music Supervisor:** This is usually the person with the specific responsibility of finding songs for the movie or television show. Watch the end credits closely, and you'll see the same names show up again and again. These are the people you need to be pitching.

- **Studio:** This is just as vague as it sounds. Most major motion picture studios are full of executives, lawyers, production coordinators, and assistants that spend much of their time trying to figure out what they're supposed to be doing and where they rank in the current corporate pecking order. Trying to determine who does what from the outside is almost impossible. Nevertheless, most studios do have someone for whom music is a focus, like Randy Spendlove, the President of Motion Picture Music at Paramount Pictures, or Mitchell Leib at Disney.

- **Production Company:** Particularly on television projects, this is usually where the powers that be reside. The good news is that these companies are usually far less Byzantine than the major film studios, and if you can forge a relationship, they may come back to you for more than one project. *The Hollywood Reporter* and *Variety* are good sources for information about what various production companies are working on. Especially with the explosive growth of companies like Netflix, the amount of content being generated around the world by these production companies opens up a myriad of opportunities for placements.

- **Soundtrack Label:** For movies in which the soundtrack will play an important role in the marketing campaign, it can also be useful to attack the project on two fronts at once. I suggest pitching the music supervisor and production company, while simultaneously working the A&R department at the record label that will be doing the soundtrack. It's never easy to figure out who's calling the shots in these situations. All you can do is cover your bases. If you have a song that's a genuine hit, the record company can exert quite a bit of pressure to get the song in the movie.

And then there's the advertising and other "product"-related opportunities. Most of the decision makers in this process are associated with either the client (which is to say, the company that the campaign is promoting) or the advertising agency. If you've got a song you think is a perfect tie-in with a particular product, it's worth pitching both parties.

Have you ever played the game Clue? Then you know that it's not always the obvious suspects—Professor Plum, Colonel Mustard, or Mrs. Peacock—that wind up being the one who did the deed. Sometimes, it's the butler or the maid. Never underestimate those in supporting roles. While it would be impossible to detail all of the assorted assistants and hangers-on that hover around every major artist, you should never count out the possibility of getting a song to someone's personal assistant, business manager, lawyer, personal trainer, or dog-walker, and having it wind up in the right hands. Links to a SoundCloud file don't cost a thing. If someone says they can get your song to someone, give it to them. Opportunity in this business is not so much about aiming your dart at the bull's eye. It's more about throwing a lot of darts. The more people that are listening, the better.

15

Making the Sales Call: "And Here Comes the Pitch . . ."

Okay, the time has come. Time to make that big sales call. The pitch. Time to put the plug in song plugging. You've got the music right and ready to go. You've got your list of who's looking, who's right for the song, and who's listening. All you have to do is send that email.

So go ahead. What are you waiting for? Get that song out there. C'mon….

Selling is hard. Maybe not for everyone. I suspect that just as there are some people who seem to have been born humming a melody, there are others who are just natural sellers. They love the challenge of it, and the occasional door slamming in their face only makes them that much more determined. Just for the record, I'm not one of those people.

I tell you this because I suspect that a fair number of readers are in the same boat—especially those who are combining the role of songwriter and creative director. There are a few songwriters who are natural sellers and they are worth their weight in gold (records, that is). They are valuable in part because they are so rare. Most musicians and writers seem to naturally shy away from the selling process, which explains all the music that's never left your hard drive. People that don't mind expressing their deepest feelings in a song that could be heard by millions are intimidated about making a simple phone call.

Fine. I long ago accepted the fact that the sales pitch is not my natural gift. I hereby grant you permission to accept your own shortcomings as well. But accepting our shortcomings doesn't mean we don't have to send the email or make the call. There's no way around that. If you want to have a publishing business, then someone has to do it. Unless there's another willing party hiding in your office, I think that someone is you. And while we may never become virtuosos at the craft, we can learn to be effective.

The goal of the next two chapters is to give you the information you need to be able to sell your songs in a competent, professional manner. Follow the guidelines, and you will be able to get past the awkwardness, the self-consciousness, and the fear of rejection. Don't be surprised if a few years from now, some colleague says to you, "Oh, but you're just a natural-born salesman. I could never do that." You can fool a lot of the people a lot of the time.

Step 1: The Approach

Now that you've got that list of potential buyers, the first element in your plan of attack is the approach. Consider the options:

The Referral

One name can mean a lot. There is nothing that better paves the way for a sales pitch than the nice ker-plunk of the right name dropping on a weasel's desk. "Your friend _____ suggested I reach out." (Fill in the name of prominent weasel, or respected songwriter, or fellow publisher, or manager, or producer, or whatever you've got that will do the trick.) Needless to say, the right name in the right situation can be something of a free pass, getting you past the receptionists and the no "unsolicited material" policy. But where do you get that name?

By now, you should already have a couple of sources to draw upon. You are part of a community, after all. And that's what a community is: people who know other people. Your first source of referrals will likely be other writers and publishers who can open doors to some of their contacts, usually on the basis that you do the same for them. Of course, co-writing can accelerate this process by offering an obvious reason for all the publishers and writers involved in a song to pool resources. Other members of the community can also be helpful. For example, singers and musicians may have relationships at record companies for whom they do session work or with artists with whom they perform.

In addition to being part of a community, by now you should also have constructed a support team around your company. Your lawyer was selected in part because of who he or she has access to. While you may need to prove yourself a bit before a prominent attorney is willing to go to bat on your behalf, it is reasonable to expect that he or she can help provide an entree to at least a few of the people you need to know. Your contacts at the performing rights organizations can also be useful. One of the nice things about BMI, ASCAP, and SESAC is that they work with almost every record company and publishing business, but do not actually compete with any of them. This makes the writer relations representatives extremely well connected and completely unthreatening to everyone in the industry (except each other).

The more pitching you do, the deeper your pool of references will become. If someone reacts favorably to a song but feels it's not quite right for their act, inquire as to whether they know of anyone else that might be interested in it. If they offer a suggestion, ask if they would be comfortable with you using their name when following up on the tip. Even when a meeting doesn't result in someone wanting one of your songs, it has been successful if it leads to an introduction to one or two more industry contacts.

The art of name-dropping requires a certain amount of finesse to pull off safely. There are two inherent dangers to be avoided. The first risk is overdoing it and annoying the person with whom you are trying to establish contact. Writers or creative directors who offer an unsolicited litany of everyone in their orbit are putting their own insecurity on display, and are generally viewed as either desperate or silly. You should use a name only when necessary. Then, use the best one or two that you've got, and let it go. Constant reminders of who you know will not make the music sound any better. It will just make you look worse.

The second risk in tossing names around is the danger of offending the person whose name you're throwing out there. Generally speaking, I would not recommend that you use anyone's name without their permission, unless it's a simple case of mentioning some of the people with whom you've worked (that falls under the category of "just the facts, ma'am"). Without making too big a deal of it, you would be wise to ask your industry contacts if it would be alright to mention their name as a reference. This may also help to ward off the possibility of using the wrong name with the wrong person. Casually dropping the name of someone's worst enemy can produce more of a thud, rather than the ker-plunk you were hoping for.

The Cold Call

Let's make this a little harder. What if you don't have any sort of referral to pave the way? This is the toughest outreach to do, but probably the most necessary. The person who is entirely outside your sphere can remain that way indefinitely, unless you open up your industry directory and take the plunge.

Wait. Not so fast. Only fools rush in. The first key to a successful cold approach is preparation. The contact should be cold only in the sense that the object of the outreach doesn't know you—not because you don't know them. There is enough information available in the industry trade magazines and the Internet for you to know what successes the person has had recently, who his or her biggest acts are, and what sort of material he or she gravitates toward. This is not telemarketing. You should not be hitting up perfect strangers just because you found their number in the *A&R Registry*. You need to know whom you're interacting with.

You also need to convey who you are. Quickly. Be prepared to identify yourself. Give a one- or two-sentence description of your company (one of those sentences should highlight your biggest or most recent success), and then get straight to the point.

So, what is the reason you are contacting this lucky A&R or music supervisor? "I have some music I'd like you to hear" is not a reason. It may be to you, but it's not to the person on the other end of the line. "I have a song I think you need to hear for your new artist and wanted to get permission to send it over." That's a reason. Whether the approach is by email, text, LinkedIn, or a phone call, the motivation is the same: you're trying to supply something the other person needs. This isn't about you. The question is always: what's in it for the weasel?

The other thing to consider about a cold approach is whether it might be warmer done in person. Most people in the music industry are far more approachable in the flesh than through email or a phone call.

The Face to Face

There's always the opportunity for the chance personal encounter, although actually leaving it to chance is not much of a strategy. The trick is to find ways to be in the right place at the right time to actually meet the person you've been trying to reach. This is not necessarily as difficult as it sounds.

The music industry loves conventions. For weasels, a convention is an escape from the office and a chance to hang out on the company's money, which pretty much ensures that everyone will be there. At the same time, for a well-organized, aggressive creative director, a convention can provide a bounty of potential contacts—like fishing in an aquarium. You know the people who you're looking for are somewhere in the vicinity; the challenge is just to find them.

Working a convention effectively is a matter of applying the same principles we've already discussed and altering them to fit this unique environment. Preparation is key. Try to get a list of attendees, panels and moderators, events, and exhibitors in advance. Utilize your community contacts and business team. Find out what friends and associates will be there and who they'll be meeting with. At many larger conventions, there may be a party sponsored by BMI or ASCAP; see if you can score an invitation. If the person you're trying to meet is on a panel of some kind then, by all means, attend. If the forum is open to questions from the audience, try to make an impression by asking an intelligent question.

This last strategy can also be used effectively at all the various industry educational and networking programs put on every month by various music business organizations. Speakers on these panels are exactly the sort of insiders that you need to meet. The inevitable question-and-answer period is an opportunity for a one-on-one dialogue, even if it is in front of a crowd of people.

Having spoken on many such panels, I will tell you that 98 percent of the people who come forward with a question completely squander what should be a golden opportunity. Whoever said there are no stupid questions has never spoken on a music industry panel. When the meeting is over, there will likely be some opportunity to approach the panelists. I guarantee that if you've asked a "smart" question, which is one that references something the panelist has done or an issue they're facing and also has relevance to both the panel discussion that preceded it and the audience in the room, everyone on the panel will remember you and will probably be willing to have a quick conversation.

Beyond the conventions and educational panels, there are also industry parties, awards events, fundraisers, and showcases that can offer a chance for an "accidental" meeting. It's up to you to make an impression. Two quick bits of advice in that respect:

1. **Keep it casual and quick.** This is not a meeting; it's an introduction. Plan on getting out three sentences, which should include who you are, who you know, and something noteworthy that you've done. The last sentence is reserved for "Is it okay if I contact you at the office next week?" In between, it's always nice to work in a little humor.

2. **Keep it to a conversation.** Leave the music at home. These sort of face-to-face meetings are not the right moment to be digging a CD out of your bag, handing the person a set of headphones, or singing them an idea (yes, I really have seen people do this). The point here is not just to make an impression; the point is to make a *good* impression. This is the wind-up. The actual pitch is still to come.

Step 2: The Pitch

You did it. Whatever method you used, you've managed to sneak past the firewall of protection, past the receptionists and assistants, and get your songs a chance to be heard. These days, that is no small feat. The truth is, most of the actual pitch is out of your hands. It's now up to the music to speak for itself. Nevertheless, it's important to understand the pitching process, and to understand the creative director's role in presenting the songs in the best possible light. There are really only two basic methods of getting your songs out there:

"Send It Right Over . . ."

Whether you get it there via a link in an email, through a service like Disco, or on SoundCloud, the fundamental nature of this type of pitch remains the same. Your music is in the weasel's office, but you're not. This freaks a lot of people out. Days go by, no response is heard, and pretty soon you're convinced that the music has been lost on the island of misfit demos, never getting even a cursory listen.

Relax. Songs are sold every day without creative directors being right there in the room. It may not happen as quickly as you would like or with the thoroughness that you would wish for, but most A&R people will listen to the material that they receive. Like it or not, it is their job.

Most cloud-based services used to send music files have the advantage of showing when the link has been opened, and in some cases, how long the recipient listened. This can be an important tracking device, particularly for people whose primary business is sending beats or toplines out to a wide variety of producers. If someone has listened repeatedly or sent the link on to others, it may be an indicator that there is a something happening with your material. However you choose to send your music, be sure that the files are downloadable and that the MP3 files have clean, clear, and correct metadata (review chapter 7 if you're not quite sure what that means). Whatever you do, *never* send links with an expiration date. Of course, you think ten days is a reasonable amount of time for someone to listen—because you don't know the projects on that person's plate already, their travel schedule, vacation plans, or anything else. Let them listen whenever they can, even if that's a month after you sent the song.

The email or correspondence you send with the material should include:

- A very brief note recalling your phone conversation, meeting or prior correspondence, highlighting your company's recent activity, and providing any pertinent information about the material. (Be sure to include the name of the project for which it's being submitted.)
- Lyrics. This can be important when pitching in the pop and country markets, or for film, television, and advertising projects. It's less important when working in the R&B or rock markets.

- A bio, discography or one-sheet can be helpful, particularly if this your first contact with this A&R person.

Most importantly, you need to consider how much music to send. If you are pitching songs for a specific project, the strongest pitch is usually one song—the one you believe is a "perfect fit" for the artist. If you're pitching for several projects, or you can't decide which songs are appropriate, you can get away with three songs on the link. But that's the limit. Unless you receive a specific request from the recipient, *never* send more than three songs at a time. Better to follow up with a few new songs three weeks later. It's the oldest rule in showbiz: Leave 'em wanting more.

"Let's Take a Meeting"

This is your big chance. Not only are you there to make sure your music really does get a fair listen, but you've got an opportunity to watch the reaction, to see how the song and the demo stand up under fire, and to make on-the-spot choices about which songs to pitch based on the listener's feedback. Even better, you have a chance to establish a relationship with this new contact—to send more material in the future, to find out about upcoming projects, and perhaps to gather a few suggestions about potential co-writers or other places to send your songs. This is your shot at putting yourself on this particular person's radar screen. You need to be at the top of your game.

Most likely, you will have somewhere between twenty and thirty minutes to make your case. Don't underestimate the first five minutes (when you're likely just making small talk) and the last five (when you're summarizing and saying goodbye). These are your moments to make a personal connection. The rest of the time, you're just sitting there listening to music.

Small talk should probably start with congratulations to the A&R person for any recent success, a quick description of your own background, and a mention of all the exciting things happening with your company. You can follow with an inquiry as to whether there's anything specific that the A&R person needs, or if there has been any change in what he or she is looking for since your last conversation. If you can do it naturally, an attempt at a personal connection is worth the effort. Take a look around the office. Anything that might suggest a shared interest in sports, art, travel, children, or hobbies can serve as a conversation starter. Even the weaseliest weasel has a human side (I think).

The last five minutes is the final impression, which is usually the one that endures. You summary should review the songs that you've played and a confirmation of which songs the A&R person would like to receive copies of (if he or she doesn't already have them), and a reiteration of the timeframes of his or her current projects. That leaves about two and half minutes for the send-off: an expression of thanks for the meeting and a promise to stay in touch. Then you should get out of the office. Overstaying your welcome will negate all the positive work you've done up to that point. By getting in and out of the office quickly, you establish yourself as a busy professional who appreciates the value of time.

When it comes to the pitch session itself, the key is to let the music speak, which means making the process as effortless as possible. Make sure all the music you're ready to share is organized clearly in a folder or playlist—no risk of accidentally playing an earlier rough demo, an initial pass at a mix, or a version with the wrong vocalist. If you're playing music from your phone, bring a cable to connect to the stereo and also be prepared to send files to the A&R in case he or she prefers to play the songs on her or his computer.

Then just hit Play. It's acceptable to preface a song with a mention of the writers or the artists who have recorded the song in the past, or projects that it's currently being considered for. That should be all that's necessary. No sales pitch and no excuses. You've already done your work getting the music right.

Don't be surprised if the A&R person listens to only a verse and a chorus. Every music person has their own idea of what they listen for in a song. Someone told me that LA Reid barely listens to a verse at all; he makes all his judgments about a song solely from the chorus.

Don't be offended if nothing you play quite hits the mark. It's understood by everyone that there are always many more misses than hits. The important thing is to demonstrate a high level of quality in the material. That should be enough to make a favorable impression.

Step 3: The Follow-Through

It's always important to finish strong. I'm amazed at how often writers and publishers fail to follow through after making their initial pitch for a project. The real art of selling lies much more in the follow-through than in the pitch itself.

If you've sent a song to someone's email to whom you've never sent in the past and not received an immediate acknowledgement, you may want to follow-up just to confirm that the file didn't wind up in the spam folder. You'll likely be told, "Yeah, I got it, but haven't had a chance to check it out." In general, I would suggest giving people one week to ten days after you send a song before you follow up to get their reaction. If the material has been reviewed, then the goal is to get any feedback you can. Positive beats negative, but sometimes negative is even more useful. Try to find out specifically what he or she liked or disliked. Then lay the groundwork to try again. "I really appreciate the feedback. I'll see if I can come up with something closer to what you're looking for. Can I touch base with you in two or three weeks to get an update on the project?" If you've missed the mark, then you need to try again. If you've hit the mark, then there's even more reason to try again. The only failure is to pitch to someone once and never send them anything else.

The post-meeting follow-through should be considerably quicker. Anything that was requested from the meeting should be sent the next day in an email thanking the A&R person for his or her time. After that, you should plan on touching base in some manner every six to eight weeks. That can mean sending a new song, but it can also mean news of some recent success of your company, a congratulatory note for a recent success at the A&R person's company, or a phone call to see what other projects are in development. The goal is an ongoing dialogue.

Keep in mind that no one expects you to show up with a smash hit in your first pitch meeting. Overnight success is a myth that is bought into largely by those outside of the industry. Those on the inside have long given up on such fantasies. I've signed many writers before they were capable of writing genuine "hit" songs. I signed them because I saw consistent productivity, and noticed that each song seemed to be a little better than the last. As long as you're moving in the right direction, you can stay in the game.

The message sent by a good follow-up is that you are in this business for the long haul. It tells the A&R community that yours is not a one-shot effort at hitting the mark, but that you intend to keep working until you can deliver what's needed. Doing so lays the groundwork for the most important element in the entire selling process: The Relationship.

16

The Song Plugging Master Class: Smooth Operator

Some of the best song salesmen that I've ever seen are not publishers (and many are not men either). They're songwriters—and often very good ones, which of course makes selling their songs considerably easier. Writers like Kara DioGuardi, Shelly Peiken, Billy Mann, Cutfather, Steve Diamond, and Gary Baker are top-tier songwriters who know how to deliver the hits that A&R people need—which is, of course, the primary factor in their success.

But they also know how to sell. Though all of these writers work in different genres and have different skill sets, they are all experts at finding their way into projects that match their skills, getting their songs into the hands of the decision-makers, and keeping their songs in consideration even when the competition gets fierce. The strange thing is, even if you're the A&R to whom they're selling, you hardly ever notice them doing it. At least not with the methods that we just discussed. That's because they're busy with something more important. They're building relationships. Tip sheets, emails to contacts out of the *A&R Registry*, and pitch meetings will get you started, but relationships are what you build a career on.

Relationship Selling

The first thing to notice about relationship selling is that it's largely invisible. When it's done well, not only is the buyer unaware that he or she's being sold, but the seller is hardly even aware that he or she is selling. Most expert practitioners of relationship selling never seem to be doing all that much. They just seem to have an uncanny ability to turn up at just the right moment or to be buddies with exactly the right person. That's precisely the point.

The truth is, the usual selling process is something of an uphill battle. The seller feels self-conscious delivering his or her pitch, and the buyer is suspicious that he or she is being "hustled." If selling is not something to which you look forward, think of your buyers. Being sold to is probably not the high point of their days, either. Relationship selling aims to take the pain out of the procedure.

This is hardly a new technique and certainly not one unique to the entertainment industry. Most companies long ago recognized the value of building relationships with their customers. This would explain the corporate season tickets to the local sports teams, the lunches, dinners, and the rest of the expense account largesse doled out in the interests of entertaining clients. The basic theory behind relationship selling is this: Let the seller and buyer develop a personal bond, let them discover shared interests and begin to consider each other friends, and they will find a way to do business together in a way that is mutually beneficial.

"Oh, I get it," you say. "He's telling me to be phony and pretend to be someone's friend just so they'll do me a favor and cut my song." No. In fact, being phony is probably the worst thing you can possibly do, in part because it's always more transparent than you think, and also because it's inherently short-term. Relationship selling is not geared toward quick results. A faked friendship will not survive the inevitable give and take that is part of any business relationship. Phony will not work.

Relationship selling is not about "favors" either. You don't build a business on the hope that someone will put your substandard song on a record or in a TV show as a "favor." The idea of building a personal relationship is that it will afford you not just opportunities, but a deeper understanding of the buyer's needs and preferences. Gary Baker's involvement in writing "I'm Already There" grew in part out of a long relationship with Lonestar lead singer and fellow writer Richie McDonald. Billy Mann has had more than a dozen songs recorded by Pink. But no one is doing anyone a favor by cutting those songs. The songs speak for themselves through their power and relevance to the artist.

So if phony and self-serving doesn't work, what does? What will it take to advance to the level of "relationship" selling? Three things: concern for others, selectivity, and patience. The best part is, they are the same sort of values that your mother said would make you a better, happier person. Relationship selling is one of the few times in the music business that nice guys can actually finish near the top of the heap.

Concern for Others

The real key to relationship selling is changing your point of view. No longer is your focus centered on you and your need to make the sale. Instead, your interest is in the people with whom you are doing business. The idea is to get to know them: their likes and dislikes, their goals for the project, their hobbies, you name it. It's all about them and what you can do for them—not because of what's in it for you but because of a friendly desire to help.

Ever see *Miracle on 34th Street*? The part where Macy's Santa refers the customers to Gimbels if Macy's doesn't have what they want—that's relationship selling. If you remember the movie, you know that Macy's business skyrockets as a result. All the happy customers write to Mr. Macy, complimenting him on the store's new, altruistic holiday spirit. As you make the transition from salesman to friend, you'll begin to see the difference. Your phone calls get answered quicker. Someone calls with a hot tip every now and then. A meeting turns into dinner. Suddenly, you're an insider rather than an outsider—and opportunities just start to come your way.

Selectivity

Make lots of friends, but choose them wisely. Some people—quite a few, actually—are simply not interested in developing a relationship. They're wary of ulterior motives. Maybe they're just not very nice. Don't waste your time. You can't force a relationship on someone; either it clicks or it doesn't. If it doesn't, continue to pitch your songs as one professional to another, and leave it at that.

Here's another concept. When you're picking your friends, pick people that you like. Or admire. Or can learn from. Avoid deadbeats, losers, users, liars, and anyone who's generally bitter and angry. Building relationships is an investment of time and energy, and successful people learn to invest wisely. Avoid the temptation to always surround yourself with friends that are less successful than you. Usually the motive in this is not to generously pull your friends up, but to make yourself feel better by comparison. Build relationships with people who challenge and inspire you to do more than what you're doing.

Patience

And then, wait. Relationship selling is not like planting a flower; it's more like planting a tree. You've got to hang on quite a while to see results. It's perfectly possible that you may develop a relationship with someone for years before anything much comes of it. I once pitched an A&R person for five years. I was just about ready to give up on him entirely when suddenly he wound up cutting a song of ours and pulling the producer/writer into several major projects. Like I said, it's an investment, and it doesn't come with a guarantee. If you've picked your friends wisely and nurtured the relationship diligently, more often than not, something good will happen.

The difficulty here is that nurturing a relationship is no easy task. That is particularly true of relationships that span decades, surviving business ups and downs, disputes, misunderstandings, conflicts of interest, changes in lifestyles and position, and all the other factors that enter into friendships. It takes a consistent effort to stay in touch, to make the small friendly gesture (a note of congratulations or a call of sympathy), to return calls promptly, or do the odd favor. It also takes a willingness to understand that business is business (and to keep disputes from getting personal), to assume the best of intentions, to accept mistakes, and to understand that changes in status, attitudes, lifestyles, or social circles is an inevitable part of everyone's life. This is indeed an investment—a long-term one—and you can't allow short-term fluctuations to make you give up on it too soon.

If there's an opposing view to the philosophy of relationship selling, it is contained in the advice dispensed more often than any other to aspiring writers, publishers, and artists:

Be Aggressive

More dangerous words were never spoken. They're dangerous not because they're false, but because they're both true and false at the same time. In a world in which "aggressive" can mean anything from sending a follow-up email to storming the office with an attack mob, the words are just too open to misunderstanding.

In fact, much of the time that you spend trying to navigate past overly vigilant receptionists and "no outside material" policies is a result of "aggressive" songwriters who simply wore out their own welcome, and yours as well. My friend David Gray at Universal Music Publishing makes the distinction between "assertive" and "aggressive," and I think it's an apt point. Relationships are built by *assertive* people. They are usually destroyed by *aggressive* people. Anyone who plans to sell anything—but particularly music—needs to understand the difference.

Being assertive means:

- doing your homework before you reach out to anyone
- developing a rapport with the receptionist and assistant, with the hopes that they get their boss to call you back

- making sure to convey the exciting things that are happening with your company
- responding to requests for changes by immediately getting the A&R person a new version that incorporates their feedback
- following up a meeting or song submission with an email
- submitting a steady flow of material that demonstrates continued creative growth
- sending out requested music immediately
- making sure that you've gotten your song to everyone who's involved with a project, including the artist, management, and label
- following up regularly about songs that are "on hold," and keeping your options open if the recording process should begin to stall
- finding every opportunity to make the professional contacts you need, and, whenever possible, to develop those contacts into long-term relationships

Being aggressive means:

- calling every name in the A&R directory until somebody takes your call
- berating or demeaning a receptionist or assistant because your call hasn't been returned
- rubbing your success in the face of someone who has turned down your material in the past
- arguing with someone who feels that your song could be improved or isn't right for their particular project
- trying to persuade the listener why the song is better without the changes they've asked for
- calling a dozen times a day to see if the song has been listened to
- vowing to call the office a hundred times a day until you get a response
- putting all your efforts behind one song and refusing to take no for an answer
- demanding a meeting so that you can play the song in person
- going back to the same person more than twice with the same song
- issuing empty threats about pulling your song from a project if your timeframe is not met

In short, being assertive should be almost synonymous with being a solid professional. Responsive, organized, well prepared, confident but realistic—

this is the image that any creative director should strive to present. It is as aggressive as you should ever need to be. What some writers call aggressive is more like amateurish and naïve, or desperate and delusional. You cannot build "relationships" with that sort of aggression.

Before I close this "master class" of selling, I want to touch on another one of those things I only learned once I got on the publisher's side of the desk:

Minding Your Office Etiquette

It never occurred to me until my first day at Zomba Music Publishing: up to that point, I had never spent a single day in an office. I worked a few odd jobs in high school (not very well), but they were never office gigs. Then I went to college. Then I started writing. Sure, I'd visit my publisher every now and then—"work" the office a bit, say hello to everyone, drop off some music. Then I'd leave. When I started my first publishing gig, I had no idea how to even transfer a call or file a check request. I knew nothing of Office Etiquette.

Most writers don't. Most writers have very little sense of the rhythms of office life or the demands of a 9-to-5 gig (well, okay . . . more like 10:30 to 6:30). As a creative director, you will be spending much of your day working with people who are not rolling out of bed at 1 P.M. or going off to work at 8 P.M. at night. This is not to say they work harder than most writers (I don't think I've ever worked harder than when I was a writer), but it does mean that they work differently. The more you can adjust your way of doing business to accommodate the unique pressures of office life, the more work you'll be able to get out of your office-bound colleagues.

- Never call or email someone at 10 o'clock on a Monday morning. Never call or email someone at 6:30 on Friday night. Never ever contact someone on Tuesday morning after a three-day weekend.

- Don't contact people more than necessary. It is not necessary to email to request permission to submit material, then again to let the A&R person know that you've sent the song, then again to see if it was received, and yet again to see if it was listened to. Request permission, then send the music. You can reach back again after two weeks to see the reaction.

- Don't call to request permission to send the song until it is written, recorded, and ready to be delivered. Then hit send immediately after the call.

- Don't expect things to happen overnight. Checks cannot be cut, contracts cannot be sent, reservations cannot be made, and demos cannot be received in an office without some sort of process. Things take time in an office. Here's a formula: 1 Day in Songwriter Life = 1 week in Office Life. Adjust your expectations accordingly.

- Do not ask more than one person in an office for the same thing. In doing so, you are not "working" the office. You're working people's nerves.

- Understand that it really is possible to spend an entire day in a meeting. I never thought it was. Unfortunately, it is.

- In an office, 2 P.M. means 2 P.M. Harsh, I know. But be on time. Not early, not late.

- Do not drop by without an appointment, or at least a call before you arrive. In an office, surprises are only good when it's a birthday party.

- Develop relationships with people's assistants or staff. If someone suggests that you speak to his or her assistant, you are not being foisted off on an underling. You are being referred to the person who actually does stuff. Make friends.

- When someone looks at his or her phone or watch, it's time to go.

Another songwriter who is an excellent creative director and very effective song plugger is my old writing buddy Jeff Franzel, who I mentioned earlier. Like the other writers I mentioned at the beginning of this chapter, Jeff's approach is based on the building of relationships, on being "assertive" but not "aggressive," and on having sensitivity to the demands of an office environment. He is the consummate professional. He always stays in contact but never barrages anyone with calls or material. He responds immediately to any request for a change or alteration in a song. He is confident but always understanding if a song doesn't work for a specific project. And he's pleasant to everyone—not just the person he's selling to but to each individual in the office.

In fact, the nice thing about joining the song plugger's Master Class is that most of the people in that class are . . . well, nice. There's a lesson in there somewhere. On some days, you will sell a song. On most days, you will experience rejection. But every day, you have the opportunity to build two things that will endure and will eventually become the foundation of your business: your reputation and your relationships. If you're going to be in it, be in it for the long run.

17

The Song Plugger's Glossary

For what should be a relatively straightforward process—you like the song, you take the song, you record the song, and we'll all meet up at the Grammys—the song pitching game can get pretty complex. Like every other game, it has its own vocabulary, constructed primarily to imply that there is a set of rules for what in reality is a lawless free-for-all, like having a referee in rugby.

The truth is, almost none of the following terms are actually applied through written agreements, beyond simple email correspondence. Even "quotes," which are customarily submitted as actual documents, inevitably emphasize that the price contained is only a "quote," not a firm offer. But in the interests of enabling you to toss legal-sounding phrases around with the best of them, and to possibly even understand the underlying issues behind those phrases, I give you:

The Song Plugger's Glossary

The Pass

Let's start with the bad news first. "Passing" is the politically correct way of conveying that your song has not found a home in this particular place. It's a shorter way of saying, "Thank you for your submission, but it does not meet our needs at this time," and a slightly kinder method than the very succinct "No." It can be delivered verbally or via email; the thundering silence of no response at all is also assumed to be a pass.

However it may be delivered, don't be offended by a pass. There's really no great method of delivering bad news, and delivering bad news is about 95 percent of an A&R person's job. Another creative manager once told me, "You could pass on 100 percent of the things that come across your desk, and statistically, you would only be wrong five percent of the time." It's true.

"No" is not rude; it's just "no." Don't argue with it, try to change it, or be emotionally crushed by it. Move on. There's always someone else to pitch to.

The Hold

This is the good news and the bad news delivered simultaneously. When executives put a song on "hold," they are saying, "I like this, but I need some time to make a decision." This is the good news. They are telling you they like it, after all. The not-so-good news is that they are asking you to temporarily refrain from committing the song to another project until they can make up their mind and review the song with the artist, manager, producer, or other decision maker. The problem is, they're not telling you how long all this could take.

I think most publishers would say that eight to ten weeks is probably a reasonable amount of time for a "hold" to last. If that seems long, remember the number of cooks in the kitchen. Try to comprehend the difficulties of decision making when an artist is on the road, filming a movie, renegotiating a contract, or doing all three at the same time. In fact, most publishers would admit that on superstar projects, "holds" invariably last much longer. Especially in Nashville, the "hold" situation can reach epic proportions, with songs staying in limbo for a year.

It doesn't take a great deal of foresight to anticipate the way "holds" can affect your song pitching efforts. Particularly with a small catalog, you can quickly wind up with your three or four best songs out of the market—waiting on a thumbs-up from one project and subsequently not available to be placed on more immediate or possibly more lucrative records. Navigating your way through the "hold" process is probably the most sensitive, difficult part of the song plugging game. A few guidelines:

Holds are about relationships, not rules.

The principle of granting "holds" is a courtesy extended by publishers to their customers; it's not a law. If someone wants to put a song on hold, you have every right to say "no." You can simply say, "If you decide to cut the song, I'm happy to let you know if it's available, but I can't take the song off the market at this point." Or you can say, "I can give you three weeks, and then I'll pay you the courtesy of letting you know if someone else is interested in recording the song." You won't make many friends in A&R this way (as most weasels consider the granting of holds a God-given right), but you will keep your options open.

You have to decide what you are comfortable with as far as the granting of holds, based on the value of the relationship, the project, the timing, and the importance of the song in your catalog. The same is true when it comes to your respect for holds. If someone believes they have a song on hold, and you give the song to a more lucrative project, you haven't broken any laws but you've probably made an enemy. Sometimes it's worth it. Sometimes it's not. Personally, I will usually keep a song on "hold" for eight to ten weeks. After that, I will grant the A&R person "right of first refusal." If someone else expresses interest, then the person holding the song gets one last chance to give a commitment. Otherwise, all "holds" are off. Superstar projects are another matter. On those, you just have to find a new level of forbearance.

Granting a "hold" does not mean that you can't pitch the song.
Some A&R people would argue this; they feel that putting a song on hold should take it off the market entirely. I don't buy it. I think it's perfectly appropriate to pitch the song, so long as you preface the pitch by letting the listener know that the song is currently on hold. The message here is, "If you like the song and are prepared to give me a commitment, I will go back to the party holding the song and ask them to make a decision as to whether they are ready to move forward." It is understood that whoever has the song on hold has "the right of first refusal." In fact, in many circles, the hold game has developed a whole hierarchy; there are "first" holds and "second" holds and dates by which one party has to commit in order to maintain the hold. My advice is: keep selling until the day the song shows up on Spotify.

Never issue empty threats.
As the "hold" process drags on, it can be very tempting to try to force an A&R person's hand. There's nothing inherently wrong with saying, "I have someone else who wants the song, so you have three days to give me a date that this is going to be recorded." As long as you really do have someone else interested. If you don't have somewhere else to take the song, be very careful about calling someone's bluff. A&R people don't appreciate being pressured by publishers. This tactic is the equivalent of threatening to leave your job if you don't get a raise. Definitely an option of last resort.

A better strategy for an appropriately assertive creative director is to focus your efforts toward consistently following up with an A&R person (every four to six weeks) as to a song's current status. Some major publishers, that might have dozens of songs on hold at any time, have formalized this process. Creative directors in such companies often put specific prompts on their calendars to follow up and at least press the A&R or manager to "renew" a hold or "release" the song to be pitched to others.

If you're a songwriter pitching your own catalog, I can only hope that you have so many holds you need to be reminded of them. Most of the time, you won't be able to stop thinking about those songs and wondering if today could be the day you get good news. I don't think you need to be tied to a specific timeframe, but a regular follow-up with everyone involved in the project is essential. Don't assume that you would have been told if it was being dropped from the list of potential songs, or if it was already recorded. You could easily find out that you've been holding something that has long since become available or pitching something that's already cut.

The Quote

When you're pitching to the synchronization world, the "quote" stage is an expression of interest not dissimilar from an A&R person putting something on "hold." Happily, a "quote" does not take a song out of the marketplace in the way that a "hold" often can. When a music supervisor or agency asks for a "quote," they are telling you that they're considering using your song in a movie, television show, or advertisement, but want to know what it will cost them. For the person looking to license the song, the "quote" stage is a toe-dip into the water, to see how deep, icy or dirty it might be. Are all the copyright owners on both the master and publishing side present and accounted for? Are they all able to agree on a price? Is there another current use of the song already in the works that would complicate matters? Can the publishers get the necessary approvals from the writers? Usually, the supervisor asking for a quote will provide a brief description, including the length, of the proposed use, and a rough idea of the budget the supervisor has to work with. A quote is an effort to find out not only how much a song will cost, but also how hard it will be to license.

Just like a "hold," a quote is only a first step on the way to a song placement. It's quite possible that the company seeking the quote is obtaining ten other quotes on alternate songs that could fit the same use. Once you've issued a quote, it's best to forget about it and go back to pitching the song. It could easily be months before you hear again from the company that was emailing you every ten minutes when they wanted a price. But of course, don't forget completely. If someone else asks for the song, it just might be worth checking back on the status of that old quote before you place the song elsewhere.

Single Commitment

This is an old idea that's taken on a whole new life in the Spotify era. In trying to gauge the value of a cut with one particular artist versus another, publishers working back in the Paleolithic era of the CD would often try to determine whether one or both of the artists intended to make the song a "single" or merely an album cut. Obviously, this reflected the relative value of a song that became track #9 on a big-selling CD and a song that actually became a radio hit.

Of course, A&R people would inevitably promise the composers of all twelve songs on the CD that their song was definitely being considered as a possible "second or third single." A few years ago, we had a song that everyone was so sure would be the next single on a very big country act that the artist actually premiered it on a major awards show the week before it was supposed to be released. Two days later, we were told that the label had decided to go with a different song as the single from that album. Case closed, no appeals.

But in the Spotify era, this particular concept has taken on a whole new gravitas. Because of the royalty rate paid by Spotify to publishers, there is absolutely no comparison to the value of having a song on a #1 album that gets 10 million Spotify streams but no radio airplay and having a hit single that is being played by radio stations all over the country. It is the difference between a few hundred dollars (from Spotify and the other digital streaming outlets) and a few hundred thousand dollars (from our friends at ASCAP and BMI who collect the radio income). Not surprisingly, then, top songwriters and the publishers who represent them have grown much more aggressive in demanding guarantees from record labels that their song will be released as a single and will be taken to radio, not just auditioned on Spotify to "see how it reacts." Of course, these "commitments" by the label are still often broken, with the knowledge that even a top songwriter or publisher is unlikely to want to take any real retaliatory action against artists or record companies with whom they do other business. But for a song that's being sought by several major artists, the negotiations between a publisher, the record label and the artist now get quite specific as to the plan for the single releases and the level of commitment for radio promotion.

Recording Commitment

Needless to say, a recording commitment is not nearly as good as a single commitment, but it's still a significant step. It's an indication from the project's A&R staff that your song is, in fact, scheduled to be recorded by the artist. Sometimes, it's the selection of a producer or a statement regarding the anticipated recording schedule. If you are a writer/producer, it might be the initial discussions regarding your production agreement. Or it could be as simple as a request for lyrics. The idea here is that you've received some sort of indication as to the company's intention to record the song—which then requires you to take the song off the market.

This sort of commitment is not a contract. At best, it might be an email exchange, to provide some written confirmation of the discussion. In many instances, it will be a phone call or a casual conversation. Understand that a commitment to record your song is no guarantee of anything. Sessions get postponed or cancelled, artists change their minds, and everything always takes longer than anticipated. Sometimes songs are recorded and simply don't turn out as well as everyone hoped. A commitment to record is a statement that the process is moving forward, and most importantly, that money is about to be spent.

Not surprisingly, this last bit is the real crux of the issue. Once the recording process is set in motion—studios booked, producers hired, musicians scheduled—money is being spent. At this point, you do have some obligation to take the song off the market. You can play it for people as a demonstration of what you do; you can even pitch it with the proviso that the song would only become available if something falls apart in the recording process. But unless you hear otherwise from the A&R person or artist manager, you really have no right to pull the song away from the artist who is planning to record it. This is not to say that it's never been done, but it's definitely a "you'll never work in this town again" move. Once an A&R person expresses an actual plan to record the song, it's more or less official, or at least as official as something can be without a written agreement: the song is sold.

First Use

Of course, just because it's sold once doesn't mean it can't be sold again later. The concept of "first use" is an acknowledgement that the first recording of a song is usually the one that defines the song in the mind of the public and therefore has a greater significance than subsequent performances.

In the United States, once a song has been released commercially, it is fair game for everyone and anyone to record their own version—from cover bands to other major label artists. So long as they pay the appropriate royalties to the publishers and writers, anyone can record and release the song. (In most European countries, there is a concept of "moral rights" for the author, which allows the writer and publisher to approve any version of their song before it is released.) If a song has never been released previously, a publisher will sometimes be asked to grant a first use license to the record company. For important artists on a major label, this can be an actual document; many European companies also prefer to have a signed agreement for any release. In some cases, a clause pertaining to the first use license will be included in the producer agreement (between the producer and artist) or the artist's recording agreement (between the artist and the label). As the term "first use" would imply, this is an exclusive license granted to only one artist. Obviously, the intent is to avoid a situation in which an artist records a song and is "beaten to the punch" by another artist who gets his or her version out at the same time.

The importance attached to the "first use" of a song also affects the publishers and their right to grant the mechanical license. The law provides that on a song with multiple writers and publishers, any one party can grant a mechanical license, even over the objections of all the other parties. This means that if there are several publishers who share one song, any one of them can grant a license without the approval of the others. At the same time, the law also recognizes that a substandard "first use" can degrade the value of a song in the marketplace.

This issue often arises when one of the writers is also a developing artist. That writer and his or her publisher may want the first use of the song to be for their own artist project, while the other publishers would prefer a more lucrative placement with a better-known act. If a writer or publisher can legitimately claim that a potential first recording will damage the song's value, they may be able to prevent the issue of a license. When a song is exploited for the first time, you will probably need the consent of all the writers and publishers involved.

Different Markets

It is also possible to sell a song in more than one place at the same time. The idea of placing a song in two different markets by two different artists has a very long history—think "Tutti Frutti" by Pat Boone (for the white pop audience) and Little Richard (for the R&B market—and all others with good musical taste). More commonly today, a song might have multiple versions by the same artist, all aimed at different audiences. Latin artist Luis Fonsi released one version of "Despacito" for his core Latin audience and then months later followed with the "pop remix" version featuring Justin Bieber. Ed Sheeran released multiple versions of "Perfect" featuring everyone from Andrea Bocelli to Beyoncé. The idea here is that the markets are different enough that one version will not detract from another.

Contemporary Christian music publishers might refer to this concept as a basis for shopping a song to a pop project, even though a Christian artist is already recording a more "Christian" version of the song. A pop publisher could feel that a stripped-down, unplugged version of their song performed by the songwriter herself is unlikely to compete with a new club-ready version by Martin Garrix and Dua Lipa. All of the publishers would probably agree that an international release in Southeast Asia, adapted into the Korean language, is unlikely to interfere with anything happening with the song in the U.S.

Unfortunately, the artists and the labels involved are often much more proprietary than you would expect. In order to preserve the relationship between your company and those who are recording your song, you need to be as open as possible about any intentions you have to place the song in a "different market." Point out the difference in the target audiences, the radio formats, and the timing of the projects. Then be prepared for dissenting and often irrational objections. I have never understood why the existence of an English-language version of a song, done in an entirely different production style, would have any impact whatsoever on a Japanese label looking to release the same song in Japanese. But it's an automatic deal-breaker, and there's no amount of persuasion that will change the situation (trust me, I've tried). All you can do is argue your position, then be prepared to retreat if necessary. Don't ever try to keep it a secret. In this day and age of rabid fans scouring the Internet, nothing stays a secret. A&R guys hate surprises.

Recording Restrictions

Recording restrictions are applicable only if one of the song's writers is either the artist or a producer on the release. In most artist or producer agreements, there is a re-record restriction, preventing the artist or producer from recording a new version of the song for another company or a different artist within a set amount of time (usually somewhere from three to five years). It's easy to understand the thinking behind this. The record company or the artist is trying to make sure that someone doesn't record the same song and put it out in competition with their version.

There's not much you can do about a "re-record" restriction. It is a relatively standard part of an artist or producer agreement. If possible, you can try to insert very specific guidelines as to what sort of re-recordings would be restricted, taking into account different markets and the differences in record lifespans. You could stipulate that the record must be released by a certain date or the re-record restriction is lifted. In the end, a re-record restriction does not mean that the song can't be recorded and released by others, after the first release has occurred. But it does mean that it cannot be produced by the same producers or recorded by the same artist within the restricted period.

When it comes to the Herculean task of getting the music out, there's one more thing I have to mention. It won't keep you from having your heart broken (that's as inevitable in song plugging as it is in love), but it might keep you from doing any financial damage to yourself or your business.

Music Business Weasel Says:
A song is never on a record until you see it on Spotify or buy it on Amazon.

No matter what assurances you've received from the A&R person, manager, artist, or producer; no matter how great the song sounds with the artist's vocal on it; no matter what you hear through the grapevine; no matter where you've seen it advertised: nothing is definite until the day the record pops up on a streaming service or a digital store. Believe it when you see it.

I heard a few years ago of a Nashville writer who, upon learning that his song was being cut by a major country/pop artist, immediately ran out and bought a boat, largely on credit. It was not until the day the album was released and he went online to buy the record that he realized his song had been dropped from the project at the last minute. He spent the next year living on his boat—as most everything else he had was gone.

When I was a writer, I tried to avoid mentioning any song of mine that was being cut until I knew the album had been released. Call it superstition, but I just felt that talking about it would jinx the whole thing. Other writers are less reticent but still prone to add caveats like, "It's supposed to be on . . . " or "They're telling me it's on . . . " when discussing upcoming releases.

Despite all the high-minded discussions of holds and recording commitments and re-record restrictions, the making of a record (or even worse, a movie or television show) is really not a particularly thoughtful, well-organized endeavor. The last few days of putting together the final sequence of an album or locking the music track to film are incredibly frenetic, filled with eleventh-hour histrionics, power plays, disputes, horse-trading, and compromises. Anything can happen—and often does. No writer or publisher should ever spend money on something that is supposed to happen. Sit tight, stay quiet, and wait till you're sure it has happened. Then you can crack open the champagne.

18

Moving the Writer Up: The Climb

Even when you've managed to get the music right and to get it out where the public can respond to it—even when you've had that thrilling first rush of success and watched the song find its audience—it's still not quite time to celebrate. Remember, there are three primary functions that make up the creative director's job. You've still got one to go. Just as an A&R person understands that the real job of making records is not to make hit records, but to develop hit artists, a savvy creative director realizes that the work is not done when a song is at the top of the charts. The publishing business is not only about hit songs. It's also about developing hit songwriters.

Of course, nothing helps in that quest more than having hits. By getting the music right and getting it out, you've laid the groundwork for any writer's career. The music always comes first, and if it's done well enough, it may be all that's necessary to lift a writer into the big leagues. Legendary songwriter and producer Mutt Lange has had more hits than almost anyone can count, and won more than ten ASCAP awards for his work, but he never showed up for an awards ceremony. You never see his picture in a magazine. You don't need to. Everybody who needs to know, knows exactly who he is. Hit songs will do that.

At the same time, there are other writers whose presence and stature in the industry seems to far exceed their actual commercial success. It can be baffling at times to watch a writer move up the industry ladder to a position of prominence when no one seems to be able to pinpoint any particular hit song that he or she has written. It's the Kardashian phenomenon—famous for being famous. How does it happen?

It happens largely because someone is thinking strategically. Whether it's the writer, the creative director, a manager, or a publicist, somebody is making a deliberate effort to raise the writer's profile, to place him or her in the right situations, to receive the right sort of media attention, and to build a powerful network of supporters within the creative community. A plan has been developed that is certainly aided by having a hit record, but is not reliant upon one. The strategies we will discuss in this chapter are not song-focused; they are writer-focused. For the next few pages, it's all about the writer, not the song.

Before we proceed, it's worth asking a simple question: why? Why should a publisher care about how a writer is perceived? After all, a publisher represents the catalog—which is to say, the songs, not the songwriter. A publisher is not a manager or agent who receives a percentage of everything the writer earns. A publisher receives a portion of what a specific song earns. If a writer becomes a celebrity, the publisher will not necessarily benefit. So why should a publisher invest effort in raising a writer to prominence? What's in it for the weasel?

You do it because you have to. Song pitching is an ancient art, but in many ways, it's also a vanishing one. It's being replaced by what we might call writer pitching (if that didn't sound quite so dangerous). Rather than finding songs one by one, most A&R people are now oriented toward a sort of "package deal"—finding writers and producers who (hopefully) can be employed to come up with several songs. Writer/producers are engaged to provide three or four songs for an album; writers are asked to co-write with the artist; or writers are put together in specific combinations to try to provide the sound that the A&R people are seeking. The goal is to find a creative "nucleus" for the project—the group of creators who can generate all or most of the material that will make up the album. The challenge is this: how do you get your writer into those exclusive settings?

Everybody Make Some Noise!

Hype. It is up to the creative director to help create around a writer the sort of heat that attracts A&R people, managers, producers, and executives, and convinces them that this hot new writer can bring something exciting to their project. Certainly, a discography of hit records helps provide that aura, but when it comes to hype, quite a bit can be done with smoke and mirrors. A creative director must find a way to create a "story" for a writer—a blend of past successes, exciting current activity, name recognition, and reputation, and general industry buzz. While it may not benefit the publisher directly, that "story" will help to get the writer in the optimum situations. You can't hit a grand slam with no one on base. A creative director's job is to get his or

her writer a chance to go to bat with the bases loaded. Given enough opportunities, a writer is bound to get a hit.

Remember, this is show business. Everything is a blend of fact, fiction,
and a little razzle-dazzle. Forget about the music for a second. Believe the
hype.

Publicity

This is an obvious place to start. There are already a myriad of books on the
market that can offer you the specifics of preparing press releases, planting
stories, and generating media exposure; I recommend Peter Spellman's *The
Self-Promoting Musician* (Berklee Press). I'm going to opt instead to simply
brainstorm a little, and consider the best opportunities out there to get
people reading and talking about your writer. I'll leave it to you to work out
the logistics.

Trade Publications, Blogs, Podcasts, and Social Media

Keep in mind that when it comes to publicizing a writer, the purpose is to
increase visibility among those in the industry, not among the general public.
You're hoping to have ten A&R people calling on the phone to try to set
up meetings, not ten thousand Instagram followers tracking what the writer
ate for dinner. Consequently, it makes sense to target your efforts at media
outlets directed toward those in the business, rather than fans. An article in
Billboard will do a lot more for you than one in *BuzzFeed*. And it will be a lot
easier to pull off.

If you read the bylines in most trade publications, you will notice that
there is a relatively small staff of writers and reviewers. It should not take
a great deal of effort to cultivate relationships with the people who might
have an interest in your writer. A feature article, a positive review, or a favorable mention or picture in the pages of *Billboard*, *Hits*, *MusicRow*, or *Music
Week* will be seen across the industry. The performing rights organizations
also have regular publications, BMI's *MusicWorld* or ASCAP's podcast *Versed*,
that highlight new writers who are starting to make waves. The good news is,
trade publications exist for the purpose of spreading industry hype. In fact,
they rely on it to fill their pages. If approached properly, they will be happy
to help you tell your story—considerably more so than the *New York Times*
or *Rolling Stone*. It's all about targeting the segment of the industry that you
are trying to reach, and building relationships with the appropriate editors
and writers.

Of course, the well-known trade publications are a relatively small
segment of the media opportunities that exist to highlight your writer. The

blog world, while probably an easier fit for writers who are performers as well, is a vast machine with an insatiable appetite for new stories. Whether it's a new release from your artist/writer, a noteworthy collaboration, or a sneak preview of an upcoming project, it's worth sending to the appropriate blogs or using SubmitHub to see who reacts. Podcasts like Ross Golan's *And The Writer Is* shine a spotlight on the creative process of songwriting and attract an audience of both industry insiders and music fans. Finally, there's the ever-expanding array of social media options, from the obvious ones like Twitter, Instagram, and Facebook to more professionally-focused platforms like LinkedIn. It makes sense for your publishing company to have an active social media presence, posting news about your writers, upcoming releases, or current success stories, while also working with your individual writers to ensure that they are strategically building their own following among like-minded musicians and artists. Even if it just means reposting, commenting, or tagging, social media offers an easy entrance to a whole community of people. With a strategic approach, your writer can often infiltrate a sector of more established artists, A&R, managers, and producers than would be accessible solely on the basis of the writer's discography.

Awards

The record industry loves to give awards. It's a bit of no-brainer, of course. Everyone likes to get them (except Mutt Lange, apparently), and even for those who don't win, it's still a night of free publicity. Which is my point. Of course, it's not just the Grammys, the American Music Awards, the Latin Grammys, and other high-profile, nationally televised awards shows. There are awards shows sponsored by ASCAP, BMI, SESAC, Billboard, and Nickelodeon. There are the CMAs (Country Music Awards), the Dove Awards, BET's Hip Hop Awards, and on and on. Then of course there are also regional awards shows sponsored by local music papers and music associations—Best Local Band, Most Likely to Succeed, etc. It's like one of those youth soccer tournaments where every kid goes home with a trophy.

A word to the wise. As you may have expected when watching some of these ego-fests on television, not all awards are presented on merit alone. If you want to win an award, or even be nominated for one, you are going to have to campaign. Now, I'm not suggesting that you should take on Sony Pictures in competition for an Academy Award. But whether it's a Grammy, a regional or local award, or something sponsored by an industry trade organization, you can certainly take steps to improve your chances. Join the organization, donate time and energy serving on committees, buy ad space in the trade group's publication or the awards show program, and network with the organization's hierarchy. Gee, I can feel your chances improving already. I know, I know—I'm a hopeless cynic. Comes with the territory.

One more bit of advice. If you win an award, or even if you're just nominated, the important thing is that everyone knows it. You're not collecting these things to decorate your walls. Hire a publicist, blast it out on your socials, take an ad in the trades (this will also help you get that feature story you've been looking for), and bask in your glory. This is no time for quiet humility.

Showcases

For songwriters who are also artists or part of a band, showcase performances are inevitable. Of course, showcases go on every night of the week in the major music centers. Most come and go with little notice. But every now and then, there are performances so strong that the repercussions reverberate around the industry and careers are established. As was depicted dramatically in the recent bio-flick *Rocket Man*, Elton John made his first impression in the U.S. playing at the Troubadour in L.A. Alicia Keys generated an overwhelming pre-release buzz on her debut album by performing a series of industry-only showcases hosted by Clive Davis. If you've got the goods, there is no question that a well-attended industry showcase can still spark a fire in the A&R community. At different stages in a career, a great showcase can say, "I'm here, put me on the map," "I'm back, put me on the map again," or "I'm still here, don't even think about taking me off the map."

Even if a songwriter is not normally a performer, showcases can be an effective means of attracting industry attention. Clubs like the Bluebird Cafe in Nashville or Rockwood Music Hall in New York often feature songwriters performing their own material. Although the writers are not always polished vocalists or instrumentalists, audiences are attracted to the intimacy of hearing a writer deliver his or her songs directly in a more casual atmosphere. Some of these shows will include several writers, each performing four or five songs, so it's not necessary for a writer to have mastered a huge repertoire. Obviously, if you can get yourself or your writer on the bill with one or two more prominent writers, you've already accomplished something. Each writer's stature increases just by being on the same stage as the others.

The most important considerations in scheduling a showcase are the timing and the guest list. For a showcase to have maximum impact, it should be scheduled at an optimal moment in the writer's career (we'll discuss this more in a second) and also at a time when it will have the most impact on the industry. At a most basic level, that means avoiding weekends, holidays, and the month of December. On a more sophisticated level, it means trying to tie in with any appropriate music conventions or events (when every A&R person will be in town).

Without question, the most difficult part of putting together a showcase is getting the right people to come out. Studies show that the average record label executive spends a third of his or her time at any showcase actually watching the show, a third noting who else is in attendance, and the final third watching the other reactions to the show. If you can get enough high-ranking A&R people in one room to make each other nervous ("Is she going after this?" "Do you think they've made an offer yet?"), your showcase is a success. If you can get one or two A&R people to actually appear excited or interested (this is almost impossible), you are sure to generate some major buzz. It is as much about who's there as what actually happens there.

It will likely take the combined efforts of everyone on your team to fill the seats with those who matter. Your lawyer should be able to help in this regard. This is his or her moment to start twisting some big, powerful arms. Your performing rights organization can also be useful; in some cases, BMI or ASCAP will even sponsor the showcase or put your writer on the bill of one of their own events. The other writers and artists in your musical community can also lend their star power. If there's a major star—or even a budding star—that is a fan of your writer, try to get him or her to come to the show or maybe even do a guest spot. That move pays double; you get the glitter of a celebrity and the credibility boost of an endorsement from a respected peer.

Another tip: the more exclusive an event appears to be, the more everyone wants in. Choose a small club, and try to fill it with top industry people. As soon as you know a few people that are committed to attending, start to let people know who else will be there. Nothing is more motivating to a weasel than pure jealousy.

If you're struggling to get the industry types to turn out, don't despair. It's always difficult to get music biz people to actually go somewhere and listen to music, as opposed to hanging out at a fancy restaurant with their friends talking about music. The day of a showcase is inevitably filled with calls from some of the most prized names on your list, explaining that "something" has come up and they'll be out of town for the next six hours. Take heart in the fact that the one thing even more impressive to A&R people than a crowd full of A&R people is a crowd full of actual fans—genuinely passionate, committed, cover-paying fans, toting merch or singing along to the songs. If you've got a true fanbase, you don't need 100 percent attendance from the guest list to get the message out.

Conventions

By holding a multitude of industry types captive in one place for three or four days, these events offer maximum-impact publicity opportunities. Of course, most industry conventions include showcases. Some, like SXSW or Reeperbahn in Germany, are almost nothing but an endless series of performances. The great part of a convention is that word of a strong show will spread like wildfire. The downside is that it can be easy to get lost among the vast array of featured acts. If you're going to perform at a convention, you usually need a story that's already building in the industry. Even then, you better be prepared to do something that can cut through the clutter.

Another convention staple is the industry panel, in which a variety of insiders discuss topics of interest. "The Ins and Outs of Music Publishing," "A&R: Looking for the Next Big Thing"—I've spoken on dozens of these panels, and they always seem to have the same subjects. With a few well-placed phone calls to the organizers of the convention, you may be able to place you or your writer on one of these panels. That means a chance to be seen with others who are more established in the industry, to talk about all of the exciting things happening in the writer's career, to make personal contact with the other people on the panel, and in many cases, to get in free to the rest of the convention.

And of course, what's a convention without a party? Or parties. Anytime there are music people gathered together, there will be companies throwing parties, which can range from a room service order of cheese and crackers in a hotel suite to a gala event. At a conference like SXSW, it can be more advantageous to play a party, where the sponsor will bring in a big and influential crowd, than to have to try to fill a showcase space on your own. Or if you're looking for a way of attracting attention, it may be worth having your publishing company consider hosting some sort of get-together and featuring your writers, whether as part of a live performance or a "listening" session for an upcoming release.

Writing Camps

In addition to the obvious creative benefits to a writer of participating in a songwriting camp, these events can be a publicity coup as well. Some camps directly affiliated with conventions, like SXSW Songs, by:Larm, or the Midem camp, will put the participating writers on an industry panel and even throw a "listening party" at the close of the camp. This provides some high visibility for the writers after days of being sequestered in the studio churning out songs. But the prestige associated even with smaller, private, invitation-only events can lift a writer's reputation among the other publishers and writers involved. A few well-tagged social media posts of a songwriter working on his or her tan (studio or beach variety) with a group of important new-found friends can do more than a carefully cultivated press placement.

Which brings up one last point: don't hesitate to draw upon the social circle that exists around even such a solitary figure as a songwriter. Posts from the studio working with a well-known songwriter or buzzing artist, an article in a college newsletter or support from an alumni group (many schools like Berklee College of Music, Syracuse University, NYU, and Belmont have active networks that promote their graduates and highlight their achievements in the industry), free shows for a charity, or congratulatory posts to another colleague having success can increase the impact of your publicity efforts. All of these simply extend your reach in the industry, touching not only your own circle of supporters but also the followers, friends, and fans of other people or organizations.

Planning the Attack: Timing Is Everything

One fundamental principle of publicity is the importance of grouping events together, in the same two- to four-week span, for maximum impact. This way, events are part of a strategic campaign rather than just isolated attempts to grab the public eye. Like advertising, publicity works largely by repeated exposure. A music supervisor receives your music in an email, then she sees your name in *Billboard*, then a colleague mentions that he went to your party last night. None of those things would be enough to make an impression on their own, but the cumulative effect can get the whole industry talking.

For example, when you have a major release coming out, that's the time to try to place a feature story in a trade publication. Then, during the same week, try to get yourself a spot on a panel at an industry convention. At the end of the week, host a party to preview the upcoming record. If you organize the events strategically, your campaign will give the impression that you're everywhere at once. It's that repeated exposure that builds industry buzz. To see this theory in action, simply watch the promotional campaign that precedes any major motion picture release. There will be a cover story on one of the stars in a national magazine, followed by a premier party covered by *Access Hollywood*, followed by a guest spot with Jimmy Kimmel—all happening in the same week that the movie is released. Coincidence? I think not.

A&R Meetings

Timing also applies to A&R meetings. The month prior to a big upcoming release, or the week of an awards show in which you or your writer are nominated, or the week that you happen to be in town working with a major artist, are all opportune moments to schedule a round of A&R meetings. Yes, I do mean a *round* of meetings. If one A&R person meets you or your writer, then talks to another A&R person who's just met you, and then runs into yet another A&R person who just happens to be seeing you tomorrow, you will have made an impact far greater than could be achieved in any one individual meeting. For that reason, try to schedule A&R meetings in chunks. Do five or six within a week, rather than one every two weeks.

Don't forget that there are weasels all over the world. If you've got an upcoming release or a hit in a foreign territory, it may be the time to cross the ocean and meet a whole new cast of characters. If your Nashville–based writer will be in L.A. to work with an artist or to accept an award—now you have a story to tell. Make sure you set up meetings with all the relevant power figures in Hollywood.

It's interesting how much easier it can be to set up meetings with people when you are coming in from out of town. Maybe it's nothing more than a certain exoticism that is conferred on the visitor ("Oh, he's from Sweden, ooh . . . "), but A&R people seem to go for the old "we're in from the coast for a week" routine. If you don't already have a network established in whatever city you're visiting, give yourself three to four weeks in advance of the trip to start filling the calendar.

A&R meetings themselves usually come in two varieties. There is the "pitch" meeting, which we've already discussed. The focus of this sort of meeting is to play songs for whatever project the A&R person is engaged in at the moment. There is also the "meet and greet," which is really just a chance to get acquainted. Some music may get listened to (or not), but the A&R person is likely to prefer songs that simply give a representative sampling of a writer's work, rather than anything specifically targeted to a project. As the name would imply, the "meet and greet" is relationship-focused rather than song-focused.

Be prepared at any time for either sort of meeting, or for a combination of both, and then try to read the vibe once you get in the room. The important thing is to go with the flow. Trying to pitch songs at a "meet and greet" will make you seem like an overzealous huckster. Likewise, too much conversation in a "pitch" meeting will give the impression that you don't have any songs to play. Your goal is to raise the visibility of yourself or your writer and establish a positive image. That means getting in the weasel's office and keeping him or her amused and happy while you're there. Selling songs is a secondary concern.

As you can see from the past few chapters, the creative director's role in the publishing company is a constant balancing act between the creative demands of getting the music right, the practical business challenges of getting the music out, and the public relations aspect of moving the writer up. It's a balance between listening and selling, between being the critic and being the "hype" person You wear a lot of hats in one day, and juggle a lot of balls in the air. Sort of like a circus clown. Like a clown, you usually drop more balls than you catch. I suspect you may have already seen how often the day-to-day demands of the paperwork, business affairs issues, and licensing questions can sidetrack your efforts as a creative director.

Our next section will deal primarily with the administrative aspects of music publishing, which are substantial, complex, and extremely important in their own right. But they are not the priority. Success in the music publishing business depends on doing first things first. That means:

- Getting the music right.
- Getting the music out.
- Moving the writer up.

Then, and only then, are you ready to proceed to part III of this book. Subject: Getting the money in. And keeping it in.

PART III
TAKING CARE OF BUSINESS

19

Fun with Administration and Licensing

On my first day in the music publishing business, I was ushered around the office to meet my co-workers. That's where I meet Gita. She was the head of the Administration Department, working and (during royalty season) maybe sometimes living in an office that was filled with stacks of paper. The piles of paper lined every wall, many of them dwarfing Gita, who was a small, bird-like woman who spoke quietly and I suspect saw the sun only when on vacation. Her desk was entirely obscured by paper. It looked like Mont Blanc in ski season, a looming mountain of white. I was terrified. I quickly retreated to the Creative Department and have approached the Administration side of the publishing business with trepidation ever since. Not only is it often maddeningly complex, and becoming more complex every day, it's also a little . . . well . . . okay, I'll say it: boring. Let's admit it, compared with getting the music right, or getting the music out, or moving a writer up, the nuances of getting the money are not all that exciting.

Until it's your money. That focuses the mind doesn't it? The world of administration becomes a most interesting place indeed when you try to figure out why your song is on the radio but you don't seem to be making any money, how thirty million Spotify streams can generate less in royalties than you spent buying the writer dinner, why that platinum album in France never brings in any actual American currency, or why the royalties always seem to be in the proverbial music industry "pipeline" but never seem to get to the desired destination. I once found out that I had several years' worth of performance payments that had been held up by BMI because they didn't have a correct address for me. (You see how competent a publisher I was at the time.) Yes, the world of administration can be much more exciting than you might think.

Administration is something of an umbrella term, encompassing three of the five functions of a music publisher: administration, collection, and protection. Each of these jobs is fundamental to music publishing, and all of them overlap and impact each other. If you fail to issue a license, you may not be able to collect the money later on. If you're not clear about what percentage of the copyright you own, you could find yourself unable to protect your interests if they're infringed upon. If you don't give BMI your correct address, you won't get your check. Two out of three won't do the job here. You've got to administer, collect, and protect.

Having acknowledged the difficulty of isolating one of these functions from another, let's make an attempt to break the "administration" of a copyright into manageable pieces. We'll begin with what we already know—always a very good place to start. Ladies and gentlemen, get out those split sheets.

Knowing What You Have

The first role of the administrator is to know exactly what you're administering and what rights you have to give away. The good news is, you should already have most of this work done. For each copyright, you should have a signed split sheet that will identify what portion of the song is owned by your writer, what portion you publish (this may not necessarily equal the writer's share), and the necessary information about the co-writers and co-publishers. You should also have a Copyright Administration Checklist in your files. That "Notes" section should tell you if there are any limitations to your control of the copyright.

If you are the only writer for your publishing company, you can assume that you publish each of your songs for the lifespan of the copyright. A copyright's lifespan begins on the date the song is written down or recorded and extends for the lifetime of the last surviving songwriter plus seventy years. (By the way, this means that if your publishing firm is a solo venture, it's invariably going to outlast you. Either you sell out in your golden years or give it to the grandkids). You can also take for granted that you have a right to make any administration decisions without obtaining approval from an obstinate writer.

On the other hand, if you publish writers other than yourself, that "Notes" section can make for fascinating reading. Depending on the agreements that you've made with your writers, there could be any number of restrictions on your control of the copyright and your right to exploit or administer a song. As I mentioned before, the more of these restrictions you agree to when trying to sign a writer, the harder you make your life later. It's not enough to know that you publish the song. You've also got to understand the details.

Knowing Your Limits

Other than in an actual purchase of the copyrights by a publisher, the publisher always has limitations on their control of the copyrights. Here are the most important conditions that any publishing agreement would cover.

Duration
Some publishing deals provide that the copyrights will "revert" back to the writer after a certain period of time. If the copyrights have been recorded and released during the term of the agreement, that reversion could occur anywhere from ten to thirty years after the deal ends, though it's sometimes even sooner. Often, the reversion may be based upon the status of a writer's account, with copyrights reverting only if the writer has "recouped," which is to say, earned back their advances. Another variation on this idea provides for the reversion of all unexploited copyrights. Those are the ones still sitting in the drawer that have never been released. Unexploited copyrights commonly revert to the writer after three to seven years.

To properly understand the issue of duration and reversions, it's essential to keep in mind the very nature of the writer-publisher agreement. In most cases, with the exception of an outright purchase of a catalog, the publisher is never actually taking "ownership" of the copyrights. The ownership stays with the writer. The publisher is "controlling" the copyrights ("managing" them, if you like) on behalf of the songwriter. It's a little like leasing a car. You can drive it however and wherever you like, but that doesn't make you the owner of it forever.

While my soft and fuzzy songwriter side empathizes with a writer's desire to limit the length of time a publisher can hang on to the copyrights, the weasel in me screams, "No, no, NO!" Publishing empires like Warner Chappell or Tree Music were built on obtaining songs for the lifetime of the copyright, with no reversions. It takes a great deal of work and an even greater amount of luck to create one classic copyright. It's hard to build a long-term business if you allow your company's greatest assets to slip away after only a few years.

In fact, even the lifetime of a copyright isn't as long as it would seem to be. While the copyright extends for the life of the composer plus seventy years, the law provides a window of time during which a songwriter can reclaim a copyright from a publisher. This window is a five-year period, beginning either thirty-five years from the date of publication, or forty years from the date the song was assigned to the publisher. The writer or heir is required to notify the publisher of the intent to reclaim the song; that notification must be made at least two years prior to the date the writer wishes to take back the copyright.

As a publisher, there's not much you can do about this, except to hope your hard work and diligence persuades the writer to let you continue to publish the song. Or you can rely on the premise that writers, being what they are, will likely forget to file the necessary paperwork. If the five-year window passes without notice, the song remains with the publisher for the rest of the copyright's lifespan.

First Use

There are some instances in which a publisher will also give the songwriter the right to approve a first-use license. This is most common with singer/songwriters or band members, in situations where most of the material is intended for the writer's own project. To keep the publisher from giving the best songs away to another artist, a writer/performer will sometimes insist on a first-use approval.

Territory

Before you start sending those songs overseas for projects you saw listed in your favorite tip sheet, be sure you have worldwide rights. Given the opportunity, a publisher should always try to sign a writer for worldwide rights. There are too many lucrative opportunities around the world—opportunities that in many cases a writer would find difficult to access on his or her own—to limit the scope of your rights based on territory.

Unless you absolutely have to. There may be instances in which a top writer is only available for certain territories, or may be hesitant to sign a worldwide deal to a small publisher that doesn't have offices around the globe. Or it may be that there's simply not a broad international audience for what your writer does. In such cases, at least give some thought as to what will likely be the most lucrative markets for this particular writer, and try to get as many of those territories as you can.

Alterations and Adaptations

When writers start referring to songs as their "babies," get nervous. Because when you sign up to publish those songs, it means that you're adopting their babies. They're now yours to care for as you see fit. Or at least, that's what it should mean.

Some writers will require approval over edits, lyric changes, or translations—in other words, you can't touch your adopted baby without Mom or Dad's approval. You can imagine what fun that is. Film placements and advertisements will often require small changes in the lyric or song structure. Pitching a song overseas will likely lead to the need for a translation. To clear every such decision with a writer can be both a logistical and creative nightmare.

Specific Uses

Many publishing contracts will require the writer to approve the placement of their baby in certain types of films, advertisements for certain products, or use in political campaigns. Make sure you know what these restrictions are before you pitch the song for this sort of placement.

Reduced Royalty Rates

More about reduced royalty rates in a second. Suffice to say, the music industry has devised a number of different ways to get songs at a discount, forcing publishers to accept less than the full statutory mechanical royalty rate of 9.1 cents. A writer's primary concern is usually to prevent a publisher who is also affiliated with a record company from licensing a song to the associated record label for less than the full rate. To guard against this, a writer will sometimes demand approval over any licensing at a reduced rate, or at least over any such licenses granted to a company in which the publisher has an interest. Fair enough.

While all of the preceding limits on your rights as a publisher may feel inconvenient to say the least, it's important to remember that the publisher derives all rights from the songwriter. Unless the songwriter actually sold his or her rights, the publisher acts *on behalf of* the songwriter, who remains the owner of the copyright. In light of that, it's only right that the songwriter should retain some control over where, when, how, and at what price the song can be used. Of course, if you're publishing your own songs, navigating these issues is pretty easy. But if you're publishing someone else's songs, be sure to read the fine print. Don't break that trust with the songwriter by overstepping the boundaries around your control of the copyright.

20

Licensing Your Music: You Get When You Give

Ironically, once you've figured out what you've got, the most important thing you can do is give it away. For a price. The very phrase "copyright" means, quite literally, the right to copy. Owning a copyright only has value if there's someone else that wants a copy. The issuing of licenses is the process by which a publisher grants the right to use a song, most often in exchange for a fee or royalty payment (we hope). Copyright licenses are like love: the more you give away, the more you get back.

Well, maybe you don't want to exactly *give* it away.

If you're wondering what all those papers were in Gita's office, most of them fall under the category of license requests or the licenses themselves, along with the accounting statements generated by all of those licenses. If you're already publishing your own catalog, you probably have your own stack starting to grow: Notices of Intent (or NOIs) from a dozen different streaming services, Music Reports requests for use on services like Amazon and Pandora, a gratis request from a school choir, and a sample request from a producer who found your song on YouTube.

License requests are signs that you're doing something right. At the very least, you're making stuff happen. But for better or worse, all of that stuff generates paperwork. Here's a breakdown of the licenses you'll most likely need to put in place.

Mechanical Licenses

Applies To: "Mechanical reproductions" of sound recordings, including vinyl records, CDs, and "interactive" digital streams (in which the listener chooses to play a specific song).

Rates: The current full statutory rate for a song of average length is 9.1 cents. Recordings over five minutes in length receive an additional 1.75 cents per minute or fraction thereof. For interactive digital streams, such as Spotify or Apple Music, the math gets a whole lot more complicated. In general, the rates reflect a percentage of the income generated by the service. But the formula takes into account not only the number of streams, but also the status of those who do the streaming (is the listener a paid subscriber or a "free" service customer?) and the total number of streams in a particular territory during that monthly period.

Who Sets the Rates: Blame it on Washington, DC. Every five years, the Copyright Royalty Board (CRB), a panel of three judges from the Copyright Office, listens to testimony from those who license music (mostly digital services and record labels) and those who control the rights (music publishers and songwriters), and sets the mechanical royalty rate. While the statutory rate has not changed since 2006, the CRB did decide in 2018 to give songwriters and publishers a big raise in regards to the mechanical rates for digital streaming. Over the next five years, the portion of income that streaming services are expected to pay out to publishers will gradually go from 10.5 percent of the revenues generated by the digital platform to 15.1 percent.

Who Issues the License: The Harry Fox Agency (primarily for physical product), the new Mechanical Licensing collective (for interactive digital streaming services or download services), or Music Reports (for non-interactive streaming or other digital services). We'll discuss these organizations in the next chapter. It's also possible for publishers to issue mechanical licenses directly on their own. You can find an example of a mechanical license in appendix E.

What the License Contains:

- song information (writers, publishers)
- record label information (including ISRC and configuration)
- representation of ownership by publisher
- accounting requirements for record company
- statement of rate
- acknowledgement by record company that the license is limited to specific artist and recording
- remedy if record company fails to account as required by license

Things to Argue About: Oh boy. This could take a while . . .

Music Business Weasel Says:
Everyone wants a discount.

If it seems like the mechanical license process should be relatively straight-forward—after all, it's a set royalty rate—you are in for a quick education in the ways of weaseldom. Legal inventions like the controlled composition clause and the three-quarter rate are little more than the record company's way of saying, "We don't like this price. We'd prefer to pay less." A nice trick if you can pull it off. Try it on your landlord or your local grocer and let me know if it works. All I can tell you is, in the record biz, it works a lot more often than it should.

Controlled Composition Clause

This is a killer. Originally aimed primarily at artist/writers, it extends to producer/writers as well. The controlled composition clause states that the mechanical rate for songs that are written or "controlled" by the artist will be 75 percent of the statutory rate (reducing 9.1 cents down to 6.825 cents). Then to add insult to injury, it usually sets a total mechanical royalty "cap" of ten times the three-quarter rate for the entire album. That multiple of ten comes from the days when albums were generally made up of ten songs. Of course, in a digital world, there's no set number of songs to which an album must conform. But the royalty cap is a statement by the label that they only intend to pay out 68 cents per album in mechanical royalties, regardless of how many songs an artist decides to include. In any case, for a controlled composition on an album with twelve songs, the royalty rate will be reduced yet again to 5.68 cents.

Wait—I'm not done yet. If some of the songs on the album are by writers who are not controlled (which is to say that they are not the artist or the producer, and are therefore not forced to accept anything less than the "full stat" rate of 9.1 cents), the rate for the controlled parties drops even further in light of that mechanical royalty "cap." If there are samples on the album, which require payments of mechanical royalties to the artists and writers whose work is being borrowed, that rate goes down yet again. It is quite possible for controlled writers subject to a cap to receive a rate that is two cents or less for each unit sold. Great system, right?

Unfortunately, there is little a publisher or writer can do to avoid this pinch. If the writer is also the artist, he or she will almost inevitably be subject to the controlled composition clause as part of the recording contract. Likewise, all but the most powerful producers will find themselves forced to acquiesce to what is now an industry standard. My advice? Suck it up, and go on. Change those things that are within your power, and accept those things that aren't.

Reduced Rates

If your song is recorded by an outside artist and you don't produce the record, you are not obligated to accept less than the full stat rate. But that doesn't mean the weasels can't ask.

Record companies will frequently ask for a reduced rate (usually 75 percent of full stat) from outside writers, under the guise of trying to be fair to the parties who are "controlled." This can often put a songwriter and publisher in a very uncomfortable position, as they are pressed to make concessions not only by the label, but also by the artist and other writers. Of course, the implied threat is that your song will be dropped off the album and your relationship with the artist or producer irreparably damaged if you won't agree to the reduced rate. And that could very well happen.

In such negotiations, the greatest factor in favor of the writer and publisher is the general ineptitude of most record companies and artist managers. Frequently, record releases will outpace a label's licensing department, which can mean that requests for reduced rates will go out to publishers when the song is already up on Apple or YouTube. At that point, the balance of power shifts drastically. There is very little reason for a publisher to agree to a rate reduction in such situations, unless you have a great deal of future business at stake with the record label or artist. The best strategy for publishers in rate negotiations is to do as little as possible and hope that the record comes out before an agreement is reached. Never call a record company to ask about a rate. Let them come to you.

Performing Rights

Applies To: Any commercial performance of the song on the radio and television; Spotify, Pandora, SoundCloud, or other digital streaming services; or in nightclubs, concert venues, restaurants, elevators, and almost anywhere else in the world, other than the comfort of your own home or car.

Rates: Once again, it's impossible to break down exact rates for the myriad of different performance situations. While rates per performance are only a few pennies, a chart-topping pop hit could easily bring in more than a million dollars in performance income over two or three accounting periods. Performances on streaming platforms or live shows (particularly in the U.S.) earn much, much less than radio and television uses.

Who Sets the Rates: Rates are negotiated by the performing rights organizations (ASCAP, BMI, SESAC, and GRM), with the broadcasters and other licensees. When you join a performing rights organization, you are authorizing them to grant the performing right license on your behalf.

Who Issues the License: The performing rights organizations issue what are called "blanket" licenses to music users. This allows the licensee to use any songs in the organizations' catalogs, rather than apply for individual licenses on a song-by-song basis. This blanket licensing system is what enables radio stations or any live performer to use any song they like without having to clear it in advance.

Things to Argue About: With some notable exceptions, this is a much more agreeable process than the one for mechanical licenses. Sure, there are always disputes about the relative merits of the performing rights organizations, as well as the validity of the Consent Decrees—those antiquated laws that often hamstring ASCAP and BMI in the negotiating process with broadcasters and digital services. But in general, the blanket licensing system is better suited to the 21st century global music industry than the song-by-song systems that apply to mechanical and synchronization rights. In the next chapter, we'll talk more about the relative merits of each organization, and how they go about collecting your money.

Synchronization Rights

Applies To: Just about any situation in which music is "synchronized" to visual images, to create an audiovisual work. This includes movies for theatrical release, television shows, videos, commercial advertising, electronic games, and nontheatrical or noncommercial works (like instructional videos or corporate presentations). There are a couple of strange exceptions: it does not include artist official videos (for which the label generally demands a gratis license) or some of the biggest user-generated streaming services like YouTube and TikTok.

Rates: Whatever you can get. Sync licenses are negotiated between the publisher and the production company, studio, or whoever wishes to use the song.

Who Sets the Rates: Rates are determined solely by what the market will bear. However, there are limits. If you ask for too much, you can be assured that the production company or studio will find another song to fill the slot. No piece of music is indispensable to a motion picture or a video game. Rates are largely determined by the following:

- **The Use:** Title and end credits and on-screen performances are considerably more valuable than non-featured uses like background instrumental spots or incidental music.

- **The Duration:** A use that extends over a minute in length is considerably more valuable than a 10 second snippet. It's also possible that a song could receive multiple uses; again, this ups the ante.

- **The Artist:** If your song is performed by a superstar artist, its value increases substantially.

- **The Soundtrack Opportunity:** If a movie studio can guarantee a placement of the song on a soundtrack album, it may be worth taking a small reduction in the sync fee. Obviously, a soundtrack can bring in mechanical royalties that will compensate for the reduction in sync money.

- **The Budget:** Even the richest producer will cry poverty when negotiating fees. The general ranking, from deepest pockets to no pockets at all, is: major motion pictures and advertisements at the top of the money heap, then network and cable television, then independently produced movies or television shows. If a producer insists that they are giving you all that is available in the budget, you could try requesting a "favored nations" clause. This provides that you will receive no less than the highest fee granted for any other song (in a similar placement). These clauses are not too popular with producers or studios, but are relatively common in licenses for major hits. No one will give you "favored nation" status for an unknown song in a background use.

Who Issues the License: In most instances, the movie studio or production company will submit the license to the publisher for approval. Some added good news: if a movie appears on television, it will also generate a performance royalty, under ASCAP or BMI's blanket performance license with the network.

What It Contains: These vary depending on the type of usage, but most will include:

- Song information
- Administrative share: This is the percentage of the song controlled by the publisher.

- Description of the movie, television episode, or game, including the performers involved (which often gives you a hint about the size of the budget), the plot, the release date, and the scope of the release or campaign.
- Duration of license: Motion pictures will generally require a license in perpetuity while television and advertising uses tend to be for five years or less.
- Limitation to specific motion picture, episode or advertising spot.
- The amount of the sync fee
- The granting of non-exclusive rights to the song (some producers will want exclusive rights, which means more money for you)
- The nature and number of uses, including timings
- The territories: For most motion pictures, the license will be for worldwide rights. Television, commercials, and other uses may be more limited.
- Requirement for producer to provide cue sheets, usually within thirty days of release

You can find an example of a synchronization license in appendix C.

Things to Argue About: Because of the wide variety of sync uses, these agreements can get somewhat complex. For instance, the licensing of a song for a small indie movie may grant the production company the right to show the film in festivals, but not in a full theatrical release. The use of the song in a movie trailer (I mean in previews, not in the star's dressing room) is a completely different transaction than licensing a song for the movie itself. Be careful to understand exactly what rights you are granting in the license, and make sure that you are receiving fair compensation for each type of use.

Master Rights

It's also important to remember that the publishing sync license applies only to the composition; it does not cover the actual recording of the song that appears on film. The licensing of the master recording is a separate issue, to be negotiated between the owner of the master (traditionally the record company) and the producer of the movie or TV show. In most cases, this "master" license generates a fee equal to that of the publishing sync license. (Most publishers will request "favored nation" status in relation to the licensing of the master recording.)

But what if the publisher is also the owner of the master? Particularly in low-budget movies or television shows, you may be able to place the "demo" version of a song directly into the production. In this instance, the publisher who paid for the demo is the owner of both the master recording and the copyright. You've just doubled your money. To this end, many publishers of important songs are now producing their own recordings of them, which can be licensed directly to film and television producers, usually for considerably less than the more famous hit recordings. It's a good argument for making sure you get your demos right.

By now, it probably won't surprise you to learn that, the movie business weasels (same animal, nicer suits) have come up with their own method of siphoning off a portion of your money. In Hollywood, everyone wants a piece of the action. Almost all of the major motion picture studios are also in the music publishing business and will likely try to grab a portion of the publisher's share of the song.

If the song was written specifically for the movie or television show, is a recurrent theme song, or was previously unexploited, you will most likely wind up giving up at least a third, and possibly half, of the song's income. You might even be forced to deem the song a "work for hire" and give up all ownership and control in exchange for a flat fee. On the other hand, if the song was already a hit before the license was requested, then you should resist any attempt to dip into your money.

Foreign Rights

Applies To: All uses of the song outside of the U.S. This means mechanical, performance, sync, and other income.

Rates: Vary significantly depending on the territory. Independent publishers commonly strike what are called "sub-publishing" agreements with local publishers in each foreign territory. Those companies then administer the rights on behalf of the original publisher. These are territory by territory administration agreements, with the local publisher taking ten to twenty percent of the income they collect in their territory.

Who Sets the Rates: Depends on which rates we're talking about. Mechanical rates for recordings are usually set by some sort of government-approved formula in each territory. For the most part, they are based on the RSP (retail selling price) or PPD (published price to dealers) of the album. Streaming rates change continually, adjusting for the size of the market and the number of total streams in the territory. Performing right rates are determined by the performance society within that particular territory.

Who Issues the License: We'll deal with the subject of sub-publishers in chapter 21. Alternatively, it is, to some extent, possible to issue licenses directly, and to collect the money through the reciprocal arrangements that ASCAP, BMI, and SESAC maintain in foreign territories.

Things to Argue About: Weasels are weasels the world over—so there are always disputes between publishers and sub-publishers. These can range from shady accounting practices, currency exchange rates, splits, and foreign taxes all the way down to failure to provide the foreign publisher with adequate demos, writer information, and release notices. In the interest of international brotherhood, it's best to have your sub-publishing agreements negotiated by your lawyer, to do business with companies of good reputation, and, if you're bringing a hit to the table, to get an advance up front.

Commercial Advertising

Applies To: Use of the song in a promotional or advertising campaign for a product or service. Most advertising uses fall under the category of synchronization: music used in conjunction with visual images in television or internet campaigns. But there are also audio-only advertising uses on the radio and Internet to be considered. Because most songs written specifically for ad campaigns are done on a work-for-hire basis (meaning that the agency or client maintain full ownership of the copyright), we'll limit our discussion to the use of a pre-existing song in an advertisement.

Rates: Subject to negotiation. There is no standard here; numbers can run from a few thousand dollars for a local advertisement to big money for a major hit placed in a national spot.

Who Sets the Rates: Rates are ultimately negotiated between the client (that is, the subject of the ad campaign) and the publisher, usually with the advertising agency running interference between the two.

Who Issues the License: This is issued by the publisher directly, though it may require the writer's approval, particularly for certain types of products.

What It Contains: An advertising license, even if it's not for a synchronization use, will cover much of the same ground as a sync license. A few things to keep in mind:

- **Alterations or adaptations:** So they wanna change the lyric, eh? Anything for a price. Remember, this may also require the writer's permission.

- **Exclusivity:** Most clients will seek to prevent the publisher from licensing the songs to similar or competitive products. More zealous marketers will seek total exclusivity, which is considerably more expensive.

- **Options:** Can be exercised as needed for extended license periods, rights outside the U.S., or increased exclusivity, provided there is additional compensation to the publisher.

Things to Argue About: You could argue with your writer about whether or not an advertising placement degrades the copyright. Or you could argue with the agency about a license for a regional or off-air test. Or you could just take the money and run. You can probably guess which option I would choose. If you get a song in an advertisement, just smile, smile, smile....

Other Uses

Oh, there's more. There are licenses for print rights, which apply primarily to the sale of sheet music, but can also include reprints of lyrics in magazines, greeting cards or advertisements, or the creation of arrangements of the song for orchestras, symphonies or choirs. There are grand rights and dramatic rights that apply to the use of a song in the context of live theater. And happily, there are licenses for special uses that grow more diverse daily. This category includes everything from karaoke, to in-flight programming, to the much-loved Billy Bass, the singing fish. All of these licenses can provide significant income, and all raise certain issues that must be resolved. When in doubt, consult your lawyer to find out what limitations you should insist on and what compensation is appropriate. But don't be too careful. Licenses are only good if you give 'em away.

Music Business Weasel Says:
In show business, there are no standards.

In case you haven't noticed, most licensing agreements (with the exception of blanket licenses through the performing rights organizations) are not locked into fixed rates. Even though there are thousands of such licenses issued every day, there are no set standards that apply uniformly. Everyone's making a deal—some good, some not so good. In the interests of trying to get more of your deals to fall into the "good" category, we'll close this chapter with a few quick negotiating tips:

- **Information is power.** The more you know about the people and project that you're involved with, and the importance of your song to the project, the stronger your position is. Prepare for battle.

- **Start with the easy stuff.** Resolve the simple issues first, and then go on to the tougher points. A little positive momentum is always helpful.

- **Use your lawyer for advice, but not for the initial negotiations.** In most instances, bringing your lawyer in will send the clients scurrying for cover. Unless it's a *big* deal, try to keep things on a personal basis.

- **Give with one hand and take with the other.** If you make a concession, try to extract some small concession in return.

- **Don't play hardball if you can't afford to lose.** Most negotiations simply come down to who needs the deal more. If you're the needy party, then avoid threats, nitpicking, and ultimatums.

- **Get it in writing.** After a negotiation, follow up with an e-mail or memo outlining the discussion and the deal points agreed upon.

- **Don't confuse principles and money.** In licensing discussions, there can be issues that really are matters of principle. Is the songwriter comfortable with the song being used to promote a particular political candidate or as part of a graphically violent film or video game? But royalty rates or a licensee's grab for a piece of the publishing are just about money. Don't get on your moral high horse about them. Get the best financial deal you can, and try not to get your feelings hurt.

If all of this feels a little overwhelming, don't give up yet. On the very next page, help is on the way.

21

The Collection Crew:
What Friends Are For

As we learned from the Music Business Weasel early on in this book, "It's never easy getting paid." After reading the previous chapter, you've had a quick look at just how challenging it can be. It's not only that you have to fight with record labels over controlled composition clauses or film studios who want your song as a work for hire. There are also the logistical challenges of collecting income from songs that may be used anywhere in the world in a hundred different ways. So when I tell you that you need some allies who will help to collect the money, you know I'm talking about teammates that are aggressive, thorough, and connected. I've already mentioned these names to you in previous chapters, but now we'll look a little harder at the role each one plays in the collection process. Publishers, meet your new best friends!

ASCAP/BMI/SESAC and GMR

We've already mentioned the support that performing rights organizations like ASCAP, BMI, and SESAC (known as PROs) can offer to writers and publishers by providing networking and educational opportunities. Now, let's talk about their day job.

The idea of monitoring the amount of airplay and other performances any one song receives is mind-boggling. Think about the thousands of radio and television stations across the U.S., then add in dance clubs, gyms, lounges, concert halls, and restaurants with stereo systems. Needless to say, it's something less than an exact science. But the systems devised by ASCAP, BMI, and SESAC have been enormously effective in compensating copyright owners for the use of their product, while continuing to encourage the public performance of music in an ever-increasing array of venues. In the United

States, ASCAP and BMI both pay out over $1 billion annually in performance income. For most publishers around the world, performance royalties constitute more than half of their annual income. How do these performing rights organizations do it?

While each organization differs somewhat in their approach, the fundamental system is relatively straightforward. All three PROs issue blanket licenses (at a variety of different cost structures) to companies that use music in a public way. As we said before, these licenses allow music users to use any song from the PRO's catalog without having to request thousands of individual licenses. The revenues from these blanket licenses are then distributed among the thousands of writer and publisher affiliates on a song-by-song basis, depending upon how many public performances each work has received. This is the tricky part.

ASCAP, BMI, and SESAC all monitor their licensees to find out what songs they are playing, using similar methods but with slightly different approaches. When it comes to radio play, BMI relies on a combination of programming logs provided by the stations and digital monitoring through services like Nielsen's Broadcast Data Systems. ASCAP and SESAC lean almost solely on digital monitoring. All of the PRO's track television uses primarily through cue sheets submitted by the networks, although digital monitoring is used here as well. Live performances are the one area in which the U.S. performance organizations are notoriously weak. Whether it's Madison Square Garden or Mo's Bar & Grill, the payments for live shows in America are far below what could be earned in similar venues in other parts of the world. If your writer is playing shows in Europe, it's important that set-lists are submitted to the local performing rights organization, usually prior to the show. In fact, most venues will insist on it. In the U.S., it's not worth the bother.

For non-commercial music, which might only receive a few hundred plays on small local stations, tracking becomes an even greater challenge. In many instances, ASCAP, BMI, and SESAC have tried to make adjustments to compensate for this. Certainly, all the organizations make efforts to track small as well as large broadcasters; they have also created payment systems to reflect the differences in the quantity of uses for music outside the mainstream. Concert music pieces, for instance, which might receive only two or three performances in a year, are monitored in a different manner and paid at a much higher rate than three-minute pop songs. Performance royalty rates are based on:

- the nature of the performance (feature, background, theme, live)
- the duration of the performance

- the size and nature of the broadcasting network (network television, syndicated radio, independent stations)
- the time of day the performance takes place (for radio in particular)

ASCAP, BMI, and SESAC distribute royalties quarterly; these include foreign distributions, which are collected through the societies' reciprocal organizations all over the world. SESAC also offers an option to receive radio royalties monthly. It's important to understand that the payments to writers and publishers are made by divvying up the big pie, which is the amount received by the organizations from their blanket licenses, minus the organization's administration charge to cover their own costs. These costs are roughly ten to fifteen percent of the gross income for both organizations. All those helpful services and great parties that BMI and ASCAP offer their members don't come for free.

Global Music Rights (GMR)

Global Music Rights is the most recent invention in the performing rights universe, having been created in 2013 as a way around what are called the Consent Decrees. These are laws that date back to 1941, originally intended to prevent ASCAP and BMI from acting as monopolies in their negotiations with those seeking to license their catalogs. Fast forward to the 21st century, and the Consent Decrees have instead become an almost insurmountable handicap for ASCAP and BMI in their negotiations with digital streaming platforms like Pandora and Spotify. This law requires the PROs to issue blanket licenses to anyone making a request, and to settle rate disputes in court, rather than through bargaining in the free market. At no point can ASCAP and BMI simply decline to license a service.

Because new organizations are not subject to the Consent Decree (SESAC is also exempt from the restrictions), music mogul Irving Azoff launched GMR in 2013 with the idea of attracting the top tier of commercial songs, offering big advances to sign up those writers who dominate the Hot 100. GMR then uses that hit-heavy catalog as leverage with broadcasters and digital platforms in order to negotiate the best possible licensing rates.

Whether it will work or not remains to be seen. Not surprisingly, music services have not been thrilled to now have four organizations from whom they need to obtain blanket licenses. Nor have BMI and ASCAP been happy to see their top writers leaving for greener pastures. So far, much of GMR's business has been fighting off legal challenges to its legitimacy, rather than putting infrastructure and licensing agreements in place. Suffice to say that unless you have massive success, GMR will not be an option anyway, as they aim for a client roster limited to the highest-earning songwriters.

By Invitation Only, Cash Prizes at the Door

Likewise, SESAC does not present itself as being open to all interested writers or publishers. In order to become a member, you will have to obtain an invitation from the Writer/Publisher Relations Department. By contrast, ASCAP and BMI are open to anyone who wishes to join, provided they have at least one song likely to generate performance income

Traditionally, ASCAP and BMI had not made advances to attract new members, but that has changed significantly over the past two decades. SESAC started the advance game with an aggressive spending strategy, only to be quickly one-upped by BMI. ASCAP does occasionally try to compete when it comes to retaining top talent, but does not usually have the deep pockets of BMI. As you might expect from an organization founded by one of the most aggressive artist representatives of all time, GMR is by far the most open to writing big advance checks, though their generosity is usually aimed solely at writers who don't need the money.

So, let's get down to the big question. Which one should a songwriter join?

I don't know. ASCAP is older and very much a society of writers, both in spirit and in fact. It is essentially run by writers, with past presidents like Hal David and current leader Paul Williams. BMI is more corporate, having been founded by the broadcasting industry that it now negotiates with. However, it has its own historical importance, particularly as the first society to open up to black American writers and the early country music and rock and roll community. Unlike the other two, SESAC is a for-profit organization, but it remains small enough that a new writer might expect more attention than at BMI or ASCAP.

As a writer, I've been affiliated with both ASCAP and BMI at different times, and I've written many songs with co-writers from either organization. To tell you the truth, I've never noticed a significant difference in what the various PROs paid in royalties for the same song. I don't think an income comparison can help you make your decision.

Instead, I would suggest you take a good look at the relationships you've developed at each organization. By now, you should have at least a passing familiarity with the writer/publisher relations representatives at each company. Who has been the most helpful, the most willing to answer questions or offer references, the fastest to return a phone call, and the one you most enjoy working with? That's your winner.

The truth is that both BMI and ASCAP, and even SESAC, are large bureaucracies. On a bad day, dealing with any of them can be like trying to work out a problem with the IRS. At times like those, the most important thing is not the history of the organization or the percentage of income that each spends on administration. The important thing is to have a human being that you can call—someone who has a genuine interest in you and your company. At the end of the day, the people make the difference.

Or you could join all of them. As I mentioned earlier, while a writer can be a member of only one performing rights group at a time, a publisher is not similarly restricted. If you represent an ASCAP writer and a BMI writer, you have no choice but to be associated with both organizations. If you subsequently take on a SESAC writer, then you'll need to join there as well. An ASCAP writer must be represented by an ASCAP publisher; a BMI writer by a BMI company. If you publish more people than just yourself, your writers will ultimately determine what performing rights organization you will be associated with.

Harry Fox Agency and Music Reports: The Mechanical Breakdown

Even with the advent of a fourth collection agency like GMR, the performing rights environment remains relatively tranquil compared to the tumultuous world of mechanical rights. Remember, mechanical rights apply to the sale of any mechanical reproduction of the song, like digital downloads, CDs, ringtones, or other sound recordings.

You've probably already guessed one reason for the chaos when it comes to mechanical income: nobody buys digital downloads, CDs, or ringtones anymore. In the space of one decade, mechanical income has gone from being the most important and reliable source of income for music publishers to something that is almost irrelevant. Almost.

Mechanical income remains meaningful primarily because streaming involves two different sets of rights for every stream: a performing right (as the music is transmitted in a public way over the Internet) and a mechanical right (because the stream is considered a mechanical reproduction, replacing the need to own the recording). That means each stream generates both performance income and mechanical income. As we've already learned, the performing rights organizations will collect the performance royalty on your behalf. But what about the mechanical royalty? The mechanical royalty rate for a single stream is only a tiny fraction of the 9.1 cents paid for a digital download, but you still have to collect it somehow. How does a publisher collect mechanical income in the 21st century?

Unfortunately, there is not one answer. There are several answers. None of them are particularly good, and as you'll see in a second, none of them are built to last. Here are the mechanical solutions out there at the moment.

Harry Fox Agency (HFA)

Once upon a time, people actually spent money on CDs and downloads. This money then flowed back to the record labels, who were obligated to pay 9.1 cents of that income to the songwriters and publishers in the form of a mechanical royalty. In order to collect those mechanical royalties from the labels, publishers turned to a company called the Harry Fox Agency (HFA), which issued the mechanical licenses, collected the money, and distributed it to those publisher/clients. In addition, HFA annually audited record companies to see if the labels' accounting was correct, collected settlement payments when they discovered the usual record business chicanery, and distributed that to the publishers as well. For all their trouble, HFA took a percentage of roughly ten percent from whatever they collected. Most publishers needing to collect mechanical royalties from a wide variety of different record companies opted to use Harry Fox, rather than trying to collect directly from the labels.

Unfortunately, as mechanical royalties have dwindled, the viability of HFA has dwindled as well. Many large independent publishers, still faced with the prospect of having to license and collect from dozens of different companies, continue to utilize the agency, recognizing that collecting royalties on record sales of 100,000 units is just not worth the effort of doing it themselves. But smaller companies, which might have only a few songs that earn mechanical income or have most of their releases with one particular artist and label, find it more efficient to license and receive royalties directly from the record company.

Not surprisingly, the changing business environment has forced major changes on HFA, which was sold in 2015 by the National Music Publishers Association to SESAC. While continuing to act as a royalty collector on behalf of its publisher members, HFA has now taken on a new role as royalty administrator for various streaming platforms, including Spotify. Rather than paying all of the income due from streaming to the record labels and allowing the record companies to pay mechanical royalties, Spotify has elected to use HFA to distribute those mechanical royalties directly to the publishers. The difference in HFA today, at least in the world of streaming, is that they work on behalf of the streaming platform, not the publisher, when paying out the mechanical portion of streaming royalties.

Unless you need to put mechanical licenses in place with ten or more different record companies, you probably don't need to join Harry Fox. You can simply issue mechanical licenses directly to the record labels and collect your mechanical royalties from them. An example of a license and description of the process can be found in appendix D.

Music Reports

In some ways, the model for the manner in which Harry Fox is trying to remake itself is Music Reports, which designates itself a rights administrator, servicing clients like Amazon and Pandora.

You don't have to be in music publishing long before you start hearing from Music Reports. Usually, it will start with a proposal for a license agreement with some new innovative technology that inevitably combines karaoke with gaming and music and virtual reality and influencers and online shopping, and which no one has ever actually used. The royalty rates proposed are invariably fractions of a penny and the statements that you receive from Music Reports are frequently worth less than it would cost to mail them if they had to be sent by post.

You don't have to agree to any or all of these requests. In fact, many larger, more established companies will hold off giving rights to unproven platforms, expecting that if the app or service achieves any level of popularity, larger organizations like the National Music Publishers Association will negotiate better licensing terms than the ones initially offered.

Nevertheless, it's still important for your catalog to be properly documented with Music Reports, just as with ASCAP or BMI. The truth of post-modern publishing is that you simply never know what obscure app will suddenly emerge as the next TikTok (also administered by Music Reports), or how any particular song might react within a certain platform. Music Reports handles a few services that are very well-established, some that are already becoming obsolete, and others that are little more than a concept in the mind of a wild-eyed twenty year old entrepreneur. It's amazing how quickly something can go from one category to the other.

A Thoroughly Modern Solution

If the preceding system for collecting mechanical income strikes you as ridiculously complex, labor-intensive, and full of yawning cracks just big enough for your money to disappear in, you're not the only one with that opinion. Every publisher, from the largest major corporation to the smallest bedroom operation, acknowledges that the system in effect over the past ten years is inadequate, both for the songwriters and publishers who depend on it to get paid as well as for the myriad of digital services who rely on it to license the music they need. It's a little like the New York City subway system: too old to handle the amount of traffic that exists in a modern metropolis, but too big and complex to be easily remodeled or expanded. Everyone winds up standing around, angry, and praying for the sight of some small light at the end of the tunnel.

Arriving now on the uptown track: the Mechanical Licensing Collective.

The Mechanical Licensing Collective (MLC)

The passage of the Music Modernization Act in 2018 represented an effort by all sectors of the music industry—publishers, songwriters, record companies and digital services, as well as the U.S. government—to rethink the music business infrastructure. The objective of the legislation was to enable the multitude of technology and media companies to efficiently access and license the music they need while allowing musicians, songwriters, and publishers to eke out more than an few micro-pennies for their efforts. The concept at the core of the bill is the Mechanical Licensing Collective, which is intended be one central database from which digital services can obtain a "blanket license" for mechanical rights, in the same way that radio stations currently obtain blanket licenses for performing rights from the PROs.

With the creation of the Mechanical Licensing Collective, publishers, including songwriters who control their own publishing rights, are now responsible for registering all of their songs and providing payment information to the MLC, which also maintains a free public database of songs and sound recordings, so that songwriters, publishers, and record labels can match up unclaimed works and settle any disputes. Requests from the digital services for blanket licenses can be approved or rejected by the MLC, who then charge the services a fee in exchange for access to this vast pool of music. Like the performing rights organizations, the MLC gathers usage reports from its licensees, divides up the income based on what songs are being used, and pays out the correct share to the publishers and songwriters. No more NOIs flooding your inbox, no more having to review the licensing terms of services unlikely ever to get off the ground, no more unlicensed songs popping up on Apple or Spotify, and no more registering songs with HFA. Best of all, the MLC is run by a board of songwriters and publishers, but paid for by the digital services like Google, Amazon, Apple, and Spotify.

When the MLC was first proposed, it sounded a little too good to be true, and many skeptics, including myself, doubted that it could be up and running by the 2021 deadline. But lo and behold, despite the challenges of Covid shutdowns and ongoing battles between streaming services and publishers, the MLC is now online and quickly establishing itself as a fully functional licensing organization. It doesn't completely eliminate the role of Harry Fox Agency or Music Reports, nor does it cover licensing challenges like physical product, YouTube, or foreign mechanical income, but it does represent a giant step forward for the American songwriting community. If you are in the business of collecting mechanical income from digital streaming or downloading platforms, whether as a publisher of other writers or of yourself, you need to join the MLC and make sure that your songs are correctly entered into their database.

Admittedly, the publisher's collection team is less than all-star caliber. You've got a couple of reliable players in ASCAP and BMI, some problematic rookies with GMR and Music Reports, and some aging veterans on the verge of retirement, like Harry Fox. Everyone is pinning their hopes on the still unproven draft pick: the Mechanical Licensing Collective. But in the here and now, where are publishers to turn when the challenge of getting the money proves beyond the reach of their collection crew? Answer: Like brothers in arms (or survivors stranded on a deserted island), they turn to one another.

22

Partnering with Your Publishing Pals: The Tag Team

As you work your way into the publishing community, especially if you start to attend some of the major music conventions and events that show up on most music publishers' calendar, like MIDEM, Amsterdam Dance Event, AIMP events, and the National Music Publishers Association annual meeting, you'll begin to notice that there's one topic that publishers like to talk about more than any other subject: other publishers.

This never struck me as particularly strange until I found myself on the record label side of the business, and I noticed that most major label record executives have only the slightest passing interest in what's happening with their competitors. Almost all of their attention is focused on the endless drama within their own office tower. Why are publishers so uniquely obsessed with each other and who's up, who's down, who's doing deals, and who's selling the shop?

Beyond the easy explanations of jealousy, opportunism, and general snarkiness, the real answer is that more than in any other sector of the music industry, publishers work together. We share copyrights, we put together collaborations, we are bound to the same royalty rates, and tied together in the same copyright lawsuits. While the sense of competition among publishers can be great, the opportunities for cooperation are often greater.

This is true not only of the creative aspect of music publishing but also when it comes to administration and collection. Looking at the crazy quilt collection system that we discussed in the previous chapter, many small publishers conclude that partnering with another publisher—hopefully, someone with more administrative expertise and infrastructure—could be the best way to keep the money coming in without taking so much time and effort that the music stops going out. Sure, they're marriages of convenience, but tying the knot with another publisher can often be the best approach to administering your songs and collecting income, whether it's a long-distance relationship limited to foreign territories or an all-encompassing partnership for the world.

Foreign Sub-Publishers: My Money Lies Over the Ocean . . .

If Harry Fox collects mechanical royalties outside of the U.S. through its international reciprocal organizations, and BMI, ASCAP, and SESAC do the same for performance monies, do you really need to give any further thought as to what's happening beyond your own borders? Why would you need to engage another publisher to administer your catalog in a foreign territory?

You might not. If your catalog is small (let's say, under thirty songs), contains few commercial releases and no hits, or is in a style with a limited appeal outside the U.S. (traditional country or underground hip-hop, for example), it is probably not necessary to think about a foreign sub-publishing deal. Not yet, anyway. The team you already have in place should be able to collect whatever foreign income your songs generate.

But if you represent a sizable catalog, or have a couple of hits under your belt, or are working in a genre that is particularly viable overseas (pop or electronic music, for instance), you may find that a foreign sub-publisher can provide a presence for your company internationally that Harry Fox or ASCAP cannot.

A sub-publisher is simply an international business partner. Ideally, this company will act as a co-publisher for a particular territory, who will not only make sure your songs are properly registered and collect your money within that territory, but also help to find local exploitation opportunities, set up collaborations and writing trips, and aggressively promote your company outside the U.S. A foreign sub-publisher's primary role may be that of collection, but many sub-publishers go far beyond that. Like I said before, if you go into the jungle, it's good to have a friend out there. Preferably one who speaks the language.

A typical sub-publishing deal involves the full passing of the baton. You license exclusive publishing rights to another publishing company (your sub-publisher) for a certain territory for a set period of time. The sub-publisher then assumes all rights to the catalog in that territory. This means that a sub-publisher can license the mechanical, performance, sync, and print rights within the prescribed territory, collect the proceeds, and then account to you, the original publisher. Note that the sub-publisher does not receive any actual ownership of the copyright; that stays with the songwriter, just as in a typical publishing agreement.

Most sub-pub deals provide a fee to the sub-publisher of somewhere between 10 to 25 percent of the earnings in the territory, depending both on the desirability of the catalog being sub-published and the extent of the sub-publishers efforts in exploiting it. Many agreements have provisions stipulating a higher percentage fee on exploitations obtained by the sub-publisher. It usually makes sense to incentivize your sub-publishing partners in this way, as the primary goal of doing a sub-pub deal is to find opportunities for your copyrights or writers in territories outside of the U.S.

A good sub-publishing deal should lead to:

- covers of your songs in the local market
- placements of your songs in local television and radio programs
- promotion of your releases in the international territories
- tips on local projects seeking material
- publicity and marketing for your company and catalog

For instance, you may be able to work with your sub-publisher in setting up a trip for your writers to collaborate with international artists or producers. It's well worth giving up a larger percentage of the income if it encourages your sub-publisher to take an aggressive approach to exploiting your catalog.

The other trick to motivating sub-publishers is to make them fork over some money as an advance. If you have one or two songs in your catalog that have generated some heat in the U.S., it is perfectly reasonable to expect an advance from a sub-publisher. The amount will depend on just how big your "hits" were, the viability of your genre in the foreign territory, and the size of the split the sub-publisher will receive. These advances can be helpful "quick" money when cashflow problems arise. But I wouldn't recommend doing sub-pub deals solely on that basis. You need a partner who is attentive to detail, responsive, active in exploitation, and honest in their accounting, not just the one with the deepest pockets.

"Mmm . . . people with exotic accents who give you money you haven't earned yet. Sounds good," you say. "Where do I sign up?"

Your lawyer will likely be the best resource when seeking a sub-publishing deal. A well-established music business attorney in the U.S. will almost surely have done sub-pub agreements for other clients and will likely have a sizable network of international contacts to draw upon, along with strong opinions as to who the reputable players are in each territory.

But if you really want to be part of the publishing network, you should think of attending MIDEM, the international music conference held in Cannes, France in June. This is the true music business melting pot and an ideal spot for networking with publishers from all over the world. Licensing and sub-publishing deals are the focal point of business at MIDEM. If you're looking to do a deal, this would be an excellent place to test the waters. Soon, you'll be sitting around the Carlton hotel trading gossip like all the rest of us.

By Territory vs. Ex-U.S.: One for All and All for One

If all goes well at MIDEM, you may soon find yourself having to contemplate the bigger issue in regards to sub-publishers: how many of them do you want? Since sub-pub deals can be done for one particular country, a whole collection of countries (like Scandinavia or Asia), or even particular songs (though this is less common), ultimately you'll need to decide if you want a lot of little deals with local publishers, or one or two big deals with large international publishers. There are persuasive arguments on either side of the equation.

The strategy of making separate sub-publishing deals for each distinct territory has a number of clear advantages. If you have a hot song in your catalog, you may be able to get advances for each small territory that in total far exceed what you could get from one large deal for the whole world/ex-U.S. (i.e., excepting the United States). Even if you haven't had that hit yet, you may find that these smaller local publishers are more accessible, responsive, and aggressive in their market than the regional office of a large international corporation. Finally, while a few of local deals could go sour, they may be balanced out by exceptional performances in other territories. At least, you haven't put all your eggs in one big multinational basket.

On the other hand, a dozen sub-pub deals around the world can be a lot to keep track of. It's far easier to have one contact person at Kobalt or Universal who can deal with any problem worldwide than it is to run down an errant sub-publisher in Singapore. If your company is having some success, there's something to be said for a coordinated effort to establish your company as a worldwide presence, rather than a piecemeal approach among a dozen different entities in a dozen different locales. Don't discount the inherent advantages of some real corporate muscle to settle local disputes over infringement, administration, and accounting issues. All of which leads us to...

One Size Fits All

You may already have been contemplating this. If a sub-publisher can administer your catalog, put registrations in at all the local societies on your behalf, collect the money and send you a check, all for a 20 percent fee, why exclude the U.S.? Could you find another publisher who would do all of those things for you around the world? You undoubtedly could. Whether or not you should is a harder question to answer.

When I wrote the first edition of this book, my intention was to help people understand how to become their own music publishers: to develop the knowledge necessary to handle on their own all of the functions of music publishing, including administration and collection. At the time, this was not only possible but reasonably common. There were a significant number of successful songwriters who administered their own catalogs, and few alternatives to self-publishing available to songwriters who had not yet had significant success.

Things change. The past two decades have brought massive changes to the publishing industry around the world, overwhelmed much of the existing infrastructure for royalty collection and licensing, and created paperwork on a scale that would have been inconceivable when this book was first published. Today, the Spotify accounting statements for a tiny twenty or thirty song catalog could be a hundred or more pages every accounting period. At the same time, new companies focused solely on the administrative functions have established themselves as viable options for songwriters and small music publishers who desperately want to get out from under that pile of paper and get back to the music.

While I still believe that it is possible to create a music publishing company that covers all five functions, I'm not sure it's necessary, cost-efficient, or wise. If administration and collection is what you excel at, then by all means you should retain those functions. There is no shortage of songwriters who will need you. But if your strength is on the creative side, you might want to consider handing off the administration and collection roles altogether. Fortunately, there are plenty of publishers who should be happy to be your worldwide partner.

The New Breed of Administrators

Administration deals have long been a part of the publishing landscape, but in the past, they were usually reserved for songwriters or publishing catalogs with a long history of consistent five- or six-digit earnings. These agreements would customarily provide for a ten to twenty percent administration fee on the total earnings collected. The administrator would be responsible for administering the songs, collecting the income, and maybe finding a few sync placements here or there.

With the arrival of Kobalt Music Group in the year 2000, that all began to change. Kobalt's original model was based solely on administration deals (only recently have they started doing co-publishing agreements or catalog purchases) and provided far greater transparency than had previously been possible, with more frequent accountings and online portals to track income and activity in real time. Rather than the usual three- to five-year administration agreements, Kobalt allowed clients to end their contract at any time with only a few months' notice. But even more significantly, they offered all of this at extraordinarily low rates, from as little as three percent for top writers to less than ten percent for many others. Surprisingly, their target clients were not only older songwriters and catalogs with ten or twenty years of earnings history, but younger, contemporary hitmakers who would have traditionally been offered co-publishing agreements.

As Kobalt and their new administration model grew in popularity, other similar companies began to move into the administration business, creating options for almost every level of songwriter and publisher wanting to hand the administration and collection duties off to someone else, while still maintaining full ownership and control of the creative functions. If your catalog is earning big money already, the major publishers as well as almost all of the large independents now offer administration deals that are competitive with Kobalt. But even if you don't yet have earnings to show, there are companies like Sentric or Downtown Music's Songtrust that can provide worldwide administration and collection for a reasonable fee. Some of the top independent distribution companies, such as CD Baby and Tunecore, also offer publishing administration.

Of course, all this could change yet again in the near future. If the Mechanical Licensing Collective that we discussed in the previous chapter works as advertised, it could reduce much of the job of publishing administration and collection, at least in the U.S., to putting registrations correctly into a database. If that were to be the case, it's hard to see why small publishers or even songwriters would be willing to give up a percentage of earnings in an administration agreement. But in the present moment, it's worth considering whether outsourcing the administration and collection functions to an administrator for something between ten to twenty percent of earnings might save you both time and money, and also increase the accuracy of your collection process.

The Rules of Collaboration Part II

Does that mean you can forget about all of that information in the previous two chapters and leave it in the hands of the experts? Not at all. You don't have to do your own administration, but you do have to understand it. The decision about which performing rights organization to affiliate with and the responsibility for establishing relationships at ASCAP, BMI, and SESAC remains yours. In order to communicate effectively with your administrator, you will need to comprehend how mechanical licensing and collection works, whether it's done through Harry Fox Agency, Music Reports, or the Mechanical Licensing Collective. Regardless of how carefully you choose your publishing partners, mistakes will happen and it will be up to you to check the registrations that are in place, trouble-shoot the problem, and in many cases, push your administrator to resolve the issue.

By the way, if your relationships with your collection crew do go wrong, you may want to take a look at your own operation before you start pointing fingers. Whether you're working with a dozen sub-publishers across a range of foreign territories, one international partner who handles everything except the U.S., or an administration company that handles your catalog around the world, lax administration on your part will invariably impact your business partners as they try to collect and distribute your money. No split letter means no license. No license means no royalties. No address means no royalty check. It all starts at home.

We talked earlier about the Rules of Collaboration for songwriters; now, it's time put on your publisher hat. When you're working with other publishers or collection agencies, here is the code of conduct that makes for a productive, positive relationship.

1. **Get it right.** Sure, mistakes happen. Just don't let them happen here. Any information you send to your partners needs to be absolutely, 100 percent correct. A misspelled name, an IPI that is off by one digit, or an incorrect split percentage will take your business partner's carefully calibrated, highly automized system and throw a giant wrench into the middle of it. This will not be appreciated.

2. **Get it right the first time.** Organizations that register and administer songs are built to quickly and efficiently assimilate new copyrights into their systems. They are not built to retract them. What may seem like a minor "update" to you—an additional co-writer who surfaced a week after you submitted the song or a change in the title—is a major headache for your partner. If you're not sure about the information you're submitting, wait. You get one shot at getting it right.

3. **Get it all.** When you're submitting a song to a publishing partner, here's what you need to provide:

- Complete splits. Names of each writer, correctly spelled, as he or she would be listed at their performing rights organization (i.e., not "Lil' Boi BuzKil").

- IPI numbers for each writer. A CAE (Composer, Author, Publisher)/IPI (Interested Parties Information) number is assigned to every writer and publisher who is a member of performing rights organization. This is that writer's unique ID around the world. If you don't know a writer's IPI, you should be able to find it by looking them up at whatever performing rights organization to which they belong.

- Release information including artist, label, release date, and the ISRC code if you can get it. The ISRC (International Standard Recording Code) usually can be obtained from the label, the producer, or sometimes by the online look-up at Sound Exchange.

- The names and IPIs of any co-publishers, if you know them.

4. **Get them music.** This of course depends on who the partner is. In the case of the performing rights organizations, HFA, or Music Reports, they're not asking for music and wouldn't know what to do with it if they received it. But in the case of foreign sub-publishers or administrators from whom you're hoping to receive some creative support, they can't get far if you don't send the music. Make sure you deliver them all versions of any new releases, including instrumental mixes or remix versions.

5. **Get them excited.** Regularly send along bios of new signings, good press, and news about awards or upcoming releases. No need to inundate anyone, but periodic updates will keep you and your writers top of mind.

6. **Get them your payment info.** Check your administration agreement, confirm that the information listed in it is the correct one for you to receive payment, and then don't forget to update your partners if you change banks. Upon signing any foreign sub-publishing agreements, it's also wise to check with your sub-publisher about any tax forms they may need you to complete.

7. **Get them your address**—and make sure they have it right.

23

Protecting Your Copyrights: Can't Touch This

Collection, protection . . . This business is starting to sound more like a Mob racket with every chapter. As any small business owner can tell you, it's not enough to get the money in. You also have to protect your income from those who would seek to take the money out and grab a piece for themselves. As a publisher, you are entrusted with protecting the family jewels (that would be your songs) and making sure they stay in the family, untarnished, for the next generation.

Understanding the Threat

The problem is that most songwriters and publishers are worrying about the wrong things. Because it's so dramatic, the risk of someone "stealing" a song is the threat that seems to occupy the minds of inexperienced writers. "Imagine my surprise when I turned on the radio, and there was *my* melody!"

I'm not going to tell you that it can't happen. There are lawsuits every day alleging this kind of thing—from Lizzo's "Truth Hurts" to Ed Sheeran's "Photograph" to Led Zeppelin's "Stairway to Heaven." But of all the possible threats to your copyrights, outright song theft is probably the least likely and the least financially damaging. By focusing protection efforts on the most unlikely scenario, publishers waste money and energy that could be put to better use. If you live in the middle of a secluded forest, it's probably more important to own a fire extinguisher than a burglar alarm. Protect against the greatest threats first. Worry about the other stuff later.

Split Disputes: Beware the Frenemies

You know where I'm going with this, don't you? The sad truth is that the greatest danger to your copyrights is not posed by a stranger or a sleazy music business weasel to whom you once submitted a song. The real threat is from people you know. Most copyright battles are fought between friends. They are disputes between people who worked together in some capacity and who now can't quite agree on exactly who did what, the "Truth Hurts" (what an apt title indeed) battle being a case in point. A musician who came up with the bass line, a singer who added something to the melody, an engineer who suggested a restructuring, or another writer who just tossed in a word or two while he was hanging out—now that the song is on the radio, they're all sure that they should own at least some small portion. If only someone had some sort of document, maybe a letter, that listed the names of the writers and their respective shares, and had their signatures on it.

As you probably suspected, split sheets are your first line of defense against the vast majority of copyright claims. While such a letter may not entirely disprove someone's claim to a portion of the song, it will certainly raise the question as to why the newly announced writer never asserted the claim earlier. In addition, the split sheet can provide you with an ally. If other writers or publishers are co-signers, they are essentially confirming your version of the songwriting process.

The Song Submittal Form that we discussed as far back as chapter 7 can also help provide a record of how a song came to be. This is a form meant to be completed whenever you bring a new song into the catalog, whether it's written by you or a writer you represent. By listing the dates the song was written and recorded and by keeping notes as to the engineer and studio, it will help you to reconstruct exactly who was involved in each step of the creative process.

It's wise to hold onto session files and other records of the writing process itself. Attorney Helene Freeman, who has defended some of music's biggest superstars in infringement cases, told me that one reason she won the case defending Mick Jagger's and Nile Rodgers' authorship of the song "Just Another Night" was that Mick habitually held onto every work tape and lyric sheet throughout the writing process. Often, these sorts of disputes boil down to one person's version of events versus another's. It goes without saying that whoever has kept the most accurate and detailed records will likely prevail.

Many publishers require any demo vocalists, engineers, musicians, or arrangers who are paid for their work to sign a letter confirming that their contribution to the demo was made on a "work-for-hire" basis. The phrase "work for hire" indicates that the signer has no ownership in the copyright; the fee received for the work itself is the sole compensation. This sort of paperwork can be extremely helpful if singers or arrangers later decide their work was really a songwriting contribution. I find it a bit heavy-handed to ask every person involved in a demo to sign such a letter, although it's probably a wise policy. But you should certainly consider such a letter if someone's behavior indicates a potential problem. Watch out for a general shiftiness of the eyes for instance, or a tendency to refer to the recording as "our song."

Split Adjustments: "Change a Word, Get a Third"

When I said that the scenario of outright song "theft" was relatively unlikely, I was referring to the possibility of people simply taking your idea and calling it their own. What is much more likely and much harder to defend against is what I call the "shakedown" scenario—and I'm not talking about a dance step. Again, this sort of fleecing is usually done between friends. In fact, it almost invariably comes from the same people with whom you've been cultivating relationships as you scramble to get your song cut. "The good news is that (artist, producer, manager, A&R guy) loves the song. But we feel it may need a few changes before we record it. We're looking for (blank) percentage of the song...." Hey, everybody, do the Shakedown.

This move has a long history (Elvis was well-known for grabbing a percentage of any song he recorded), and it appears to have a solid future. If anything, it becomes more prevalent each year. Producers demand a piece of the publishing when all they did was purchase a beat from someone else; artists insist on a piece of the writing for changing two words in the bridge; movie studios want a cut for putting the song in a movie; labels want you to give your share to their related publishing company; even presidents of A&R at major record labels are now muscling their way onto the copyrights.

Sometimes, the threat is explicit: "Give me a piece, or the song doesn't get cut." Sometimes, the coercion is more subtle: "There are just a few lines that the artist had some concerns about...." Sometimes, it means an artist showing up for a co-write, spending fifteen minutes in the room (on the phone the whole time), and expecting a third of the song. This joker has a thousand faces, but it all amounts to someone trying to grab a piece of your song in exchange for an exploitation opportunity.

Sadly, there's almost nothing you can do to prevent it. After all, you need to get the song on the record or in the movie. Sure, whoever is twisting your arm might be bluffing. Then again, they might not be. Copious record keeping will not do much for you on this one, because no one is claiming that they were legitimately a part of the writing process. This is a power play, pure and simple. More often than not, the publisher is not the one holding the heavy weapons. The best protection you can muster in this situation is to try to limit the damage.

Strategy #1: Stall

But don't let them know you're stalling. Give the impression of being responsive (so no one gets nervous), but adjust your speed to slow motion. Return calls in two days, rather than an hour, and call after you know the office has closed. Drag things out.

The point here is to buy some time, and see whether someone is really prepared to pull your song from the project. In the meantime, try to use whatever contacts you have to find out:

- if your song has already been recorded
- if the artist is shooting a video to the song
- if the song is a possible single (if so, you've got a little more power, but also a lot more at stake)
- if the DJ/artist is playing it at live shows or the artist is mentioning it in their social media

As I mentioned before, your primary advantage is the weasel's natural tendency toward disorganization. Sometimes, you can wait it out and hope the balance of power changes.

Strategy #2: Draw Some Lines

If you have to give something away, then at least try to establish some limits. Offer to give up a share of the income from the specific release but not a share of the copyright. This requires you to share any money generated by the project in question, but still allows you to place the song in other venues without giving up a portion. If that doesn't work and you have to give up a percentage of ownership, try asking for a "reversion." This would mean that the percentage you give up would revert back to you after a set period of time, should the song never be released or never achieve a minimum level of sales. If all that fails, try to at least hang on to the right to publish and administer whatever share you keep.

Strategy #3: Keep Pitching

One of the problems with placing a song "on hold" is that it leaves a publisher vulnerable to the Shakedown. By continuing to play the song for other executives and projects, even with the proviso that it's currently committed to another artist, you can at least be aware of whether there are other places to take the song.

Strategy #4: If You Lose, Do It Gracefully

If you're in a losing battle, the worst result is not surrender. The worst result is that you continue to fight until you lose not just the battle but the whole war. No one enjoys being coerced into giving money away, and no one in the industry expects you to be happy about it. But if you let the negotiations become acrimonious and ugly, you will have only increased the damage. You'll still lose a piece of the song, and you'll also lose the relationship with the artist, label, producer, or manager. Keep your exchanges on a friendly, businesslike level. Get the best deal you can, and then put on a happy face. If you're in the ring with a bigger, stronger opponent, it's best to just get knocked out quickly and get it over with. Don't get them mad at you.

Unauthorized Use: The Silent Killer

At least in the Shakedown, they ask your permission before they rip you off. In this technology-driven era, there are plenty of characters and companies operating on the theory of "what the publishers don't know won't hurt them." These are not small-time, shady operators doing business at the fringe of the industry. These are some of the biggest players in the game. Whether it's YouTube, SoundCloud, TikTok, Peloton, or even to some extent Spotify, the evolutionary process of music-related tech companies always seems to follow the same pattern:

Stage One: Platform launches with a model that infringes copyright on a mass scale.

Stage Two: A few years later tries to patch things up with an eye-popping settlement payment to the National Music Publishers Association.

Stage Three: Finally puts some actual licensing systems in place and hires a publicist to blast out to the media how much the service pays annually to the industry.

Be assured, if you have a hit, you will find your copyright turning up in all sorts of places, usually without a license, proper compensation, permission, or even credit. At least, you hope you find it.

The first difficulty in combating this type of infringement is that you have to catch someone at it. With the online platforms, the problem is one of scale. It's not hard to find one unauthorized use of your song on YouTube, but it's very hard to find all of them. Conversely, many other unauthorized uses are difficult to spot because they're obscure: a song shows up in a foreign television production or an independent film, is used in a local advertisement, or gets sampled for an underground hip-hop record or club track. Unless you spend your days scanning the airwaves and your nights hitting the clubs, it's unlikely you'll find everyone who's "borrowing" your song. For optimal protection, you may need to add some players to your team.

Luckily, the same tech community that invented the platforms infringing your copyrights has also been busy developing ways for you to find those infringements. Audiam is most popular with publishers for helping to license and collect income from YouTube. But Audiam also searches out unauthorized uses of your music and obtains payments for uses on other interactive streaming services as well. Similarly, companies like TuneSat and BMAT, which use audio fingerprinting technology, can help publishers monitor usage on radio, television, and even nightclubs.

Given that your greatest vulnerability is often outside of the U.S., the benefits of a vigilant foreign sub-publisher are obvious. Sub-publishers can be your eyes and ears in their individual territories. It is an important part of their role to uncover and pursue cases in which your song is being improperly exploited in their market. Within this country, you need to rely on your network of industry contacts to help uncover what may be happening right under your nose. In my experience, most of the time you find out about this sort of thing from an excited friend or collaborator calling to congratulate you: "Wow, you must be really excited. My daughter Tiffany just told me the song was going viral on TikTok!"

Then what? Once you've uncovered an unlicensed exploitation of your song, the next challenge is to figure out the most effective way to take advantage of the situation. Note my words. I did not suggest that you try to stop the use of the song. On platforms like YouTube, the standard procedure is to confront the user who has posted the video with a choice: either they allow the video to be monetized (meaning advertising will run before the video appears) and you will claim your percentage of the publisher share of income, or you will issue a takedown notice. For an unauthorized sample or unlicensed sync use, you should get your attorney's advice. Depending on the significance of the infringement, you may need to at least threaten a lawsuit. When it comes to TikTok, there's not much at all you can do. But most of the time, you don't want to stop the use of your song, at least not right away.

In fact, you may have unwittingly hit the mother lode.

Music Business Weasel Says:
If someone is in the process of making your song a hit—don't get in the way.

Once you are aware of the infringement, your best strategy will be to wait until the unlawful user has maximized his or her ill-gotten gains before you swoop in for the kill. There is no profit in taking legal action against a small company with no money. Wait until the violators have made some money. Then go claim your share, plus some.

Several years ago, a friend of mine wrote and recorded a song that he released on an independent label. The record was a minor underground success, but did not generate any serious royalty income. Nevertheless, it was discovered a year later by two European dance producers, who borrowed a line from a tag section just after the final chorus and used that vocal part as the basis for a whole new song. While the producers found a new vocalist to re-sing the original lines, eliminating the master recording infringement, the melody and lyrics were still directly lifted from the original composition. which meant that it remained a copyright infringement on the publishing side.

As you might have guessed, the song became a huge hit throughout Europe and eventually crossed over to the U.K. as well. It was only then, more than two years after the release of the original record, that my friend learned what had happened. What should he do?

Exactly what he had done up until that point. Absolutely nothing. It was only when the song was picked up by an American label and peaked at the top of the dance charts here that he spoke up and filed a copyright infringement claim. With little choice but to pay up, the European producers handed over a big portion of the worldwide income and all was forgiven. Like I said, if someone's making a hit out of your song, let 'em. Someone using your song without permission is not necessarily bad news.

Copyright Infringement: The Tables Turn

Conversely, being accused by someone else of infringing on their song is never fun. The unfortunate reality is that when it comes to outright theft of a song, you are much more likely to be the accused than the accuser.

Thanks to the increasingly litigious nature of our society and some recent game-changing court decisions, these sorts of cases are spreading like a virus. Should you have a big worldwide hit, it's likely that someone will show up with an infringement claim.

Many of the most high-profile battles are between established industry professionals, as in Katy Perry versus Flame over "White Horse" or Charlie Wilson and the Gap Band versus Mark Ronson and the other writers of "Uptown Funk." These disputes have proliferated in part because of the "Blurred Lines" decision, in which the heirs of Marvin Gaye were able to take legal action against Pharrell Williams and Robin Thicke, not on the basis of a specific melodic or lyrical appropriation, but a more general imitation of "the vibe" of Marvin Gaye's classic "Got to Give It Up." Rulings like this have left even many veteran, professional songwriters unsure of what now constitutes an infringement.

Most infringement cases however are not between dueling superstars or the estate of one Hall of Fame songwriter versus another. Instead, the vast majority of claims come from unknown (and usually unsuccessful) song-writers and are directed toward writers and producers whose track record alone would indicate that they are unlikely to pilfer songs from amateurs. Many of these inexperienced songwriters have their own misguided ideas about what can legitimately be called an infringement. On top of that, there is a growing cadre of opportunists who have made vocations out of filing spurious copyright claims and collecting payouts from publishers who figure it's easier to pay than to fight. In case you haven't noticed, there are a lot of crazy people on the fringes of show business.

These sorts of legal fights require enormous efforts to resolve. You'll need:

- work tapes from the writing sessions, to show the process of creation
- testimony from co-writers, engineers, musicians, or singers that were in the room while the song was written
- records of when the song was completed, demoed, and where it was pitched
- possible testimony from others in the industry who may have heard the song in pitch meetings or other venues
- supporting analysis and testimony from expert "musicologists" explaining the similarities and differences between the songs in question

You also need a good lawyer, which is never cheap. While the publisher is responsible for protecting the copyright, the costs of fighting such a case are recoupable from the writer's share of income. As soon as such a claim is filed, the publisher will begin to place the writer's royalties into an escrow account, pending resolution of the case. The publisher reserves the right to settle the claim, with the writer's approval, such approval "not to be unreasonably withheld."

Now, if you're the songwriter as well as the publisher, none of that is particularly helpful. Should you find yourself in this exasperating predicament, the best advice I can offer is to make sure you're wearing your publisher hat and not your writer one. There is nothing more upsetting to a writer than the implication (legitimate or not) that he or she has lifted someone else's work. In order to maintain a positive and productive mental state, you must learn to deal with these issues as business arguments, rather than creative ones. Try to take the emotion out of it. If your lawyer tells you to settle, then settle, regardless of how convinced you are of your innocence. It's just business.

One key issue in this sort of infringement claim is that of access. It is not copyright infringement if, purely by chance, you happen to write a song almost exactly like someone else's song. In order to prove that you purposely copied his or her work, the plaintiff must show that you had access to his or her song at some point prior to completing your composition. Could you have heard it on the radio or on a commercially available recording? Was a band in a live venue actively performing it? Or did you at some point receive a demo of the song? If the plaintiff can show that you received a demo of his or her song prior to writing yours, any hope you had of a quick dismissal of the claim is probably gone. When you wonder about the origin of the "no unsolicited material" policy that most record and publishing companies have adopted, there it is. It can be very dangerous to accept demos from people you don't know.

I'm not suggesting that you draw the shades and lock the doors. I am counseling you to be careful about taking CDs or clicking on links from obviously amateurish writers or people that appear to be mentally unstable. If you receive something that makes you uncomfortable, return it immediately. Finally, make sure that your record keeping is accurate and comprehensive. Try to keep a list or a folder of all incoming material, and if possible, your response to it.

Admittedly, the vast sea of user-generated content circulating on platforms like YouTube and SoundCloud has made the concept of access hard to comprehend. If I put my song on YouTube, it may only have a hundred views, but the whole world has access to it. At the same time, the digital world can provide precise data about who is listening to any particular song and when or how many times they listened. In the end, it's up to the plaintiff to prove access to a jury, as there can be no infringement without it.

Copyright Infringement: There Goes My Baby

Only now do we come to the subject that seems to be the greatest fear of most new writers and publishers. What if someone takes your song? What if you send your song off to Sally Superstar, and six months later, you realize you know all the words to her new single the very first time you hear it? What should you do?

First, be sure you're right. A song with the same title does not equal copyright infringement, nor does a song with the same chord progression. (You didn't invent A minor to G major to F major.) A similar shape to the melody will not usually constitute infringement (although it could, if that shape is so unique, or combined with the same lyric, or if that shape is the only melody in the song). A similar lyrical subject matter is certainly not enough to justify a claim.

There is no set rule here. Because of the nature of music, it remains a subjective judgment. For instance, it is generally not possible to claim an infringement for a similar drum pattern. But in the case of a rap record, in which the drum pattern might be the sole distinguishing musical element, it could be possible to claim ownership of a drum part in the same way that Joe Perry can own the riff in "Walk This Way." Ultimately, musical experts will make the call.

As the marquee names in one of the fastest growing fields in the industry, musicologists are the most important element in building a case for or against copyright infringement. Without strong supporting testimony from a respected musicologist, any lawsuit is doomed. These highly educated music nerds will do an in-depth analysis of every note of the song, the chord progression and the arrangement, examine the melodic shapes of the phrases, and give you a description of the compositional techniques used in the song that will leave the songwriter thinking "Did I do that?" When they've done all their work, they will come back with a judgment of the viability of your claim. Listen to them. Whether you agree or not (and I frequently disagree with the analysis of musicologists), theirs is the last word. Don't waste your time and energy on pointless claims. More importantly, don't make all the rest of us waste our time and energy on pointless claims.

If you really do have a legitimate infringement case, then gather all your paperwork and lay it quietly in the hands of your attorney. If your attorney is wise, he or she may quietly contact the publishers of the song in question, quietly present your evidence, and quietly negotiate an appropriate settlement.

If that sounds like a rather unsatisfying response to such a dastardly deed, remember, this is not about punishment or revenge. It's about getting what's yours, nothing more. The last thing you want to do is go public with this in any way, least of all in court. That's not because you might lose (which is always possible). It's because the last thing you need is the publicity of leveling a copyright infringement claim, especially if the accused is a well-known figure. One front-page article in *Billboard,* and you'll never get any weasel in town to accept your demos again.

Or your lawyer may choose to wait a while. As we discussed, sometimes you're better off letting the record have its run. There's no sense in strangling the goose before it lays the golden egg. If the song is shaping up as a hit, just sit tight and wait until it peaks. Then you can speak up. Quietly.

Registering Your Claim for Copyright

If it seems strange that we're this far into a chapter on protecting copyrights and we're just now taking a look at the actual copyright process itself, there's a reason for that. It's not that I feel that copyrighting your material is unimportant. Historically, it has been and continues to be the role of the publisher to register the copyrights in a timely manner. But you should be aware of two things:

First, an original song is protected as a copyright as soon as it is fixed, which is to say, written down or recorded in some manner. Your rough worktape version of the song is copyrighted. In the eyes of the law, you already own your song. What most people are referring to when they discuss the copyright process is the act of registration. Registration is simply the submission of your claim to copyright with the Copyright Office at the Library of Congress. It's a public record of your statement of ownership.

Secondly, registration does not mean your statement of ownership is valid. It does not stop anyone from disputing your claim. The point is, copyright registration alone will not protect you from any of the threats we've discussed in this chapter. It will not stop a collaborator from wanting a bigger share; it will not protect you from a greedy artist's shakedown; it will not prevent someone from using the song without your permission. It won't even definitively establish your ownership of the song. All it will do is indicate that on a certain date, you claimed to own a particular song.

Why bother, then? There's a $35 fee (if you write ten songs annually, that's $350 every year) and forms to fill out. Why not just use the old-school method of mailing a copy of the song to yourself and keeping the unopened, postmarked envelope as proof of the song's existence?

Unfortunately, the old trick known as the "poor man's copyright" is just that—a trick. It has no legal value. There is nothing that replaces the formal process of registering a copyright. This is especially true when things get ugly. You cannot take action against an infringement of your copyright until the song has been registered, and you could lose your claim to any monies earned by that unauthorized use prior to the date your claim was filed. If there is a dispute as to who actually owns a song, the party who first registered the copyright claim will likely carry the day. The question then is not whether or not to register your songs with the Copyright Office. The questions are how and when.

The process of registering copyrights is straightforward. It can be done online at copyright.gov, where you'll probably want to create an account at Electronic Copyright Office (eCO). You can then enter the portal and select the category "Performing Arts." Do not register the song as a sound recording. This harkens all the way back to the discussion in chapter 2. The copyright for the sound recording would belong to anyone acting as the record label. The publisher controls the composition, which falls under the broader Performing Arts category. You can register works individual (at $35 a pop) or as a "group" (a better deal at $55).

As you go through the process, you will need the title and writer information, and it will prompt you as to whether or not the work has been "published." This generally refers to a public distribution of the work. As publishers don't normally file copyrights until or unless something is going to be released, the answer here will usually be yes. Once you've submitted the form, along with your payment, the Copyright Office will review your application. Several months later you should receive your certificate with the official copyright number. This form should go in the song file, along with the validated registration forms from your performing rights society and your mechanical licensing organization. That's it. You're now in the Library of Congress.

Feel safer now? I've noticed that one can often proceed through life feeling relatively secure (probably falsely so) until a single event or warning triggers panic Suddenly, evil-doers are everywhere. Don't get paranoid. Yes, there are many threats to your copyrights, but there is also a danger in being overprotective. For instance, being sampled could be the best thing that ever happens to you. If you take the necessary precautions, stay on top of your paperwork, and keep your eyes and ears open, you can sleep comfortably at night, knowing your songs are as safe as possible.

Here's a shortlist of protection fundamentals:

DO:

- Include a (c) notice, the year of publication, and your name on any physical copies or lyric sheets. You can write either: © (or the word "Copyright") 2020 Ima Weasel. All rights reserved.
- Keep all work tapes, studio records, and invoices relating to any original compositions.
- Have a standard "work for hire" acknowledgement letter to be signed as necessary by musicians, singers, engineers, and others who may have worked on the song, but will not receive a portion of the copyright. You can find a sample in the appendix E.
- Keep records of all incoming and outgoing material, as well as notes as to where a song has been pitched.
- Find vigilant sub-publishers to protect your copyrights outside of the U.S.
- Listen to your lawyer. Avoid wasting time on infringements that are frivolous, or on matters in which little money is at stake. If your lawyer says it's time to settle a dispute, do it.
- Get signed split letters from all of your co-writers. There—you knew I had to say it.

DON'T:

- Have large groups of people hanging out at a writing session. More people, more problems. Keep it private.
- Ask someone to sing, play, or engineer on a demo with a vague promise of "taking care of them" if and when something happens with a song. Make your promises clear and specific.
- Discuss concerns about similarities between your song and a previously existing one in an email or text. In any lawsuit, your written communications will be the first thing you're required to turn over to the opposing side.
- Send out music without adequate metadata, which should include your contact information.
- Assume that a musical idea that you "borrowed" is so small or obscure that no one will know or care. Somebody cares.
- Personalize copyright disputes. This isn't about anything except money. Save your moral crusades for things like world peace.

24

Acquisition: The Final Frontier

For any business built on the unique talents of one person, there is an inevitable moment of truth. Whether you are a songwriter, a business consultant, an architect, or a hairstylist, sooner or later you will hit a wall that can't be broken through by fortitude and a few sleepless nights. It's a simple fact of life: a business built around one individual can only get so big. If your publishing company is built around your work as a songwriter, you may already be seeing the wall looming in the distance.

No matter how well you try to manage your time, throwing the publishing ball in the air with one hand while simultaneously catching the songwriting ball with the other, there comes a time when the only way to grow your business is to add more hands. It's time to sign some new writers and songs. This is at once the greatest opportunity and the greatest risk your enterprise will face.

In a simpler world, adding songwriters would be like buying another machine for a factory. Let's imagine that your efforts as a publisher are showing some big results for you as writer. You've got a hit record climbing the charts, and everyone is calling. Artists want to work with you; weasels want to take meetings; Hollywood wants you to write the big ballad for *Frozen VI*. It's good, but it's too much of a good thing. You need another you.

Adding another songwriter is not adding another you. The new writer can't necessarily write the hits that you're writing. They certainly can't write the same hit that you would write. This new machine in the factory doesn't really get you more of an already popular product. It gets you a new product line. That is both a benefit and a risk.

In addition to providing more hands to carry the workload, one of the benefits of expanding your roster is the chance to diversify. No matter how "hot" you may be as a writer at any moment, there will be times when you are equally cold. Whatever is "in" fashion must eventually be "out," if only so it can later be brought back "in" again. The value of having several writers on the roster is that when one's sound is fading in popularity, another's may be ascending. Diversity is an insurance policy against the fickle nature of popular taste. If you want to have the flavor of the month, you need more than chocolate and vanilla in your fridge.

Diversity can also counter the natural creative ups and downs that are part of any writer's career cycle. Most songwriters will struggle at times, often for a year or two, searching for a direction or a sound. Then suddenly they'll hit their stride and get on a bit of a roll. Then, just as quickly, they get distracted, overly self-conscious, or just plain bored, and start the whole process again. If you only have one writer in your publishing company, those struggling periods can be tough to weather. Ideally, different writers will peak at different times and in different market environments. There is indeed some safety in numbers.

But there's some risk too. Here's the most obvious one:

Picking "hits," whether it's hit songs or hit songwriters, is the single hardest thing to do in the entire music industry. No one, and I do mean no one, can do it consistently. Certainly there are executives that have built a reputation on discovering talent, and deservedly so. But if you looked at all of their signings, you would still find more misses than hits.

I've always thought that other writers, musicians, and artists should make the best judges of talent. There is some evidence to support that idea, as songwriters like Max Martin, Dr. Luke, Stargate, or Luke Laird have all launched publishing companies that have successfully developed the next generation of superstar songwriters. Still, taking into account the much larger number of failed record label imprints and publishing joint ventures tied to artists or record producers, I think the creative community's batting average is only slightly higher than the music weasel side. Regardless of how convinced you may be about the merits of a song or songwriter, you are much more likely to be wrong than right. Over 90 percent of the acts signed to major labels lose money. The statistics of songwriters signed to publishing companies is slightly better, but not by much. If you're a betting person (and if you're paying advances to sign writers, that's exactly what you are), you can't like the odds.

There are risks beyond just betting on the wrong horse. While additional writers may carry some of the workload on the creative side, they also create additional work on the publishing side. Many successful writers and producers have attempted to increase their career longevity by signing a staff of writers to their publishing company, only to find their own creative energy sapped by the pressures of managing three or four other writers.

Diversity can easily lead to a loss of focus, pulling you away from what you excel at into an area in which you're less effective. If it's your strength as a writer that's driving the publishing company, you need to keep writing. Your company can't afford for you to sacrifice your own writing time in the interests of developing the other writers on your roster.

My suggestion? When checking out the pool of talent, don't dive in. Test the waters first. Stick one toe in, then another, moving a little deeper all the time. I admit it lacks the drama and bravado of a big belly flop off the diving board. But it stings a lot less too.

Unless your company has extensive funding, you need a cautious growth strategy, starting with a few sure things (or as close as you can get in this business). These can provide a steady income stream, enabling you to move on to one or two low-risk, short-term ventures. Only when you have had some success with these initial signings should you consider gambling on the more high-risk, long-term deals. This will reduce your financial exposure and allow you to see how much you can handle as a writer/creative director/administrator.

The Single-Song Deal: Betting on the Sure Thing

Maybe we should call this the *pretty* sure thing. Single-song deals involve very little risk or effort. While they won't make you millions, they can provide some additional income. Surprisingly, there are more of these opportunities out there than you might think. It's all about knowing where to look.

Collaborators

I tipped you off on this one way back at the beginning of the book. This strategy is not so much about creating additional catalog as it is about increasing your share of those songs in which you already have an interest. Here's the way it can work.

Let's say that your writer (that is, you, or someone else that you represent) collaborates with a writer who is not affiliated with another publisher; the song is a 50/50 split between the two writers. And let's suppose too that the unaffiliated collaborator has not yet read this invaluable guide and is not actively engaged in being their own publisher. You can make a simple proposal: if the song is commercially released as a result of your publishing efforts, the collaborator agrees to sign all or part of his or her publishing share (for this one song) to you.

From your standpoint, it's a no-brainer. After all, you're the one who's going to be pitching the song anyway. If you get it cut, you'll already be administering part of it as well. This deal could allow you to double your income without doing substantially more work than you were already committed to. In fact, your job actually becomes easier when you control 100 percent of the publishing, as you no longer have to obtain approvals from another publisher, should you want to license the song in a movie, television show, or other venue.

At the same time, it's not a bad deal for the collaborator either. If the song is released, they would have to go to someone to administer their publishing share. Most large publishers aren't interested in handling a single song and would be unwilling to offer much of an advance. Better then to offer you an incentive to try to get the song placed. If you succeed, at least they will be administered by a company for whom this song is an important copyright.

In most instances, it's not necessary to offer an up-front advance for this type of deal. As I said, advances for single-song deals are rare, even from large publishers, unless the song is placed on a platinum-level artist. Since you're only taking the publishing share if you exploit the song, there is almost no risk for the writer. If you get a placement on a major artist, you could consider offering an advance of $500 to $1,000 as a gesture of good faith.

Foreign Publishers

If you or your writers regularly collaborate with others outside the U.S., there may be additional opportunities to increase your share of the copyright. Even if a foreign writer is signed to a local publisher in their territory or running their own publishing company, they may not have a sub-publishing deal in America. If you are able to place a song in which you share an interest, it is worth suggesting that you sub-publish their share for the U.S. Such an arrangement would allow you to administer the song in this country and keep a portion of the income collected here. Again, you're going to be administering the song anyway on behalf of your own writer.

In 2007, the company where I worked, Shapiro Bernstein, was representing a songwriter named Chris Willis, who at the time was a co-writer and featured artist on a dance hit called "Love Is Gone" by a not terribly well-known French DJ/producer named David Guetta. While representing Chris, we noticed that the French company representing David Guetta did not have a sub-publisher in place for the U.S. The agreement we made to represent David's share of that song led to a relationship that has lasted more than a decade and yielded six Top Ten U.S. pop hits and nine Grammy nominations. It's always a wise practice to look at the co-writers on any copyright in your catalog and see if someone is in need of a helping hand.

The only drawback to this approach is that it won't do much to diversify your catalog. You simply own more of something that you already had. Still, it allows you to begin working with new writers in a structure that involves very little risk, which makes it an excellent starting point.

Outside Songs

The next logical step in developing your catalog is to consider publishing outside songs in which you don't already have a collaborative interest. Again, I recommend that you approach this on a single-song basis, with the agreement that you will pitch the song and if you place it, receive all, or a portion of, the publisher's share. If you hear a song that you feel would be right for a specific project, you can simply gain the writer's approval to the general terms of the deal, then put the song forward for consideration. Only when there is a commitment to record the song do you need to execute a single-song contract.

A few precautions:

Be careful about telling the writer where you intend to send the song. It's a little too easy for a songwriter to take your suggestion and get the song there before you do . . . and then decline to cut you in. Likewise, don't give out too much information about the unsigned writer to the A&R person you're pitching to. You may later see the song on the record, with the publishing share going to the A&R guy instead. Finally, make sure that you get a healthy portion of the pie for all your efforts. Don't waste time on songs where the writers are willing to give up less than 50 percent of the publisher's share.

By proceeding on a single-song basis, you're able to watch a writer develop, see how their work is received in the marketplace, and get a glimpse as to how they might fit into your company, all without putting any money at risk. It's a nice arrangement, but it's a little like a courtship. It can only last so long.

The Not-So-Sure Thing: The Writer Deal

Let's say you first meet New Kid in Town through a collaboration. The two of you write a song that you subsequently manage to place in a movie and on the related soundtrack album. Being the new kid, NKIT is thrilled by this first taste of success and agrees to give you her share of the publishing. Next week, she brings you a song she's written all on her own. Again, she offers to give up her publishing share if you can get the song recorded. Soon enough, you've placed this new song as well. So you execute a second single-song agreement.

Now you're approaching a crossroads. New Kid is eventually going to resent giving up the publisher's share of her most successful songs to a publisher who has made no financial investment in her long-term career. With a couple of cuts under her belt (thanks to you, of course), New Kid has some choices to make. She might be able to go to a larger publisher, do a co-publishing deal (which means she could keep half of the publishing), and probably collect some advance money on top of it all. But if she continues to give away her publishing to you each time a song is placed, she'll never own enough catalog to interest another publisher.

You're in a bit of predicament as well. Sure, you've made out okay so far, but not without a fair amount of effort. You've invested time in New Kid's career, and helped her make a name for herself. (She's now known as "Hot New Kid in Town.") But if other people are talking about her, you run the risk that another publisher will step in and capitalize on the groundwork you've laid. What if some other company throws her an advance check and takes her away, just when she's on the verge of big success?

This is when the game gets interesting. It's easy to feel trapped in such a situation, especially if your company is low on cash and larger players are offering New Kid some big money. Never let another company force you into making an offer that doesn't make sense for your business. It's all good to be creative in your deal making and to find ways to structure proposals that are competitive with those from more cash-rich publishers. But it should never be done at the risk of your own financial future. The primary thing to keep in mind is that there are a wide variety of options open to you. Consider a few possible responses to the NKIT scenario:

You could walk away. This is sometimes the best possible strategy. You have to ask:

- Is New Kid's success a product of her skill as a writer or a result of your connections as a publisher?

- Is New Kid's work improving or do you have a sense she may have peaked creatively?

- Is there a specific market in which New Kid has had her success? Is that market growing or shrinking?

Small publishers have survived for years by discovering talented young writers, grabbing their early and best work, and then letting a large Johnny Come Lately corporation overpay for what turns out to be a quickly fading career. In the proverbial pool of talent, it's just as important to know when to get out as to know when to get in. If you've made good money and acquired some solid copyrights, you could walk away with no hard feelings.

Or you could find a way to share. If New Kid were to sign a co-publishing deal with another publisher, she would be giving up half of her publishing share. But that still leaves the other half available. You could suggest that you continue doing what you've been doing for her, with the agreement that she will give you her half of the publishing, or perhaps a portion of her half, for any song that you place on a commercial release. Remember too, you already own two of New Kid's presumably valuable copyrights. If you would be willing to share those with the other prospective publisher, both New Kid and the other publisher might be willing to give you a small piece in future copyrights.

Or you could sell. Those two copyrights might be worth a lot more to NKIT's new suitor than they are to you. Your advantage here is access to the books. You know how much the songs are earning and should have some sense as to whether the bulk of the income has been collected. If you believe that the pipeline is running dry for these two copyrights, or that the musical style of the songs is sliding out of fashion, it may be more lucrative to contact your competitor and offer to sell them your publishing share. This gives them ownership of New Kid's entire catalog, including her two commercially released songs. Meanwhile, it gives you some quick cash to invest in some other younger, fresher New Kid.

Or you could compete. If you really believe that New Kid is an exciting talent on her way up, then it's time to fight for her. You will most likely want to counter by offering some type of exclusive songwriter contract. There are countless ways in which these contracts can be structured, but most fall into three basic types:

- **Full Publishing:** This requires New Kid to assign 100 percent of her publishing share to you for any songs written during the contract term. (NKIT of course retains her full writer's share of the song.) You have full control over licensing and administration and, unless you agree otherwise, retain your share for the life of the copyright.

- **Co-publishing:** This allows New Kid to keep a portion (usually 50 percent) of her publishing share, while you take the other 50 percent. In most instances, you should insist on administering both New Kid's publishing share and your own. This allows you to issue all the licenses and collect all the income, which you will then distribute. Again, you retain your share for the life of the copyright.

- **Administration:** This is a much more limited structure. In an administration deal, New Kid holds on to her entire publishing share. She does not assign to you any long-term share in the copyrights, but rather hires you to administer them. Your job is merely to issue the licenses and collect the money. For your administration service, you charge a fee, somewhere between 10 and 20 percent of the money you collect. This arrangement lasts only for the duration of the contract (usually three or four years), after which New Kid can take her copyrights somewhere else.

So what sort of deal do you offer?

For a small, independent publisher, there is no question that a full publishing deal is the best of all options. It is very difficult for a modestly sized company to make a sufficient profit with less than 100 percent of a writer's publishing. Remember, when New Kid collaborates, you own 50 percent of whatever her share is in the composition. For instance, if she writes with two other people and they split the song evenly, you own only 16.6 percent of the song's income.

If you then factor in the possibility of reduced mechanical royalty rates, you can see the income dwindling fast. In many cases, a full publishing deal is the only way to make the entire exercise worth your effort. This is partic- ularly true if you work in a genre somewhat outside the commercial main- stream. Publishing is a business built on pennies. You can only split a penny so many ways and still have money in your hand.

But you can't always get what you want. In the pop, rock, R&B, and country genres, the co-publishing deal has become the industry standard. Many writers are simply unwilling to give up their entire publishing share, and in some instances, for good reason. As I said at the beginning of this book, many of the most successful writers have embraced their role as a publisher, and while they may be willing to share the labor, they are unwilling to step out of the role altogether. If a writer is active in exploiting their own work or is an artist that records and releases their own songs, then it's not unreasonable that they should have a piece of the publisher's share.

So how valuable a co-publisher is NKIT Music? If New Kid is genuinely engaged in the business, then a co-pub deal may make sense. Otherwise, you can't afford to give up half of the income. Your best solution may be to vary the split on a song-by-song basis. If NKIT Music gets the song cut, then you split the publishing 50/50. If you get the song cut, then you take 75 percent, and give NKIT Music 25 percent. If you place the song in a movie or a television production, you take the full publishing share of the sync fee. However you structure the percentages, you must make sure that the poten- tial income justifies the labor involved.

For this reason, it rarely makes sense for a small publishing operation to offer an administration deal. In most instances, only a large corporation can achieve the economies of scale necessary to make an admin deal profitable. Publishers who build their business on administration services have invested heavily in technology to process registrations and accounting statements for hundreds of writers. They have offices full of workers that they already employ and need to keep busy. The cost of administering one more catalog is very low. It's just the opposite for you.

An administration deal would only make sense if New Kid writes exclusively with you or one of your writers. If that were the case, you would be administering those copyrights anyway (on behalf of your writer). It would not be much more work to administer New Kid's share as well. Still, I would suggest a fee in the neighborhood of 15 percent, just to make it worth your time.

The Details: Where the Devil Lives

As you probably suspect, there is much more to any songwriter/publisher contract than just the percentage received by each party. There are a myriad of books available that discuss songwriter agreements in detail and offer samples of the various types of contracts. *This Business of Music* by William Krasilovsky and Sidney Shemel or *All You Need to Know About the Music Business* by Donald Passman can give you a good idea of how these sorts of deals are structured. For my part, I'm simply going to touch on a few of the terms that will need to be negotiated. This is not a comprehensive list. Just a quick heads-up on issues that can sometimes be contentious:

Term of Contract/Contract Period. Most songwriter agreements are structured as one contract period, plus options. This means that a writer is signed exclusively for the duration of the first period, at the end of which the *publisher*—not the writer—has an option to renew the agreement for additional contract periods (usually three or four periods of similar duration).

So what's a contract period? That's the big question. In some contracts, the first period is specified as a calendar year. But in many contracts, particularly co-publishing agreements, the first period ends upon fulfillment of the minimum delivery requirement. This does not necessarily equal a year.

Minimum Delivery Requirement. This is the specific number of compositions a songwriter is required to write during their contract period. In most cases, the amount is between eight and twelve songs. But that number is only a small part of the story.

First of all, the Delivery Requirement refers to whole compositions, owned 100 percent by the songwriter. A collaboration in which the writer has a 50 percent share only counts as a half a song. So if the minimum delivery is ten songs, and a writer normally writes only 50 percent of any composition, they will have to write twenty songs to fulfill the requirement for the contract period. It gets even heavier.

"Record and Release" Requirements. Many contracts will require that at least a portion of the minimum delivery be made up of songs that have not just been written and demoed, but have been *recorded and commercially released*. Again, this is particularly common in co-publishing agreements, especially when there is a significant advance being paid. For instance, a minimum delivery clause might require that five of the ten compositions be recorded and released during the first contract period. Remember, that's five songs owned 100 percent by the writer. If the writer collaborates, that number increases.

For a publisher, the general effect of the "record and release" clause is to lengthen the duration of the contract period. Not even a very successful writer (unless he or she is an artist or producer) is likely to have five songs recorded and released in one year. After all, many records can take a year or more in production. With a "record and release" clause, a contract period can extend up to two or three years, regardless of whether or not the writer has recouped the advance. Multiply that by options for three additional contract periods, and you start to see how long a long-term relationship can be.

Not surprisingly, "record and release" requirements are one of the most contentious subjects between writers and publishers. As a former songwriter myself, I don't like them.

These requirements are largely a reaction by publishers to the insistence of writers on co-publishing deals (which cuts the publisher's income by half), accompanied by exorbitant advance payments. If a songwriter is willing to agree to a full publishing agreement and a reasonable advance, I think the minimum delivery requirement should be eight to twelve songs, with no "record and release" requirement. If a writer insists on a co-publishing deal and demands a hefty advance, then make the "record and release" requirement commensurate. Fair is fair.

Back to our New Kid story for a second. If New Kid has been offered a deal from a large publisher for what seems like an awful lot of cash, make sure that our young friend understands this concept of "minimum delivery." Upon closer look, she may realize that she's better off taking a much lower advance from you. This way, she writes eight songs during the year and can get another advance twelve months later. If she takes the big money, she better be sure it can last her three or four years.

Retentions/Reversions

Life of copyright (seventy years after the death of the last surviving song-writer) is a very long time, especially to a twenty-two year old new kid in town. Consequently, it's hard to get songwriters to agree to contracts that allow publishers such a lengthy retention, particularly in the U.S. or U.K. Most will demand a ten or fifteen year reversion, provided the writer has recouped all advances. At that point, the songs will revert back to the writers, who can use those copyrights as their pension plan, either living off of the income or selling the catalog to the highest bidder.

Advances

Now we're talking real money. Advances are a loan against future earnings, paid by the publisher and then recouped as the writer begins to generate income. For the publisher then, this is not money lost. The plan is to get it back eventually. But, as we said before, there are no guarantees. Very rarely will a publishing deal require a writer to repay the advance if the songs fail to earn back the money. It's a gamble. So how brave are you?

Writer advances vary wildly, from as low as $500 to $1,000 on a single-song deal, to well into seven figures for a superstar writer with a proven catalog. For the purposes of this book, I will assume that few readers are going to find themselves in the middle of a million-dollar bidding war for a songwriter. Try to come up with a number that is within your financial capabilities, is sufficient to meet the basic needs of the writer, and most importantly, is in line with what you can reasonably expect to earn back. Here's a basic formula:

Pipeline Income: Does the writer already have songs in the market earning income that has not been collected? If so, you need to figure out roughly how much is out there. This means knowing what songs have been released and the share controlled by the writer. You will need to know whether the writer licensed the song at a full or reduced rate. And you'll need an accurate report of the number of records sold, the number of streams or YouTube views and some sense of how much radio airplay the song received.

Projected Income: This is the same exercise, but done on a hypothetical basis. Does the writer have songs that are scheduled to be released? If so, go through the same "pipeline" process, but simply estimate what you think the project can be expected to generate. This is not the time for optimism. If an act did 20 million streams on their last single, and the industry buzz says the new record will do 100 million, figure on 30 million. Remember to take into account the mechanical royalty rate. If the writer is a producer or artist, he or she will almost certainly receive less than the full rate. Unless the writer is well established, assume that the rate is between three-quarters and half of the full statutory rate.

Future Income: This one's pure guesswork. What do you think this writer is capable of in the first contract period? One or two cuts? Five or six? Be sure to keep in mind how long it takes for a song to be written, demoed, pitched, recorded, and released. Other things to consider:

- **Percentages:** How much of each song is the writer likely to have?
- **Output:** How prolific is the writer?
- **Genre:** What is the commercial outlook for the genre the writer works in?
- **Rates:** Is the writer likely to be "controlled"?
- **Mechanical Income:** Does the writer work in a genre that still sells physical product or downloads (this means a mechanical royalty per unit), or is it all about Spotify? Streaming earns a tiny fraction of the mechanical royalty per stream.
- **Sync and Performance Income:** How likely are you to place songs in an advertisement or television show? How likely is radio airplay?
- **Full or Co-Pub Deal:** What sort of share will you have of the income?

Once you've looked at the numbers for pipeline, projected, and future income, you should be able to approximate what you are comfortable offering as a writer advance. But don't get too generous. Only the pipeline number has real substance. Everything else is an educated guess.

There's one other essential thing to keep in mind. The advance is recouped from the writer's share of the income, not the gross (the combination of the writer's s and publisher's share). After all, at least part of the gross income already belongs to you. If you pay an advance of $2,000 for a full publishing share on a single song, that copyright will have to generate $4,000 in gross income in order to recoup the writer's advance.

Just to warn you, the back-and-forth nature of contract negotiations can be very frustrating. It will likely lead to several crisis points, where you begin to question whether this new, unproven talent is worth the financial risk and the emotional investment. In fact, that's part of the value of the negotiation process. It forces you to continually reassess your initial judgments about the writer and the catalog. As the wheeling and dealing drags on and the stakes keep rising, the weaknesses of the writer, or at least their limitations, may become increasingly apparent. Don't be afraid to change your mind. You can walk away at any time.

The Character Test

One of the most interesting aspects of my work in publishing has been the opportunity to observe what qualities go into making a writer successful. Musical talent certainly helps, although there's many different levels of musical skill represented on the Hot 100 each week. Clearly, some musical and lyrical talents are more valuable than others. For composers, a great sense of melody far outweighs harmonic knowledge. When it comes to lyricists, the ability to think conceptually is more useful than a vast knowledge of rhyme schemes.

Ultimately, many of the most important qualities in a songwriter are personal rather than musical. A writer doesn't need to have hit songs to be worth taking a chance on. You just need to believe that he or she has the qualities of a hit songwriter.

What are those qualities?

- **Confidence.** A songwriter must believe that they have something to say that's worth hearing, and be able to convey that confidence to others.

- **Realism.** In show business, most things fail most of the time. The songwriter you want to sign understands the risks, knows the odds, and can accept criticism.

- **Desire.** An A&R colleague of mine calls it the "eye of the tiger." Successful songwriters are entirely focused on making hits, and nothing but.

- **Grace under pressure.** Songwriting is not always a laid-back gig. Try sitting in a studio with a superstar artist or someone who was once your musical hero. Great songwriters can raise their game under pressure.

- **Productivity.** Writers write. When a writer explains to me why they haven't been writing, I know he or she isn't really a writer. A real writer can't stop doing it.

- **Savvy.** I call this knowing how to get lucky. Successful songwriters know how to work a room. They know intuitively who can help their career. They know how to make and keep friends.

- **Salesmanship.** Great songwriters can sell their songs better than any publisher. That's why they are their own best publishers.

- **An inexhaustible supply of positive energy**. Successful songwriters are always up. Up for a challenge. Looking up. Moving up. There is no place for cynicism and negativity in this business. The moment it sets in, the game is lost.

Fortunes are not made in this business by signing proven writers with hits already in their catalogs. Such writers are too expensive for you to ever really make much money with them. Small companies become big companies by identifying good writers before they are fully developed. You can't always do that by listening to music, because the hits may not have been written yet. You have to look at songwriters on a personal level. If you believe in a writer's determination to succeed, that's about as much of a guarantee as this business offers.

No matter how careful you are, entering the pool of talent is always a leap of faith.

Conclusion: The End of the Road

A couple of hundred pages later, we end up back where we started: with all those MP3s or WAVs scattered across your desktop. At the very least, I hope this tome has empowered you to take ownership of your song catalog, and has opened your eyes to how much you can do on your own to transform those songs into money-making assets. Every songwriter needs a publisher, and now you have one. I'd like to think that this book could inspire you to roll up your sleeves and step into the role with confidence.

But I'm not that naive. I was once a songwriter too. I'm guessing that mixed in with your newfound ambition is another feeling, something a little different....

Call it pure dread. "Wow man, that's a lot of information. There's a lot to this whole publishing gig." Yup. The truth is, there's a lot more to it than what's in this book. There was quite a bit I left out, because I just couldn't fit it in. Then there's still more that I just don't know anything about. On top of that, the business is changing all the time.

Question: "So how am I ever gonna deal with all this stuff anyway? Exploitation, administration, protection, collection, acquisition . . . How'm I gonna do all this?"

Answer: Poorly, probably. At first anyway. Then you'll get better. Each day, each week, you'll improve. Every time your business moves up to another level, you'll learn a little more. If you start. If you do something to begin the process of building your business, you'll begin to generate some momentum. Things will start to happen. If you don't do anything, then nothing will happen.

Something is better than nothing. Do what you can.

You are not alone in feeling overwhelmed. As I mentioned earlier, every creative director in every publishing company feels the same way, every day. There is always one more song that should have been pitched or call that should have been returned. Every Administration Department has a pile of split letters that haven't been signed, or registration forms that haven't been submitted. This is not a sign of failure. This is success. This means things are happening.

Of course, some of the paperwork will fall through the cracks. But if you've done the important things—if you've organized your catalog and set up proper systems—you'll be able to spot the mistake and quickly clear up any confusion. Certainly, you will find yourself in situations where you don't know all the answers. If you've set up a solid team to support your business, you'll have experts you can call for advice. Trust me, as one creative director to another: no one has ever said that song-pitching was easy. But if you've gotten the music right, and if you are tenacious about getting it out to those who need it, you will find opportunities. Step-by-step, you will move your writer up the ladder of success.

The truth about most businesses is that a little success can cover a lot of failures. All of those things you never got around to doing will fade in importance if you get a few big things right. The one thing that you can't afford is inaction. It's not necessary to do all of the things I've suggested in this book. Nor is it necessary to do any of these things perfectly. But you have to do *something*. Don't wait until you think you have the time or the knowledge or the money to start your publishing company. Just start it. Set the wheels in motion and let momentum take care of the rest.

Once you begin this venture, you'll find there are some areas in which you excel and other areas in which you struggle. If you're a songwriter, you may find that the creative director's role comes quite easily to you, while the administration function always feels like drudgery. Or it could be just the opposite. Perhaps you are highly organized and efficient, but the thought of meeting with A&R people gives you nightmares. Nobody can do it all equally well. Luckily, nobody has to.

Play to your strengths. Everyone has strengths and weaknesses.

Even the largest corporate monoliths are nothing more than collections of human beings. That means they too have their areas of excellence and of vulnerability. If you're frustrated by your inability to handle all the demands of running your company, rest assured that there are managers in other larger, well-established companies who are equally frustrated with their employees. Granted, your one-person operation is limited by the fact that you are good at some things and not very good at others. Someone else's company is plagued by the fact that the vice-president of Administration just quit, and the creative staff in New York won't speak with the one in London, and the Royalty Department is backlogged by an antiquated computer system. Everyone has problems.

Focus on what you do well. Certainly try to fix those things that are holding back your company's progress. As you grow, you'll be able to hire people who can compensate for your own shortcomings. But your business will be built on your strengths. Some companies excel at pitching songs, others focus on acquiring talent, and still others survive by finding niche markets that they can exploit. Some publishers have their success in the film and television world; others find their opportunities in foreign territories. Some people are dealmakers, others are innovators, and some are team-builders. Whatever works. The key is: once you find something that does work, build on it.

The exploitation opportunities and strategies outlined in this book are not a laundry list of tasks to be completed. They are suggestions of what might work and explanations of what has worked for others. Pick the ones you like and use them. Or try them all, and see which ones pay off. As soon as you sense that something is clicking, put your energy into that. A small company can't afford to pursue every possible avenue of opportunity. You need to go where the action is, for as long as it's there. If you can achieve a few small victories, that success will begin to open doors in other areas.

Independence is power. Make them come to you.

It's a funny thing. The more you need people, the less they want to help you. Ignorance, helplessness, and desperation are not big turn-ons. On the other hand, if you can show people that you are able to achieve some success on your own, suddenly everyone wants to be your friend. Any banker will make a loan to a guy who's already got money. Every weasel wants to work with a songwriter who's already got something happening.

The primary purpose of this book is to give songwriters a sense of the power they have over their own career. One of the most difficult aspects of a writer's life is the feeling that one's destiny seems to be in the hands of others. Life is spent always waiting for a phone call or hoping for that big break. Becoming your own publisher means educating yourself about the industry, creating a network of contacts, pursuing opportunities, and managing your own business. It means creating an enterprise that stands on its own. Once you show that you can survive and prosper independently, everyone will be calling, wanting to help you take your business to the next level.

As I mentioned in the introduction to this book, I've never intended to suggest that a writer should avoid affiliation with a larger publishing company. There are obvious benefits to having a business partner that can provide a worldwide network to administer your copyrights, or access to superstar artists through a well-connected creative director. But by establishing some record of success as an independent company, you can make these deals on your terms. You can pick and choose what offer best meets your needs. Most importantly, you will know how to get the most out of such a partnership, should you decide to enter into one.

Many inexperienced writers view the chance to sign with a major publisher as an opportunity to escape responsibility for their own career. Upon inking the deal, all control over their own fate is deposited immediately into the already full hands of their creative director. Not surprisingly, the publisher usually drops the ball. Most writers come out of such deals worse off than when they went in. Most publishers have learned to avoid doing these types of deals altogether.

A successful publishing relationship needs to be a partnership—not necessarily between equals, but between two self-sufficient, independent enterprises with a common goal. A large international publishing company can certainly be effective in providing money to help your business grow, or administrative services to alleviate the demands of paperwork, or creative support to bring you into projects otherwise beyond your reach. But such a company cannot afford to provide the day-to-day attention that will keep your business alive. That part is up to you. To ask a major publisher to organize your catalog, collect split sheets, or tell you who's looking for songs is to misunderstand the relationship. Your business should already be up and running. You can call on your partner for help with the things that you can't accomplish on your own.

There are no invitations to the big dance. You're going to have to crash the party.

In case you haven't noticed, the music business is not the most welcoming of industries. It's been quite a few years since I came to New York to begin my own career as a songwriter, but this is one aspect of the experience that remains quite vivid in my memory. Just to get someone (anyone) to listen to my songs meant somehow circumventing a thousand closed doors, unreturned phone calls, "no unsolicited material" policies, hostile receptionists, and a teeming mass of other equally frustrated songwriters. I work with enough of today's young writers to know that it hasn't gotten any easier. The entrance to the music industry has not only gatekeepers but armed guards standing watch outside.

If you're waiting for someone to come along, take you under their arm, flash some credentials, and escort you safely through those gates, you are waiting in vain. No one is going to discover your songs, hidden away on your hard drive, and decide to make you a songwriter. No one is going to ask to hear your music.

So stop waiting. Luckily, you don't need someone's permission to become a songwriter or a music publisher. You just need to do it. When someone asks me how I got started as a songwriter, I usually say that I simply started writing songs. Then I had to figure out how to sell them. So I did that too. My story is not unique. It's true of every working songwriter. The only way to enter the music industry is to decide to be a part of it. As soon as you start playing, you're in the game.

I hope this book can provide you with some useful information about the music publishing industry. It should offer a little bit of insight and some strategies to get the ball rolling. It will not teach you everything you need to know. Only experience can do that. Most of all, I hope it will inspire you to action. Let this be your official invitation to join the ranks of music publishers everywhere. I hereby declare you a member of the grand fraternal order. Now grab your demos and get busy.

Happy Weaseling.

Appendices

A. Split Sheet

Date:

To Whom It May Concern:

This is to confirm that we are the sole writers of the composition listed below (the "Composition") and hereby agree between and among ourselves to the following writers' and publishers' divisions:

SONG TITLE: _____

WRITERS	WRITERS SPLIT % (based on 100% share)	PUBLISHERS	PUBLISHER SHARE (based on 100% share)

Month/Year in which creation of this work was completed: _____

(month/year)

If any samples are contained in the Composition for which the sampled writer(s) / publisher(s) are to receive a copyright interest in the Composition and/or income attributable to the Composition, then we agree that: (circle one of the following)

all of the above shares shall be reduced proportionately, or

the shares of _____ only will be reduced proportionately.

The following list of samples represent all of those samples which are embodied in the above composition:

SAMPLE TITLE	SAMPLE ARTIST/WRITER	SAMPLE PUBLISHER	SAMPLE LABEL

If the composition has been or is scheduled to be released, please provide the following:

Recording Artist: _____

Record Label: _____ ISRC: _____

Your signature below will indicate your agreement of the above.

READ AND AGREED:_____

Name: _____   Name: _____

Address: _____   Address: _____

IPI/CAE#: _____   IPI/CAE#: _____

B. Song Submittal Form

Date of Submission: _____

Date Song Was Written: _____

Title: _____ Project: _____

HOLDS/FIRST USE RESTRICTIONS: _____

WRITER	PUBLISHER	CONTACT

Split Sheet Completed: (Yes/No) _____   Date: _____

Studio: _____

Engineers: _____

Mixes Available: (instrumental, TV, clean/explicit) _____

Status: (rough mix, final, master, work tape): _____

ISRC: _____

For Digital Media

Software : _____

Version: _____

Types of Files: _____

Sampling Rate/Bit Rate: _____

Additional Comments: _____

_____

_____

_____

_____

_____

C. Sync License

This Music Synchronization License (this "Agreement") is entered into as of *[date]* by *[Production house, Film studio]* (the "Licensee"), and by *[Publishing entity]* (the "Licensor") and shall confirm the terms according to which Licensee may use a musical composition for which Licensor is an owner or copyright holder ("Composition") in a film (the "Program"), defined as follows:

Program: *[name of production]*
Composition: *[name of song]*
Songwriter: *[name of songwriter, PRO affiliation, % of authorship]*
Publisher: *[name of Publisher, PRO affiliation, % of control]*
Type of Use/Duration: *[Type of Use] [Timing of Use]*

1. **Territory.** The territory covered by this License is worldwide.

2. **Term.** All licenses and rights granted in this Agreement shall commence on the Effective Date and and extend for the duration of the Publisher's copyright to the composition.

3. **Grant of Rights.** Licensor hereby grants to Licensee the non-exclusive right to use the Composition in the soundtrack of the Program, in television and radio spots and in the advertisement, promotion, publicity and exploitation thereof, subject to the terms and conditions set forth herein. Licensor grants to Licensee the non-exclusive and irrevocable right and license to record, dub and edit the Composition in synchronization or time-relation with the Program, to copy the Composition in any form, including but not limited to, negatives, prints and/or tape and to publicly distribute, exploit, market, perform, broadcast, transmit and exhibit the Composition as embodied in the Program, perpetually, throughout the territory, in all media by any means or methods now known or hereafter devised excluding Theatrical, (including without limitation, pay television, free television, home video, Internet, mobile devices and non-theatrical distribution) worldwide.

4. **Limitations.** The license herein does not include the right to use the title of the Composition as the title of any Program or to use the story of the Composition as the subject of the Program.

5. **Payment.** In consideration of the license and rights granted herein for the Composition used in the soundtrack of the Program, Licensee shall pay to Licensor the aggregate amount of [sync fee] if and only if the Composition is included in the Program.

6. **Clearance.** Licensee shall be responsible for obtaining appropriate performance licenses and shall make all payments required to be made in connection with Licensee's use thereof. In this sentence, the Licensor preserves its right and the right of the Author/Composer to collect public performance royalties. Licensor agrees to inform Licensee if the permission of any other person in connection with this License is required.

7. **Limitation of Rights.** Notwithstanding anything contained in this License to the contrary, Licensee hereby acknowledges and agrees that this License does not grant to Licensee the right to include the Composition or any part thereof in any soundtrack phonograph record album (whether disc form, prerecorded tape form or digital media) or in any other phonograph record, without Licensor's prior written approval thereof.

8. **Credits.** Licensee shall use best efforts to credit the Publisher and songwriter, and to include such credit in the final edited version of the Program and in each case in which screen credits for music are included in the Program, to read as follows:

[Title of Song/Name of songwriters (Name of publishers)]

No casual or inadvertent failure by Licensee to comply with the credit requirements set forth above, nor any failure by third parties to so comply, shall constitute a breach of this Agreement by Licensee.

9. **Representations and Warranties.** Licensor represents and warrants that Licensor owns or controls the following percentage of the composition and has the full right, power and authority to enter into and fully perform this License and to grant the rights granted herein; that the consent of no other person, firm or corporation is required to grant such rights; that there are no outstanding liens, encumbrances, nor any claims or litigation, either existing or threatened, which may in any way interfere with, impair or be in derogation of the rights herein granted to Licensee; and that Licensee's use of the Composition will not infringe the rights of any person, firm or corporation.

[Publisher o/bo Name of Composer: Percentage of Ownership]

10. **Indemnification.** Licensor assumes liability for, and shall indemnify, defend, and hold harmless Licensee and their partners, distributors, and assigns (the "Licensee's Indemnified Parties") from and against any claims, actions, losses, penalties, or damages (including, without limitation, legal fees and expenses) of whatsoever kind and nature imposed on, incurred by or asserted against any of the Licensee's Indemnified Parties arising out of any breach or alleged breach by Licensor of any representation made, or obligation assumed, by Licensor pursuant to this Agreement. The provisions of this section 9 shall apply, without limitation, to claims brought by Licensee against Licensor.

11. **No Obligation to Use the Composition.** Nothing contained herein shall obligate Licensee to actually use the Composition in the soundtrack of the Program or in connection with the exploitation of Licensee's rights in the Program

12. **Assignment.** Licensee may assign or transfer this License or all of any portion of the rights granted herein to any of Licensee's affiliated companies (collectively an "affiliate") or to any licensee, distribute or transferee of any affiliate or to any person, firm or corporation which acquires the Program or the right to sell, distribute, exhibit or otherwise exploit same or any rights therein. This License shall be binding upon and inure to the benefit of Licensor's and Licensee's respective heirs, successors, licensees, transferees and assigns.

13. **Entire License.** This License constitutes the entire agreement between Licensor and License and cannot be modified except in writing with signatures by the parties hereto.

14. **Applicable Law and Jurisdiction.** This License shall be governed by and interpreted in accordance with the laws of the State of New York applicable to agreements made and fully to be performed therein, and Licensor consents to the exclusive jurisdiction of the courts of the State of New York and the federal courts located in New York.

15. **Severability.** The provisions of this Agreement shall be severable and if any provision of this Agreement is held to be invalid or unenforceable, it shall be construed to have the broadest interpretation which would render it valid and enforceable, or be

limited only to the extent necessary to permit compliance with the minimum legal requirement, and no other provisions of this License shall be affected thereby, and all such other provisions shall continue in full force and effect.

IN WITNESS WHEREOF, the parties have executed this License as of the day and year first above specified.

LICENSOR   LICENSEE

By:_____   By:_____

D. Mechanical License Agreement

AGREEMENT made and entered into _____ day of _____, 20___ between [*publisher name*] ("Licensor") and [*record label*] ("Licensee").

1. **Ownership and Compositions.** Licensor warrants and represents that it is the owner of a valid United States copyright in the following musical composition:

   "[title of composition]"

   (hereinafter referred to as the "Composition"), and has the right to grant the license herein provided.

2. **License.** Licensor grants to Licensee the non-exclusive right to use the Compositions, in the manufacture and sale of sound-recordings in all forms, whether now or hereafter devised or discovered ("Records") throughout the world ("Territory"), for the release entitled below.

3. **Royalty.** For such records made and distributed, the royalty shall be the statutory rate in effect at the time the record is released. All royalties and fees for recordings of the composition shall be paid as follows, unless contrary instruction shall be issued:

   [Percentage of Ownership in Composition (songwriter & publisher share) — Name of Publishing Company] [ex. 50%- Ima Weasel Publishing]

   All mechanical royalties payable hereunder shall be paid on the basis of net Records sold hereunder for which royalties are payable to Artist pursuant to Artist's Recording Agreement with Company.

4. **Accounting.** Licensee shall render to Licensor quarterly statements and payments thereof, of all royalties payable hereunder, within 45 days after March 31, June 30, September 30, and December 31, for each period for which any such royalties accrue pursuant to the terms hereof. Licensee shall account and pay for all royalties due to Licensor accruing from the release date of the below referenced product.

(a) Licensor shall have the annual right, on thirty (30) days written notice, at Licensor's expense, to audit Licensee's books and records with respect to royalties payable in accordance to this agreement.

(b) Upon Licensee's failure to account to Licensor and pay royalties as herein provided, Licensor may give Licensee written notice, by U.S. certified Mail, return receipt requested, that, unless the default is remedied within thirty (30) days from the date of the notice, the license will automatically terminate. Such termination shall render either the making or the distribution, or both, of all records for which royalties have not been paid, actionable as acts of infringement under the United States Copyright Act.

5. **Credit.** In regards to all records manufactured, distributed and/or sold hereunder, Licensee shall include in the label copy of all such records, or on the permanent containers of all such records, printed writer/publisher credit in the form of the name of the writers and the publishers of the copyrighted work as listed below.

[Songwriter name/Publisher name (PRO)]

6. **Warranty and Indemnity.** Licensor indemnifies and holds harmless Licensee, its successors and assigns form any and all loss, damage, cost or expense, including attorney fees, by reason of any adverse claims by others in and to the subject matter hereof, or by reason of any breach of any of the expressed warranties herein contained, or by reason of any adjudication invalidating said mechanical rights or copyright privileges under which this license is granted.

7. **Assignment.** This agreement is assignable by either party and shall be binding upon the heirs, legal representatives, successors and assigns of the parties hereto.

8. **Term.** This license shall continue in effect for the life of the copyright on the Compositions.

9. **Effective Law.** This agreement shall be construed in accordance to the laws of the State of New York.

10. Licensing Information:

Artist:
Song Title:
Song Timing:
Album/EP Title:
Release Date:
Label Name:
ISRC:

Agreed and Accepted:

_____   _____

Licensor   Licensee

E. Work for Hire Agreement

[Address of Service Provider]

Date: _____

Dear _____:
This will confirm the understanding between you and *[your name or publishing entity]* (hereinafter, "Client") regarding work done by you as more fully described below:

[Description of services provided] on the following sound recording: *[Title of Song/Recording]—[Artist on Recording if applicable]* (hereinafter, the "Work").

1. With this letter, you expressly acknowledge that the services contributed by you hereunder were ordered and commissioned by Client for use in connection with the Work, in exchange for a payment of [amount paid for service].

2. The Work contributed by you hereunder shall be considered a "work made for hire" as defined by the copyright laws of the United States. Client shall be the sole and exclusive owner and copyright proprietor of all rights and title in and to the results and proceeds of your services hereunder. If for any reason the results and proceeds of your services hereunder are determined at any time not to be a "work made for hire," you hereby irrevocably transfer and assign to Client all right, title and interest therein, including all copyrights, as well as all renewals and extensions thereto. Client shall have the sole and exclusive right to exploit the Work in all media around the world, in perpetuity.

3. You agree that Client may make any changes or additions to the Work prepared by you, which Client in its sole discretion may consider necessary, and may engage others to do any or all of the foregoing, with or without attribution to you. You further agree to waive any so-called moral rights in the Work.

4. You represent that your designs embodied in the Work are yours in their entirety, and do not replicate or infringe on any property created by any other party or contained in any other prior existing work.

5. You agree that the above referenced payment shall constitute full payment for the work and that you shall be entitled to no additional compensation, regardless of the manner or medium in which the Work may be used.

6. Client shall use its best efforts to ensure that you are properly credited for the Work, insofar as that is possible. Any credit shall read:

[Agreed upon text for credit]

If the above reflects your understanding, please sign below to reflect your agreement to the above terms and your intention to be bound hereby.

Sincerely,

_____

"Client"

Agreed to as of [date]:

_____

[Signature of recipient of letter]

Index

B

"... Baby One More Time," 129
Babyface, 61
"Baby Shark," 44
backing up data, 81
Backstreet Boys, 56, 135
"Bad Guy," 134
Baker, Gary, 168, 169
ballads, 33, 133
the Beatles, 108
beat market, 19–20
BeatStars, 16, 66, 106, 139
Belmont University, 138
Benny Blanco, 113–14
Berklee College of Music, 55, 138
Berlin, Irving, xi
BET Hip Hop Awards, 187
Beyoncé, 181
Bhasker, Jeff, 121
Bieber, Justin, 67–68, 113, 117, 181
Big Machine Label Group, 17
Billboard, 64, 150, 186, 191, 239
    Top Music Lawyers list, 95–96
"Billie Jean," 131
biographies, 165
"Blank Space," 17
Bluebird Cafe, 119, 188
Blume, Jason, 143
"Blurred Lines," 236
BMAT, 234
BMI, 4, 6, 19, 21, 71, 76, 86, 90–91, 119, 196, 212–14, 227
    programs of, 98
Bocelli, Andrea, 181
Bon Iver, 108
Boone, Pat, 181
Borchetta, Scott, 17
Box, 78
boy bands, 56
branding, 44
Braun, Scooter, 17
Brill Building writers, 115
Brown, Chris, 116
Bruno Mars, 116, 154
BTS, 113
business planning, 46–47
    changes in, 54–58

communication in, 56–57
deadlines in, 57–58
exploitation in, 54, 56
focus in, 55
goal setting in, 48–51
for new markets, 56
partners in, 56–57
Pop Quiz, 52–54
business strategy, 51–54
focus and, 42–43
BuzzFeed, 186
by:Larm, 190
ByteDance, 24

C

Cabello, Camila, 104
Cage the Elephant, 121
capitalization, 13. *See also* exploitation
Cardi B, 116
Carter, Aaron, 56
Cash, Johnny, 40–41
catalog diversification, 45
catalog evaluation, 31
    bottom drawer items in, 34, 80
    demo quality in, 33–34
    lyrics in, 33
    middle drawer items, 32–33
    organization in, 34–36, 73
    ownership issues in, 27–31
    tempo in, 33
    top drawer items, 32, 114–15
CD Baby, 226
CDs, 78, 179
Chapin, Harry, 98
character test, 254–55
chemistry, 140
Chic, 19
chorus, of singles, 115
Christian music, 124, 182–83
City Girls, 117
clichés, 130
Clive Davis school, 138
clubs, performance at, 109–10
Coach K, 46
collaboration, rules of
    for co-writers, 147
    for publishers, 227–28

About the Author

Eric Beall is the author of *Making Music Make Money (An Insider's Guide to Becoming Your Own Music Publisher)* as well as *The Billboard Guide to Writing and Producing Songs That Sell,* and a music industry veteran, having held senior A&R jobs at Zomba Music, Jive Records, Sony/ ATV, and Shapiro Bernstein. He's worked with a wide variety of artists, writers, and producers, ranging from David Guetta and the Script, to Stargate Productions and the Jonas Brothers, and brought in hit songs like "I Gotta Feeling" with the Black Eyed Peas, "Titanium" by David Guetta feat. Sia, "Put Your Records On" by Corinne Bailey Rae, and "Am

Photo by Cyndi Shattuck

I Wrong" by Nico & Vinz. Currently, he heads up the international music management and publishing company Adesso.

Prior to joining the executive ranks, Eric was a songwriter and record producer, writing and producing the pop hits "Nothin' My Love Can't Fix" for Joey Lawrence (Top 10 Billboard Hot 100) and "Carry On" by Martha Wash (#1 Billboard Dance Chart) along with songs for Diana Ross, the Jacksons, Samantha Fox, and many others. He is also the author of *Music Publishing 101,* one of the longest-running course offerings at Berklee Online, the continuing education division of Berklee College of Music.

In demand as a speaker and facilitator, Eric has spoken at key industry events like SXSW, Amsterdam Dance Event, New Music Seminar, Bogota Music Market in Columbia and the SPOT conference in Denmark. He has led workshops for ASCAP's "I Create Music" Expo, Medimex, and the Recording Academy.

More Fine Publications  Berklee .Press

GUITAR

BLUES GUITAR TECHNIQUE
by Michael Williams
50449623 Book/Online Audio $27.99

BERKLEE GUITAR CHORD DICTIONARY
by Rick Peckham
50449546 Jazz – Book $14.99
50449596 Rock – Book............................ $12.99

BERKLEE GUITAR STYLE STUDIES
by Jim Kelly
00200377 Book/Online Media..........$24.99

CLASSICAL TECHNIQUE FOR THE MODERN GUITARIST
by Kim Perlak
00148781 Book/Online Audio...............$19.99

CONTEMPORARY JAZZ GUITAR SOLOS
by Michael Kaplan
00143596 Book...$16.99

COUNTRY GUITAR STYLES
by Mike Ihde
00254157 Book/Online Audio...............$24.99

CREATIVE CHORDAL HARMONY FOR GUITAR
by Mick Goodrick and Tim Miller
50449613 Book/Online Audio $22.99

FUNK/R&B GUITAR
by Thaddeus Hogarth
50449569 Book/Online Audio $19.99

GUITAR SWEEP PICKING
by Joe Stump
00151223 Book/Online Audio...............$19.99

JAZZ GUITAR FRETBOARD NAVIGATION
by Mark White
00154107 Book/Online Audio...............$19.99

JAZZ GUITAR IMPROVISATION STRATEGIES
by Steven Kirby
00274977 Book/Online Audio...........$24.99

JAZZ SWING GUITAR
by Jon Wheatley
00139935 Book/Online Audio...............$19.99

MODAL VOICINGS FOR GUITAR
by Rick Peckham
00151227 Book/Online Media $19.99

A MODERN METHOD FOR GUITAR*
by William Leavitt
Volume 1: Beginner
00137387 Book/Online Video...............$24.99
Other volumes, media options, and supporting songbooks available.

A MODERN METHOD FOR GUITAR SCALES
by Larry Baione
00199318 Book..$12.99

TRIADS FOR THE IMPROVISING GUITARIST
by Jane Miller
00284857 Book/Online Audio...........$19.99

BASS

BASS LINES
Fingerstyle Funk
by Joe Santerre
50449542 Book/Online Audio $19.99
Metal
by David Marvuglio
00122465 Book/Online Audio $19.99
Rock
by Joe Santerre
50449478 Book/Online Audio $22.99

BERKLEE JAZZ BASS
by Rich Appleman, Whit Browne, and Bruce Gertz
50449636 Book/Online Audio...........$22.99

FUNK BASS FILLS
by Anthony Vitti
50449608 Book/Online Audio...........$22.99

INSTANT BASS
by Danny Morris
50449502 Book/CD $9.99

READING CONTEMPORARY ELECTRIC BASS
by Rich Appleman
50449770 Book...$22.99

VOICE

BELTING
by Jeannie Gagné
00124984 Book/Online Media $19.99

THE CONTEMPORARY SINGER
by Anne Peckham
50449595 Book/Online Audio $27.99

JAZZ VOCAL IMPROVISATION
by Mili Bermejo
00159290 Book/Online Audio...............$19.99

TIPS FOR SINGERS
by Carolyn Wilkins
50449557 Book/CD.......................................$19.95

VOCAL WORKOUTS FOR THE CONTEMPORARY SINGER
by Anne Peckham
50448044 Book/Online Audio..........$24.99

YOUR SINGING VOICE
by Jeannie Gagné
50449619 Book/Online Audio $29.99

WOODWINDS/BRASS

TRUMPET SOUND EFFECTS
by Craig Pederson and Ueli Dörig
00121626 Book/Online Audio...........$14.99

TECHNIQUE OF THE SAXOPHONE
by Joseph Viola
50449820 Volume 1.....................................$19.99
50449830 Volume 2.....................................$22.99
50449840 Volume 3.....................................$22.99

PIANO/KEYBOARD

BERKLEE JAZZ KEYBOARD HARMONY
by Suzanna Sifter
00138874 Book/Online Audio...........$29.99

BERKLEE JAZZ PIANO
by Ray Santisi
50448047 Book/Online Audio $22.99

BERKLEE JAZZ STANDARDS FOR SOLO PIANO
Arranged by Robert Christopherson, Hey Rim Jeon, Ross Ramsay, Tim Ray
00160482 Book/Online Audio............ $19.99

CHORD-SCALE IMPROVISATION FOR KEYBOARD
by Ross Ramsay
50449597 Book/CD....................................$19.99

CONTEMPORARY PIANO TECHNIQUE
by Stephany Tiernan
50449545 Book/DVD $29.99

HAMMOND ORGAN COMPLETE
by Dave Limina
00237801 Book/Online Audio...........$24.99

JAZZ PIANO COMPING
by Suzanne Davis
50449614 Book/Online Audio $22.99

LATIN JAZZ PIANO IMPROVISATION
by Rebecca Cline
50449649 Book/Online Audio...........$29.99

SOLO JAZZ PIANO
by Neil Olmstead
50449641 Book/Online Audio...........$42.99

DRUMS/PERCUSSION

BEGINNING DJEMBE
by Michael Markus and Joe Galeota
00148210 Book/Online Video...............$16.99

BERKLEE JAZZ DRUMS
by Casey Scheuerell
50449612 Book/Online Audio...........$24.99

DRUM SET WARM-UPS
by Rod Morgenstein
50449465 Book...$14.99

DRUM STUDIES
by Dave Vose
50449617 Book..$12.99

A MANUAL FOR THE MODERN DRUMMER
by Alan Dawson and Don DeMichael
50449560 Book...$14.99

MASTERING THE ART OF BRUSHES
by Jon Hazilla
50449459 Book/Online Audio...........$19.99

PHRASING: ADVANCED RUDIMENTS FOR CREATIVE DRUMMING
by Russ Gold
00120209 Book/Online Media $19.99

WORLD JAZZ DRUMMING
by Mark Walker
50449568 Book/CD $22.99

Berklee Press publications feature material developed at the Berklee College of Music.
To browse the complete Berklee Press Catalog, go to **www.berkleepress.com**

STRINGS/ROOTS MUSIC

BERKLEE HARP
Chords, Styles, and Improvisation for Pedal and Lever Harp
by Felice Pomeranz
00144263 Book/Online Audio...........$24.99

BEYOND BLUEGRASS
Beyond Bluegrass Banjo
by Dave Hollander and Matt Glaser
50449610 Book/CD $19.99

Beyond Bluegrass Mandolin
by John McGann and Matt Glaser
50449609 Book/CD $19.99

Bluegrass Fiddle and Beyond
by Matt Glaser
50449602 Book/CD $19.99

CONTEMPORARY CELLO ETUDES
by Mike Block
00159292 Book/Online Audio...........$19.99

EXPLORING CLASSICAL MANDOLIN
by August Watters
00125040 Book/Online Media $24.99

FIDDLE TUNES ON JAZZ CHANGES
by Matt Glaser
00120210 Book/Online Audio $16.99

THE IRISH CELLO BOOK
by Liz Davis Maxfield
50449652 Book/CD.....................$27.99

JAZZ UKULELE
by Abe Lagrimas, Jr.
00121624 Book/Online Audio $22.99

BERKLEE PRACTICE METHOD

GET YOUR BAND TOGETHER
With additional volumes for other instruments, plus a teacher's guide.

Bass
by Rich Appleman, John Repucci, and the Berklee Faculty
50449427 Book/CD $19.99

Drum Set
by Ron Savage, Casey Scheuerell, and the Berklee Faculty
50449429 Book/CD $14.95

Guitar
by Larry Baione and the Berklee Faculty
50449426 Book/CD $19.99

Keyboard
by Russell Hoffmann, Paul Schmeling, and the Berklee Faculty
50449428 Book/Online Audio $14.99

MUSIC BUSINESS

CROWDFUNDING FOR MUSICIANS
by Laser Malena-Webber
00285092 Book.........................$17.99

HOW TO GET A JOB IN THE MUSIC INDUSTRY
by Keith Hatschek with Breanne Beseda
00130699 Book.........................$27.99

MAKING MUSIC MAKE MONEY
by Eric Beall
50448009 Book.........................$29.99

MUSIC LAW IN THE DIGITAL AGE
by Allen Bargfrede
00148196 Book.........................$22.99

PROJECT MANAGEMENT FOR MUSICIANS
by Jonathan Feist
50449659 Book.........................$34.99

THE SELF-PROMOTING MUSICIAN
by Peter Spellman
00119607 Book.........................$24.99

MUSIC THEORY/EAR TRAINING/ IMPROVISATION

BEGINNING EAR TRAINING
by Gilson Schachnik
50449548 Book/Online Audio $17.99

THE BERKLEE BOOK OF JAZZ HARMONY
by Joe Mulholland and Tom Hojnacki
00113755 Book/Online Audio.............$29.99

BERKLEE CORRESPONDENCE COURSE
00244533 Book/Online Media..........$29.99

BERKLEE EAR TRAINING DUETS AND TRIOS
by Gaye Tolan Hatfield
00284897 Book/Online Audio...........$19.99

BERKLEE MUSIC THEORY
by Paul Schmeling
50449615 Rhythm, Scales Intervals $24.99
50449616 Harmony....................$24.99

CONDUCTING MUSIC TODAY
by Bruce Hangen
00237719 Book/Online Video...........$24.99

IMPROVISATION FOR CLASSICAL MUSICIANS
by Eugene Friesen with Wendy M. Friesen
50449637 Book/CD $24.99

JAZZ DUETS
by Richard Lowell
00302151 C Instruments......................$14.99

MUSIC NOTATION
by Mark McGrain
50449399 Theory and Technique....$24.99

REHARMONIZATION TECHNIQUES
by Randy Felts
50449496 Book......................$29.99

MUSIC PRODUCTION & ENGINEERING

AUDIO MASTERING
by Jonathan Wyner
50449581 Book/CD.....................$29.99

AUDIO POST PRODUCTION
by Mark Cross
50449627 Book.........................$19.99

CREATING COMMERCIAL MUSIC
by Peter Bell
00278535 Book/Online Media $19.99

THE SINGER-SONGWRITER'S GUIDE TO RECORDING IN THE HOME STUDIO
by Shane Adams
00148211 Book/Online Audio...............$19.99

UNDERSTANDING AUDIO
by Daniel M. Thompson
00148197 Book......................... $42.99

WELLNESS/AUTOBIOGRAPHY

LEARNING TO LISTEN: THE JAZZ JOURNEY OF GARY BURTON
00117798 Book.........................$27.99

MUSICIAN'S YOGA
by Mia Olson
50449587 Book.........................$19.99

THE NEW MUSIC THERAPIST'S HANDBOOK
by Suzanne B. Hanser
00279325 Book.........................$29.99

SONGWRITING/COMPOSING/ ARRANGING

ARRANGING FOR HORNS
by Jerry Gates
00121625 Book/Online Audio.............$19.99

ARRANGING FOR STRINGS
by Mimi Rabson
00190207 Book/Online Audio...........$22.99

BEGINNING SONGWRITING
by Andrea Stolpe with Jan Stolpe
00138503 Book/Online Audio $22.99

BERKLEE CONTEMPORARY MUSIC NOTATION
by Jonathan Feist
00202547 Book.........................$24.99

COMPLETE GUIDE TO FILM SCORING
by Richard Davis
50449607 ....$34.99

CONTEMPORARY COUNTERPOINT
by Beth Denisch
00147050 Book/Online Audio...........$24.99

COUNTERPOINT IN JAZZ ARRANGING
by Bob Pilkington
00294301 Book/Online Audio...........$24.99

THE CRAFT OF SONGWRITING
by Scarlet Keys
00159283 Book/Online Audio...........$22.99

CREATIVE STRATEGIES IN FILM SCORING
by Ben Newhouse
00242911 Book/Online Media...........$24.99

JAZZ COMPOSITION
by Ted Pease
50448000 Book/Online Audio $39.99

MELODY IN SONGWRITING
by Jack Perricone
50449419 Book.........................$24.99

MODERN JAZZ VOICINGS
by Ted Pease and Ken Pullig
50449485 Book/Online Audio.........$24.99

MUSIC COMPOSITION FOR FILM AND TELEVISION
by Lalo Schifrin
50449604 Book.........................$39.99

MUSIC NOTATION
50449540 Preparing Scores & Parts...$24.99
50449399 Theory and Technique...........$24.99

POPULAR LYRIC WRITING
by Andrea Stolpe
50449553 Book.........................$16.99

SONGWRITING: ESSENTIAL GUIDE
by Pat Pattison
50481582 Lyric and Form Structure $19.99
00124366 Rhyming $19.99

SONGWRITING IN PRACTICE
by Mark Simos
00244545 Book.........................$16.99

SONGWRITING STRATEGIES
by Mark Simos
50449621 Book.........................$24.99

THE SONGWRITER'S WORKSHOP
by Jimmy Kachulis
50449519 Harmony $29.99
50449518 Melody $24.99

Prices subject to change without notice. Visit your local music dealer or bookstore, or go to **halleonard.com** to order

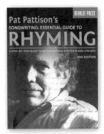